Software Architecture and Design Illuminated

Kai Qian
Southern Polytechnic
State University

Xiang Fu
Hofstra
University

Lixin Tao
Pace
University

Chong-wei Xu
Kennesaw State
University

Jorge L. Díaz-Herrera
Rochester Institute
of Technology

JONES AND BARTLETT PUBLISHERS

Sudbury, Massachusetts

BOSTON   TORONTO   LONDON   SINGAPORE

World Headquarters

Jones and Bartlett Publishers	Jones and Bartlett Publishers	Jones and Bartlett Publishers
40 Tall Pine Drive	Canada	International
Sudbury, MA 01776	6339 Ormindale Way	Barb House, Barb Mews
978-443-5000	Mississauga, Ontario L5V 1J2	London W6 7PA
info@jbpub.com	Canada	United Kingdom
www.jbpub.com		

Jones and Bartlett's books and products are available through most bookstores and online book-sellers. To contact Jones and Bartlett Publishers directly, call 800-832-0034, fax 978-443-8000, or visit our website www.jbpub.com.

Substantial discounts on bulk quantities of Jones and Bartlett's publications are available to corporations, professional associations, and other qualified organizations. For details and specific discount information, contact the special sales department at Jones and Bartlett via the above contact information or send an email to specialsales@jbpub.com.

Production Credits

Acquisitions Editor: Timothy Anderson
Editorial Assistant: Melissa Potter
Production Director: Amy Rose
Associate Production Editor: Melissa Elmore
Senior Marketing Manager: Andrea DeFronzo
V.P., Manufacturing and Inventory Control: Therese Connell
Composition: Northeast Compositors, Inc.
Cover Design: Kristin E. Parker
Cover Image: © Eyewire, Inc.
Interior Images: Java logo courtesy of Sun Microsystems.
Printing and Binding: Malloy, Inc.
Cover Printing: Malloy, Inc.

Library of Congress Cataloging-in-Publication Data
Software architecture and design illuminated / Kai Qian ... [et al.].
    p. cm.
  Includes bibliographical references and index.
  ISBN-13: 978-0-7637-5420-4 (pbk.)
  ISBN-10: 0-7637-5420-X (pbk.)
  1. Software architecture. I. Qian, Kai.
  QA76.754.S64434 2008
  005.1'2—dc22

                2008027309

6048
Printed in the United States of America
13 12 11 10 09 10 9 8 7 6 5 4 3 2 1

Contents

Preface

For decades, software architecture has received primary focus in the field of software engineering. With the growth of the software industry, it has become clear that an early and careful architectural design can greatly reduce the failure rates of software projects. A good architectural design partitions the functional requirements of a software system into a manageable set of interacting elements. Quality attributes such as efficiency, usability, modifiability, reliability, and security can be verified and estimated with respect to the design before any code is produced. As the blueprint of a software system, the architectural design allows system analysts and software architects to communicate effectively with one another and with other stakeholders. It also sets the foundation for the subsequent design and development processes. The detailed design process furnishes the specifics of each architectural element, which can then be implemented via coding, followed by debugging, testing, and maintenance. All of these software development activities greatly benefit from an architectural design that clearly depicts the structure of the software being built.

The new standards for baccalaureate Software Engineering (SwE) education require that software architecture and design be taught as part of the core curriculum. For example, the Software Engineering Volume (SE 2004[*]) of the ACM/IEEE computing curriculum project[**] recommends software design (which includes architecture) as one of its ten essential

---

[*] http://sites.computer.org/ccse/

[**] http://www.acm.org/education/curricula.html#CC2005

areas. Software design ranks as the second highest concentration for software engineering majors and the fourth highest for computer science (CS) majors. Other computing degree programs, such as computer engineering and information technology, also offer software architecture classes.

Approach

Software Architecture and Design Illuminated provides a coherent and integrated approach to the discipline of software architectural design. It is based on rich practical examples and case studies. The book covers a complete set of important software design methodologies, architectural styles, design guidelines, and design tools. Java is used throughout the book to explain design principles and present case studies. All of the authors have taught these topics in related undergraduate and graduate courses, and have practiced software architectural design in many research and industry projects in the past. Self-review questions with answers, exercises, design exercises, and challenge exercises appear at the end of most chapters.

Audience

This text is intended for software architecture and design courses for upper-level undergraduate or graduate students. It can also be used as a reference book for software engineering courses. Students majoring in any of the computing disciplines, who have completed the introductory programming course sequence (CS1, CS2), can read and work through this book without difficulty. Professionals in the software industry who desire a coherent introduction to software architecture and design will also benefit from this book.

Organization

The book is organized into four parts. Part 1 includes Chapters 1, 2, and 3 and serves as an introduction to software architecture design. This part covers general software architecture concepts and guidelines, including software system structure decomposition, subsystems, software attributes, taxonomy of software architectural styles, the Unified Modeling Language (UML), and Architecture Description Languages (ADL).

Part 2 consists of a single chapter (Chapter 4) and is dedicated to the object-oriented software design methodology. The OO methodology can be applied to all architecture styles. It can be used in detailed design and is well-supported by UML tools.

Part 3 contains Chapters 5–11. This part covers all architectural styles in detail, including but not limited to: data flow architectures (e.g., batch sequential, pipe and filter, and process control), data-centered architectures (e.g., data repository and blackboard), hierarchical architectures (e.g., main-subroutine, master-slaves, layered, and virtual machine), implicit asynchronous communication architectures (e.g., event-based and buffered message-based), interaction architectures (e.g., model-view-controller), distributed architectures (e.g., client-server and service-oriented architecture), and component-based architectures.

Part 4 contains three chapters. Chapter 12 covers a comprehensive case study that integrates heterogeneous architectural styles. Chapter 13 addresses architecture of Graphical User Interfaces (GUI). Chapter 14 was prepared by Jorge L. Díaz-Herrera, Dean of B. Thomas Golisano College of Computing and Information Sciences at Rochester Institute of Technology. This chapter discusses Product Line Architectures (PLA) and large scale software domain analysis and design.

Student and Instructor Resources

The PowerPoint lecture slides, test items, and solutions to odd exercises are available at http://www.jbpub.com/catalog/9780763754204/. The supplemental materials for instructors can also be downloaded from the instructor's website.

Your feedback is welcome. You can submit your questions or comments at http://computerscience.jbpub.com/softwarearchitecture.

Acknowledgments

Thanks to all reviewers of this book—Mike Lutz, Rochester Institute of Technology; Hossein Saiedian, University of Kansas; and Richard C. Holt, University of Waterloo—for their constructive comments, suggestions and encouragement. We appreciate the supporting work by the Jones and Bartlett staff: Tim Anderson, Melissa Potter, and Melissa Elmore. We are also grateful to our students who used earlier drafts of this book and provided valuable feedback or helped in the preparation of this book. In particular, we thank our families for their support, patience, and tolerance of the interruption of their vacation plans.

Kai Qian   Xiang Fu
Lixin Tao   Chong-wei Xu
Jorge L. Díaz-Herrera

CHAPTER 1

Introduction to Software Architecture

Objectives of this Chapter

- Introduce the relationship between software requirements and architecture
- Introduce the relationship between architecture styles and architecture
- Introduce the elements of software architecture
- Describe quality attributes and tradeoff analysis

1.1   Overview

The goal of software design is to build a model that meets all customer requirements and leads to successful implementation. As software systems continue to grow in scale, complexity, and distribution, their proper design becomes extremely important in software production. Any software, regardless of its application domain, should have an overall architecture design that guides its construction and development. The success of a software product or system largely depends on the success of its architecture design.

What is the architecture design? "The architecture design defines the relationship between major structural elements of the software, the styles and design patterns that can be used to achieve the requirements defined for the system, and the constraints that affect the way in which architecture can be implemented" (Garlan and Shaw, 1996). The architecture design representation is derived from the system requirement specification and the analysis model.

Who is responsible for developing the architecture design? Software architects and designers are involved in this process. They translate (map) the software system requirements into architecture design. During the translation process, they apply various design strategies to divide and conquer the complexities of an application domain and resolve the software architecture.

Why is software architecture design so important? There are several reasons. A poor design may result in a deficient product that does not meet system requirements, is not adaptive to future requirement changes, is not reusable, exhibits unpredictable behavior, or performs badly. Without proper planning in the architecture design stage, software production may be very inefficient in terms of time and cost. In contrast, a good software design reduces the risks associated with software production, helps development teams work together in an orderly fashion, makes the system traceable for implementation and testing, and leads to software products that have higher quality attributes.

When is software design conducted? Software design is an early phase of the Software Development Life Cycle (SDLC). During this phase, software designers model the system and assess its quality so that improvements may be made before the software goes into the production phase. As shown in Figure 1.1, SDLC consists of the following stages: software requirements analysis; software design (architecture and detailed); software development

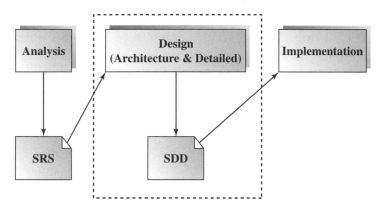

Figure 1.1
A simplified software development life cycle

and implementation; and testing and quality assurance, maintenance, and evolution. The dashed box in Figure 1.1 depicts the scope of software design. The Software Requirements Specification (SRS) provides the input necessary for design. SRS is the result of requirements analysis; it records the functional and nonfunctional requirements that must be met by the software system.

What is the outcome of the software architecture design? Simply put, it is an overall representation of the software to be built. The IEEE Std 1016-IEEE Recommended Practice for Software Design Descriptions (SDD), shown in Figure 1.1, describes an organization for software design descriptions. The SDD serves as the blueprint for the implementation phase. It describes the elements of a system, the modules that compose each element, and the detailed information (such as data attributes, operations, and algorithms) of each module. The SDD is used as a template for software design description.

The following is a sample outline of SDD based on IEEE 1016.

- design overview, purpose, scope
- decomposition description (module, data, process)
- dependency and connection description (between modules, data, and processes)
- attributes
- user interface description
- detailed design (module and data)

Notice that the architecture design is a front strategy design for the detailed design. During the architecture design stage, a designer must specify user-accessible elements and the interconnections that are visible to stakeholders. Detailed design, also called tactical design, is concerned with local design constraints and the internal details of each element. For example, in the architecture design of a city traffic controller system, the designer can specify a priority queue that stores and dispatches incoming requests. In the detailed design, the designer must choose internal data structures from alternative solutions. For example, the priority queue can be implemented using a singly linked list, a doubly linked list, or an array. The designer must then document his reasons for selecting a particular internal data structure. In large-scale software design, the software architect may perform subsystem design before the detailed design.

We will now elaborate on the concepts of architecture design, which is the emphasis of this book. Take house construction as an analogy. Before construction begins, the builders need to know the requirements from customers and the architects must design blueprints. The architects have many options to choose from, such as the style (e.g., Victorian, Colonial, Cape Cod, etc.), functionality (e.g., vocational or residential), and features of the house (e.g., basement or sunroom). Similarly, the specifications of software elements, connectors, constraints (space, time, budget, etc.) and desired quality attributes (such as availability and performance) must be addressed in software design, and this is called the "software architecture," or high-level design.

In practice, designers designate architecture styles by separating out common features of elements and connectors into "families of architecture." Each style represents a layout topology of elements, and connectors and interactions among them. Each style also describes its semantic constraints and behaviors relating to data transfer and control transfer among the elements in the system, as well as the quality attributes tradeoff.

Software quality attributes include nonfunctional requirements such as performance, reliability, portability, usability, security, testability, maintainability, adaptability, modifiability, and scalability. Quality attributes are closely related to architecture styles in that each architecture style supports some quality features. An architecture style encapsulates the tradeoffs among many conflicting quality attributes. For example, with system performance, there is always a tradeoff between time/resources and system reliability and availability.

The rest of Chapter 1 is organized as follows: Section 1.2 elaborates on the notion of software architecture; Section 1.3 presents a general discussion of architecture styles; Section 1.4 discusses quality attributes; and Section 1.5 enumerates guidelines for software architects. The chapter concludes with a brief summary in Section 1.6.

1.2 Software Architecture: Bridging Requirements and Implementation

Software architecture plays a very important role in the Software Development Life Cycle. The architecture design provides a blueprint and guideline for developing a software system based on its requirement analysis specification. The architecture design embodies the earliest decisions that have a decisive impact on the ultimate success of the software product. The design shows how the system elements are structured, and how they work together. An architecture design must cover the software's functional and nonfunctional requirements as well. It serves as an evaluation and implementation plan for software development and software evolution.

The box-and-line diagram in Figure 1.2 shows what an architecture design typically looks like. Notice that it does not contain the complete set of information found in a development blueprint. For example, it does not provide enough guidelines for programmers to follow, nor does it describe any quality attributes. In Figure 1.2, each element (also called a "subsystem") symbolizes a sole responsibility such as business logic processing,

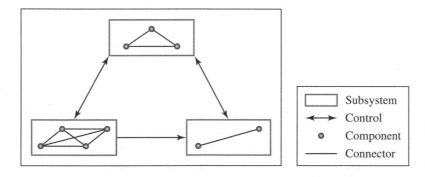

Figure 1.2

Box-and-line diagram showing subsystems

logic control, interface presentation, data gathering, and service brokering and mediating. This division of elements is based on their functionality, location, and runtime images. The elements may be in the form of modules, objects, packages, deployed elements, tasks, functions, processes, distributed programs, etc. The topology of the *static* structure focuses on the system composition configuration such as layered, flattened, star-typed, centralized, or distributed. The *dynamic* runtime connectors may be batch-sequential, multithreaded, explicit direct invocation, implicit indirect invocation (such as message queue or event notification), synchronous or asynchronous communication, peer-to-peer message exchange or message broadcasting, or another applicable coordination and cooperation mechanism among the elements.

Figure 1.2 illustrates the idea of software architecture, but what is its formal definition? Here we list two definitions, one by IEEE and the other by Garlan and Shaw (1996).

IEEE Std 1471 defines system architecture as "the fundamental organization of a system embodied in its elements, their relationships to each other, and to the environment, and the principles guiding its design and evolution" (Maier, Emery, Hilliard).

Garlan and Shaw define software architecture as "the description of elements that comprise a system, the interactions and patterns of these elements, the principles that guide their composition, and the constraints on these elements" (1996).

In these definitions, the architecture elements can be a module, subsystem, object, or binary software such as a DLL component; a JavaBean, EJB, CORBA, or web component; or even a whole system. In this book we use "elements" to refer to the generic units of software architecture, and we use "component" as its synonym in discussions related to software architectures. Don't confuse this software component term with "component-based technology."

Software design depends on the Software Requirement Specification (SRS) produced by analysis in the first step of SDLC. The requirements process covers information domain modeling, data modeling, function modeling, behavioral modeling, and user interface modeling. There are two aspects of software requirements: functional and nonfunctional. A functional requirement specifies the functionality of the software system whereas a nonfunctional requirement specifies system qualities, constraints, and behaviors.

There are many mechanisms used to specify a software requirement. The well-known box-and-line diagram in Figure 1.2 shows the conceptual analysis model of the system, which may be a starting point for software architecture design. However, a box-and-line diagram cannot fully capture the semantics of software architecture design because it does not provide the information necessary for software development in the next phase. Other descriptive notations also report the results of requirements analysis; these include Unified Modeling Language (UML) use-case specifications, Data Flow Diagrams (DFD), and State Transition Diagrams (STD). All these notations and tools can help software designers better understand the software requirements. However, they are conceptual models for analysis and not descriptions of the software architecture.

A complete software architecture specification must describe not only the elements and connectors between elements, but also the constraints and runtime behaviors so that developers know what and how the design should be implemented.

The following lists a software architect's tasks:

- Perform static partition and decomposition of a system into subsystems and communications among subsystems. A software element can be configured, delivered, developed, and deployed, and is replaceable in the future. Each element's interface encapsulates details and provides loose coupling with other elements or subsystems.

- Establish dynamic control relationships among different subsystems in terms of data flow, control flow orchestration, or message dispatching.

- Consider and evaluate alternative architecture styles that suit the problem domain at hand.

- Perform tradeoff analysis on quality attributes and other nonfunctional requirements during the selection of architecture styles. The selection of element type and connector type will have a direct impact on system properties and its quality attributes. Many quality attributes must be taken into account early in the design phase. For example, in order to increase a distributed system's extensibility, portability, or maintainability, software components and Web services may be the best choice of element types, and a loose connection among these elements may be most appropriate. The architects need to have stakeholders involved in this process.

The most important job of a software architect is to map the Software Requirements Specification to the software architecture design and guarantee that functional and nonfunctional requirements are met. If it is not possible to satisfy all requirements, system analysts and software architects can use the architecture designs to communicate with stakeholders.

1.3   Architecture Styles

An architecture style (also known as an "architecture pattern") abstracts the common properties of a family of similar designs. An architecture style contains a set of rules, constraints, and patterns of how to structure a system into a set of elements and connectors. It governs the overall structure design pattern of constituent element types and their runtime interaction of flow control and data transfer. The key components of an architecture style are:

- elements that perform functions required by a system
- connectors that enable communication, coordination, and cooperation among elements
- constraints that define how elements can be integrated to form the system
- attributes that describe the advantages and disadvantages of the chosen structure

For example, in the data-centric style, the data store plays a central role and it is accessed frequently by other elements that modify data. In the dataflow style, input data is transformed by a series of computational or manipulative elements. In the call-and-return style, functions and procedures are the elements organized in a control hierarchy with a main program invoking several subprograms. In the object-oriented style, elements are represented as objects that encapsulate data and operations, and the communication among them is by message passing. In the layered style, each module or package completes tasks that progress in a framework from higher-level abstractions to lower-level implementations. All of these styles will be discussed in detail in later chapters.

For now, let us take a look at the multi-tier architecture style in detail. Multi-tier architecture is commonly used for distributed systems. It usually consists of three element types: client, middleware server, and data server.

Each element type serves a distinct function. The client element is responsible for GUI interface presentation, accepting user requests, and rendering results. The middleware element gets the requests from the client element, processes the requests based on the business logic, and sends a data request to the back-end tier. The data store server element manages data querying and updating. All three types of elements are connected via a network (e.g., the Internet). Many enterprise software architectures are of the multi-tier style because they share the same set of constraints.

Why are architecture styles so important? Because each style has a set of quality attributes that it promotes. By identifying the styles that a software architecture design supports, we can verify whether the architecture is consistent with the requirement specifications, and identify which tactics we can use to better implement the architecture.

Theoretically, an architecture style is a viewpoint abstraction for a software structure that is domain-independent. In most cases, a software system has its own application domain such as image processing, motor control, Web portal, expert system, or mail server. Each domain may have its own reference model. For instance, the Model-View-Controller (MVC) is widely adopted by designers of interactive systems. Such a reference model partitions the functionalities of a system into subsystems or software components. In many cases, a system can adopt heterogeneous architectures, i.e., more than one architecture style can coexist in the same design. It is also true that an architecture style may be applied to many application domains.

1.4 Quality Attributes

Each architecture style has its advantages, disadvantages, and potential risks. Choosing the right style to satisfy required functions and quality attributes is very important. Quality attributes are identified in the requirement analysis process. Quality attributes can be categorized into the following three groups:

1. Implementation attributes (not observable at runtime)

   - *Interoperability:* universal accessibility and the ability to exchange data among internal components and with the outside world. Interoperability requires loose dependency of infrastructure.

   - *Maintainability and extensibility:* the ability to modify the system and conveniently extend it.

- *Testability:* the degree to which the system facilitates the establishment of test cases. Testability usually requires a complete set of documentation accompanied by system design and implementation.

- *Portability:* the system's level of independence on software and hardware platforms. Systems developed using high-level programming languages usually have good portability. One typical example is Java—most Java programs need only be compiled once and can run everywhere.

- *Scalability:* a system's ability to adapt to an increase in user requests. Scalability disfavors bottlenecks in system design.

- *Flexibility:* the ease of system modification to cater to different environments or problems for which the system was not originally designed. Systems developed using component-based architecture or service-oriented architecture usually possess this attribute.

2. Runtime attributes (observable at runtime)

- *Availability:* a system's capability to be available 24/7. Availability can be achieved via replication and careful design to cope with failures of hardware, software, or the network.

- *Security:* a system's ability to cope with malicious attacks from outside or inside the system. Security can be improved by installing firewalls, establishing authentication and authorization processes, and using encryption.

- *Performance:* increasing a system's efficiency with regard to response time, throughput, and resource utilization, attributes which usually conflict with each other.

- *Usability:* the level of human satisfaction from using the system. Usability includes matters of completeness, correctness, compatibility, as well as a friendly user interface, complete documentation, and technical support.

- *Reliability:* the failure frequency, the accuracy of output results, the Mean-Time-to-Failure (MTTF), the ability to recover from failure, and the failure predictability.

- *Maintainability (extensibility, adaptability, serviceability, testability, compatibility, and configurability):* the ease of software system change.

3. Business attributes

- *Time to market:* the time it takes from requirements analysis to the date a product is released.

- *Cost:* the expense of building, maintaining, and operating the system.

- *Lifetime:* the period of time that the product is "alive" before retirement.

In many cases, no single architecture style can meet all quality attributes simultaneously. Software architects often need to balance tradeoffs among attributes. Typical quality attribute tradeoff pairs include the following:

- *Tradeoff between space and time.* For example, to increase the time efficiency of a hash table means a decrease in its space efficiency.

- *Tradeoff between reliability and performance.* For instance, Java programs are well protected against buffer overflow due to security measures such as boundary checks on arrays. Such reliability features come at the cost of time efficiency, compared with the simpler and faster C language which provides the "dangerous," yet efficient, pointers.

- *Tradeoff between scalability and performance.* For example, one typical approach to increase the scalability of a service is to replicate servers. To ensure consistency of all servers (e.g., to make sure that each server has the same logically consistent data), performance of the whole service is compromised.

When an architecture style does not satisfy all the desired quality attributes, software architects work with system analysts and stakeholders to nail down the priority of quality attributes. By enumerating alternative architecture designs and calculating a weighted evaluation of quality attributes, software architects can select the optimal design.

1.5 Software Architecture Design Guidelines

In the following section we provide several rules of thumb to help software developers better understand requirements, identify the right architecture styles to decompose a complex system into its constituent elements, choose the proper element and connector types, meet stakeholders' requirements for quality attributes, and provide proper execution tactics for efficient implementation.

- *Think of what to do before thinking of how to do it.* Functional and nonfunctional requirements should be identified, verified, and validated before architecture and detailed design work is done. Using an abstract architecture design to communicate with stakeholders helps avoid the need to overhaul the system design in later stages of the software development cycle.

  A successful architecture design relies on inherent iterative requirement analysis. Notice that different stakeholders of software systems have their own concerns. Software architects need to confirm what is needed and what can be traded off. For example, the investors of a project are usually concerned with the system release date, budget, usability, and so on; whereas the end users of the same project are concerned with performance, reliability, and usage scenarios. Thus, the software architect must be concerned with tradeoff analysis of the quality attributes, as well as the completeness and consistency of the architecture. Software developers, on the other hand, focus on implementation and are concerned with whether the software design is detailed enough for coding. Software project managers may be concerned with software architecture evolution and maintenance in the future.

- *Think of abstract design before thinking of concrete design.* Always start with an abstract design that specifies interfaces of components and abstract data types. Use multiple levels of abstraction if necessary. Make implementation decisions based on the abstract interfaces instead of the concrete ones because those are more stable—they are the contracts between service providers and service requesters, so they are defined at the early stages of the software development cycle.

- *Think of nonfunctional requirements early in the design process.* When you map functional requirements to an architecture design, you should consider nonfunctional requirements as well. Communicate with stakeholders and document their preferences for quality attributes. If it is not possible to find a design that meets all quality attributes, try to find the right balance of quality attributes and consider heterogeneous architecture styles when necessary.

- *Think of software reusability and extensibility as much as possible.* For most software systems, it is likely that new functionalities will be added after the systems are deployed. You need to consider how to reuse existing software components to increase the reliability and cost-effectiveness of new systems. Always try hard to make software extensible in the future.

- *Try to promote high cohesion within each element and loose coupling between elements.* A highly coherent subsystem, component, or module performs one sole function. For example, in object-oriented design, if a class is assigned to bear two unrelated responsibilities, it is regarded as incoherent. You must consider cohesion factors during the very early stages of the design process. Low cohesion of a system implies that functional composition is not designed well; for example, a single function can be scattered across a large number of different components, making it very hard to maintain.

    Each architecture style should show a clear division between elements to guarantee loose coupling. In most cases, loose coupling means less interdependency between components, so the change of one component is not likely to cause ripple-changes of other components. The coupling attribute can be measured by interface signature counts. Message passing and asynchronous communication are good examples of loose coupling between the service requestor and the service provider. For example, an email conversation has a much looser tie than that of a phone conversation.

- *Tolerate refinement of design.* Never expect to have software design completely perfect in one step. You may need to use prototyping and iteration to refine the design.

- *Avoid ambiguous design and over-detailed design.* Ambiguous design lacks constraints and over-detailed design restricts implementation.

How are architecture designs described? UML notation is one of many solutions, in addition to text documentation, that are available to designers. UML provides graphic notations that are available to architects and designers in nearly every stage of SDLC, e.g., use case diagrams for documenting system requirements, class diagrams for describing the logical structure of a system, and state machine diagrams and interaction diagrams for specifying the dynamic behaviors of a system. The "4+1" view model, developed by P. B. Kruchten, is a way to show different views of a software system, from the perspective of different stakeholders. It is especially useful in describing a complete set of functional and nonfunctional requirements. Another choice is to use Architecture Description Languages (ADL) to formally specify the structure and semantics of software architecture.

1.6   Summary

Software architecture design has emerged as an important part of software development. A software architecture specification consists of software elements, connectors and collaborations among the elements, and desired quality attributes. An architecture style is a set of rules, constraints, or patterns that guide how to structure a system into a set of elements and connectors, and how to govern overall structure design patterns of constituent element types and their runtime interaction. One specific architecture style may not satisfy all of the system's desired quality attributes, in which case tradeoffs must be made. Thus, how to properly balance quality attributes is an important design issue.

1.7   Self-Review Questions

1. The constituent elements of software architecture are software elements and their connections.

   a. True

   b. False

2. Software architecture design involves many software design methodologies and architecture styles.

   a. True

   b. False

3. The purpose of the software design phase is to produce a software requirement specification.

   a. True

   b. False

4. Object-oriented design is a design methodology.

   a. True

   b. False

5. Pipe-and-filter is one of the architecture styles.

   a. True

   b. False

6. Software architecture is a static software structure description.

   a. True

   b. False

7. Software quality attributes must satisfy functional requirements.

   a. True

   b. False

8. Architecture styles contribute to software quality attributes.

   a. True

   b. False

9. Software architecture = software architecture styles.

   a. True

   b. False

10. Software architecture design is based on the software requirement specification.

    a. True

    b. False

Answers to the Self-Review Questions

1. b   2. a   3. b   4. a   5. a   6. b   7. b   8. a   9. b   10. a

References

Garlan, David and Mary Shaw. *Software Architecture: Perspectives on an Emerging Discipline.* Upper Saddle River, NJ: Prentice Hall, 1996, 1–4.

Maier, M.W., D. Emery, R. Hilliard. "Software architecture: introducing IEEE Standard 1471." IEEE Xplore. Vol. 34, No. 4 (April 2001), http:// ieeexplore.ieee.org/Xplore/login.jsp?url=/iel5/2/19820/00917550.pdf? temp=x.

Suggested Reading

Reekie, John and Rohan McAdam. *A Software Architecture Primer.* Angophora Press, 2006.

CHAPTER 2

Software Architecture Design Space

Objectives of this Chapter

- Introduce major perspectives on, and structures used in, software architecture

- Introduce major element and connector types used in software architecture

- Introduce the iterative refinement process for software architecture design

2.1   Overview

A software architect is responsible for proposing a concrete architecture that best supports the detailed design and implementation of a specific project. Software architects must know what design alternatives are available to them, and which one will best support the functional and non-functional requirements. To put it another way, a software architect must understand the software architecture's design space.

In its simplest form, a software architecture design is a set of software elements connected by a set of connectors. From a dynamic structure point of view, a software element can be a process, an object, an instance of a software component, or a service. Different software elements may run on different hardware and software platforms and may be implemented in different programming languages or on different software frameworks. Two software elements can run in the same process, on the same computer system, within an intranet, or distributed over the Internet. Depending on their relative location, the connectors between a pair of software elements can be implemented in various forms including local method invocations, remote method invocations, service calls, and messaging through a message queue. The connectors can also work in synchronous or asynchronous nodes.

In terms of the static structure, a software element can be a package, a class, a component, or a loadable library. Correspondingly, a connector can be an import clause, inheritance clause, interface specification, pipe, or filter.

Today's software industry is characterized by constantly changing project requirements. An organization's expansion or merger may lead to heterogeneous intranet IT infrastructure, just as B2B (business-to-business) integration may make integration across the Internet critical to its smooth operation. A good software architecture should be able to easily adapt to these changing environments without the need for major reengineering of corresponding software systems.

Over the last decade, information technology has gone through significant changes. Component-based software engineering calls for the use of software frameworks. For example, technologies such as .NET and J2EE (Java 2 Enterprise Edition) have greatly enhanced the level of encapsulation. Web services and service-oriented architectures have brought us more flexible connector implementation technologies and software architecture varieties.

In the rest of this chapter we discuss the design space for software architectures and put in perspective the fundamental concepts behind the latest implementation technologies.

2.2 Types of Software Structures

As indicated previously, a software architecture design can be described with various software structures, each from a different perspective. It may be described in terms of software code units like source/binary code files, software modules, or software component deployment units; this is known as the static structure. It may also be described based on the runtime dynamic structure, in which the software elements are threads, processes, sessions, transactions, objects, or software component instances at execution time. Furthermore, an allocation structure may also be used to describe the project management structure of an architecture design. These different types of structures use different connector types and different performance attributes. We provide more details about these structural perspectives in the following subsections.

2.2.1 Software Static Structure

A software project is typically implemented in multiple files. This includes static file types such as executable files; library files; binary software component modules (usually in the form of DLLs [dynamic linking libraries], JavaBeans, and Enterprise JavaBeans); deployment descriptors; and other resource files.

At software development time, the main software elements are source code modules or files. Each module has assigned functional and nonfunctional attributes, and the public APIs (application programming interfaces), defined for each module separate the module's interfaces and implementations. The connectors at this level are module dependent. Module A is connected to module B if, and only if, A needs to invoke some methods in B during execution. Such connectors may exhibit the following attributes:

- *Direction:* If module A invokes a method of module B during execution, there is a unidirectional connector from module A to module B.

- *Synchronization:* A method invocation can be synchronous or asynchronous.

- *Sequence:* Some connectors must be used in a particular sequence. For example, module A may invoke a method of module B and pass a callback reference during the invocation. Later, some events in module B may trigger a callback to module A. Both of these method invocations are represented by their connector abstractions, and a sequence attribute associated with them consists of a sequence ID and number. In this case both connectors will have the same sequence ID but different sequence numbers, which indicates the order of method invocation. Note that the terms *method* and *method invocation* are used in a very general sense in this chapter. Normally, classes and methods will only be available at the detailed design phase, which takes place after a software architecture design has been chosen.

At software deployment time, the elements are binary versions of the project modules and files. Several source code modules may be packaged into the same deployment unit, but the connectors in the deployment structures are the same as those for the source module structures. Let us look at the software structure Java.

Classes are the basic building blocks of Java software. A Java program is a hierarchical collection of one or more *classes*. A large program consists of thousands of classes. *Files* are the *compilation units* in Java; that is, each file can be separately compiled. Packages allow the grouping of closely related classes and interfaces. Thus, they support the hierarchical and static organization of a large Java program as "logical and name space" managing units.

Package declarations are file-based, meaning that all classes in the same file belong to the same package (name space), if the source file contains a package declaration. When the package declaration is absent from a file, all the classes contained therein belong to an unnamed (anonymous) package. When packages are used, source and class files must be placed in directories whose structures match the structures of the packages. Naming the classes inside a package can be done by fully qualifying the name as follows: `package-name.class-name`. Alternatively, we can *import* a package, one of its subunits, or all of its classes.

Java units declared inside other units, such as packages, classes, or interfaces, yield a tree-like hierarchy. In contrast, importing separately compiled units defines a linear partial ordering which, when combined with the tree structure of subunits, defines the *software static structure*.

The software static structure refers to the organization of physical software modules and their interrelations and this structure plays a critical role in software architecture design. Static structure affects the architecture's clarity, construction strategy, maintenance, reengineering, reusability, etc. It plays a crucial role in the management of large software systems because it deals with the packaging of software modules in order to facilitate system construction and maintenance through a clear portrayal of intermodule relations. The fact that systems are developed incrementally increases the need for tight control of this structure in the physical software element.

Managing static structures involves layers of abstraction and of refinement showing visibility and encapsulation, respectively. These two notions define different kinds of hierarchical relations as described in the following:

- A linear client-server relation is formed when a component provides primitive abstractions to another component. In this sense components may refer to abstractions that, once defined, may be used throughout the entire design (at all levels). Layers of abstractions are connected when a module, the client, explicitly requests to use the facilities or abstractions provided by another module, the server. This relationship forms a linear hierarchy, whereby visibility is not transitive. Note that in support for reusability, server units must not know the identity of the client modules.

- A tree-like hierarchy of refinement relations is formed when an abstraction (i.e., a component) is implemented, and recursively divides into subcomponents. A refinement relation specifies how a module (parent) is decomposed into a refinement module (child). This relationship always defines a tree-like hierarchy. Inheritance is a special case of refinement relations.

Figure 2.1 illustrates the client-server and refinement relations essential for specifying the static structure. A server unit is an independently compiled

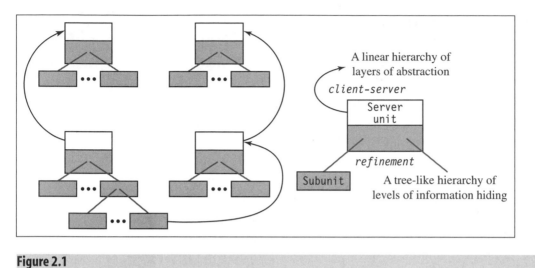

Figure 2.1

A summary of client-server and refinement relationships

unit available for use in the given scope, whereas a subunit (and its sub-subunits, and so on) is a refinement component of another unit, and hence exists only within the context of that unit.

2.2.2   Software Runtime Structure

At runtime a project consists of one or more threads, processes, functional units, and data units. These elements may run on the same computer or on multiple computers across a network. The same element in a code structure may implement or support multiple runtime elements. For example, in a client-server application, the same client module may run on many client computers. Conversely, several code structure elements may implement or support a single runtime element. For example, many threads will run multiple methods from different classes that may be packaged in different code units.

The connectors at this level inherit attributes from their source-code structure counterparts, along with the following other attributes:

- *Multiplicity:* One element can be connected to multiple elements if it needs to invoke methods of multiple elements at runtime.

- *Distance and connection media:* Two connected elements may communicate in the same thread, in the same process, on the same computer, or on different computers across a network. Based on the distance between two elements, the communication media may vary from copper/optical cable or wireless based LAN to the Internet.

- *Universally invocable:* A connector with this attribute set to true allows any external software system, no matter what hardware/ software platforms they run on and in which programming languages or software frameworks they are developed, to invoke the method at the connector's target. This attribute is critical for heterogeneous enterprise information systems that must be integrated efficiently.

- *Self-descriptive:* A connector with this attribute set to true can allow an external software system to invoke its target method without the pre-installation of any software specific to the method. This attribute allows clients to choose service providers dynamically. It also allows software systems developed at different companies at potentially different times to dynamically interact with each other. For example, agents from different companies may be able to collaborate without special software installation.

2.2.3   Software Management Structure

A large software project is normally designed and implemented by several project teams, each having its well-defined responsibilities at specific SDLC process stages. At this level, each element consists of manipulation (design, implementation, debugging, etc.) of specific code units assigned to each project team, and the connectors are derived from runtime dependency among the code units and software process dependencies. Some software architectures are best implemented by a particular software management structure. Software management structures are also used for project resource allocation.

Software runtime structures serve as the technical backbone of architecture designs and provide the basis from which other structures are derived.

In this book we focus on software runtime structures and their efficient mapping to the best implementation technologies.

2.3   Software Elements

At runtime each software element has well-defined functions and connects to the other elements into a dependency graph through connectors. The elements of a software architecture are usually refined through multiple transformation steps based on their attributes and the project requirement specifications.

Depending on each software element's assigned function, there may be different synchronization and performance constraints. For example, some elements are reentrant objects or software components (meaning that multiple threads can execute in an element concurrently without interfering with each other) while some elements are not reentrant and no more than one thread may execute in it at any time. Depending on the multiplicity of an element, it could be invoked by a limited number of other elements at execution time, or it could be invoked by unlimited elements, as in the case of a server element. In the latter case, scalability, response time, and throughput become important performance constraints and must be considered during the element's implementation.

The following are the basic guidelines for mapping runtime elements into their implementations:

- If an element is reentrant, it can be implemented by a thread or a process. Reentrant elements are usually more efficient because they avoid many synchronization issues and support shared thread or process pools. However, business logics may not allow some elements to be reentrant.

- If an element is not reentrant and multiple threads or processes need to communicate with it, it must be run on separate threads or processes in order to be thread-safe (meaning that the system behavior is not affected by the multiplicity of threads executing concurrently).

- If an element has high multiplicity and its performance is important to the global system performance, an application server (a software system running business logics) should be used for the element's implementation so that it can take advantage of thread and resource pooling, data caching, and dynamic element life cycle management to conserve resources.

- If the elements contain heavy computations for deployment at a particular location, a cluster of processors will enhance CPU data processing power. The cluster size and the elements' mapping to the cluster computers should be done carefully to balance each cluster's computation load and minimize the total communication traffic on the cluster's network.

- If an element is assigned complex but well-defined functions, similar to those of some commercial off-the-shelf software components, and the performance of this element is not critical, then it is more cost-effective to use an existing software component to implement the element's functions.

- A complex element can be expanded into a subsystem with its own elements and connectors. A well-defined interface should be used to encapsulate the subsystem's design and implementation details from the existing architecture.

- A complex element can be transformed into a sequence of vertical layered elements if each layer provides a virtual machine or interface to its immediate upper-layer element, and each layered element hides away some low-level system details from the upper layers.

- A complex element can be transformed into a sequence of horizontally tiered elements if the business logic can be achieved by processing data with a sequence of discrete processing stages, and these processing stages can be implemented by tiered elements with well-defined interfaces and balanced workloads.

2.4   Software Connectors

The connectors in a software architecture are refined during the design process and are heavily influenced by a project's deployment environment. In the most abstract form, a connector indicates the necessity during system execution for one of the elements to send a message to another element and potentially get a return message. During software architecture refinement, if two elements are mapped to a single process, the connector can be mapped to a local method invocation. If two elements are mapped to two different processes on the same computer, the connector can be mapped to a local message queue or a pipe. If the two elements are mapped to two different computers, then remote method invocation or web service invocation can be used to refine the connector between them.

Software connectors are classified according to many attributes, including synchronization mode, initiator, implementation type, active time span, fan-out, information carrier, and environment. Based on the connector's *synchronization mode*, we can classify all connectors into two categories: *blocking connectors* and *non-blocking connectors*, as shown in Figure 2.2 (a). A blocking connector allows one of its incident elements to send a request (method call or message) to another and wait for a response (method return value or message). The element will be blocked from further execution until it receives a response. A non-blocking connector allows one of its incident elements to send a request (method call or message) to another and then continue its execution without waiting for a response.

Based on the connector's *initiator*, we can classify all connectors into two categories: *one-initiator connectors* and *two-initiator connectors*, as shown in Figure 2.2 (b). An initiator is an incident element of a connector that can make a request to its partner. A one-initiator connector allows only one of its two incident elements to make a request to the other element, but not the another way around. A two-initiator connector allows either one of its two incident elements to make a request to the other element. For a system to support callback between its two subsystems, the two subsystems must be connected by a two-initiator connector.

The information flow on a connector can be implemented using various *information carriers*, as shown in Figure 2.2 (c). If the two incident elements are in the same process, say as two threads, they may use a shared variable to exchange information. If they are mapped to different processes on the same processor, then resources like pipes, files, or local message queues may be used to implement the connector. *Method* invocations and *message* passing are more common and more structured ways for carrying information. Remote method invocation and messaging can also allow communication among elements deployed on different processors. Figure 2.3 shows that a message system, consisting of a message sender module and a message receiver module connected by a network, is used to implement a one-initiator connector for subsystem 1 to send messages/requests to subsystem 2. A message format must be defined so both the sender and the receiver can understand the messages, and a protocol must be adopted to determine the proper handshaking and synchronization between the two parties. The two small circles in the arrows connecting the message system to the two

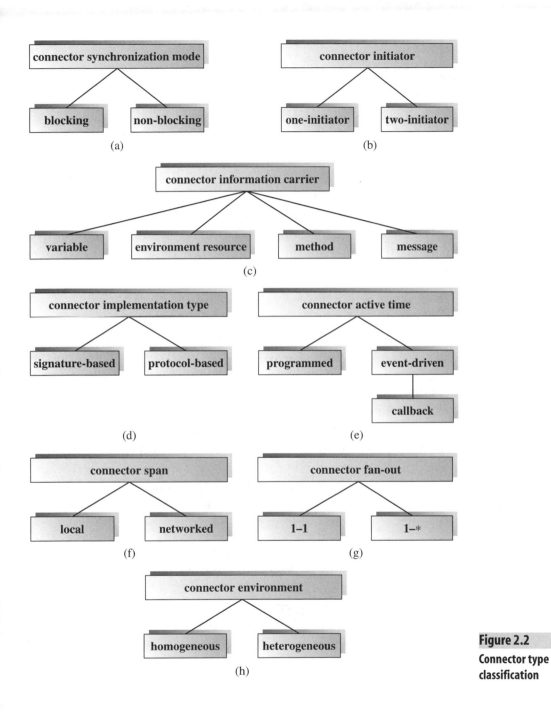

Figure 2.2

Connector type classification

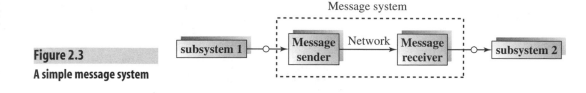

Figure 2.3

A simple message system

subsystems represent the two interfaces that connect the message system to its incident elements.

Based on the *implementation type*, a connector may be classified as *signature-based* or *protocol-based*, as shown in Figure 2.2 (d). For signature-based connectors, the method's name indicates an operation, and the parameters carry argument values for the operation's execution. If we assign one or more method parameter to indicate operation types, the connector can be used to implement protocols.

Whereas signature-based connectors can only be used to request one type of operation, a protocol-based connector can implement multiple operation types with a single binding signature. Furthermore, a protocol-based connector can support new operation types after the system interfaces are fixed. The connectors between an interpreter subsystem and its client subsystems are protocol-based. Message-based connectors support more flexible forms of protocols where all information about operations, arguments, and return values are coded in message formats and handshaking conventions among the involved parties. The HTTP protocol between web servers and web browsers is a familiar example of implementing a protocol-based connector.

Connector active time refers to when an operation request or message is sent over a connector. Connectors may be classified into *programmed connectors* and *event-driven connectors*, as shown in Figure 2.2 (e). Normally a method call will be made at a time specified during programming time: When execution comes to a line in a particular method, a call is made to another method. But for real-time systems, reactive systems, and any system with graphic user interfaces, an event-driven programming model becomes a much more flexible connection mechanism. One element will function as an event source, and all elements that need be notified of the event will register as listeners of the event source. When the event happens, all the registered listener elements will be notified for potential reaction.

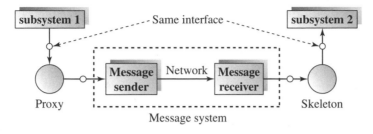

Figure 2.4
**Networked connector
implemented with the
proxy design pattern**

Method callback can be considered a special case of this event-driven mechanism. One element calls a method of another element, with one of its parameters passing a callback object/method (listener object) reference. When some event happens in the latter element, it will use the saved reference to call back and notify the first element. Event-driven connectors support late binding among subsystems.

Based on the *connector span* between incident elements, we classify the connectors as *local connectors* or *networked connectors*, as shown in Figure 2.2 (f). This connector attribute depends on whether the incident elements are located in the same processor. This attribute has major impact in the connector's implementation technologies. Networked connectors are normally implemented with the proxy design pattern to support object-oriented programming paradigm in a distributed environment. Suppose that there is a one-initiator and networked connector from subsystem 1 to subsystem 2, and subsystem 2 exposes an interface for subsystem 1 to invoke. A pair of proxy and skeleton objects will be generated from the interface by some technology-dependent tool, and they will be connected by a message system, as shown in Figure 2.4. The proxy object exposes the same interface as subsystem 2, and it is located in the same process as subsystem 1. Subsystem 1 gives the illusion that the proxy object is subsystem 2 deployed in the same process. When subsystem 1 invokes a method of the proxy object, the method body will send the operation and arguments to its skeleton partner, which is deployed in the same process as subsystem 2, over the network through the message system. The skeleton will then make the corresponding local method call against subsystem 2 and send the return value or any exceptions back to the proxy object over the message system. The proxy object will then send the received return value as its own to subsystem 1. One major advantage of this approach is that neither of the subsystems need be network-enabled at their design and implementation time.

Based on *connector fan-out* (the number of elements one element can connect to) we classify connectors as *1–1 connectors* and *1–* connectors*, as shown in Figure 2.2 (g). The 1–1 connectors are for connecting two elements only. The 1–* connectors are for connecting one element with a variable number of elements of the same type. For example, a web server and web browsers are connected with a 1–* connector, as are the server and clients in a client-server architecture. A connector's fan-out attribute may significantly impact connector implementation technology and performance.

Based on *connector environment*, which is the implementation technology or supporting platforms of a connector's two incident elements, we classify connectors into *homogeneous connectors* and *heterogeneous connectors*, as shown in Figure 2.2 (h). The incident elements of a homogeneous connector are implemented with the same programming language and software framework and run on the same operating system. The incident elements of a heterogeneous connector may be implemented with different programming languages or software frameworks and may run on different operating systems. CORBA, web services, and messaging are typical implementation technologies for heterogeneous connectors.

Heterogeneous connectors are usually implemented with the broker design pattern. This means that a message system might be implemented with the message sender and receiver modules implemented in different programming languages or on different platforms. Suppose that the two subsystems in Figure 2.4 are implemented in different programming languages and deployed on different platforms of two networked computer systems. This illustrates the broker design pattern with the following modifications.

First, the proxy object and the message sender module will be implemented in the same programming language, and run on the same computer system, as subsystem 1. The skeleton object and the message receiver module will be implemented in the same programming language, and run on the same computer system, as subsystem 2. Second, an application-level protocol will be defined to represent operations and argument values in a platform- and language-independent way. Both the proxy object and the skeleton object will support data marshaling (transforming data from a platform- or language-dependent form to the platform- and language-independent form) and unmarshaling (transforming data from the platform- and language-independent form to a platform, and language-dependent form). When the proxy object receives a method call from subsystem 1, it will marshal the argument values and send the resulting values and operation name to the skeleton object on the other side of the network, which will unmarshal the argument values into the form used by subsystem 2. Upon receiving the return value, the skeleton object will marshal it and send it back to the proxy object, which will then unmarshal the return value into the form used by subsystem 1 and return it as its own return value.

2.5 An Agile Approach to Software Architecture Design

Traditional software architecture designs, fundamentally based on a waterfall model (a linear process without integrating feedbacks), do not emphasize the iterative refinement nature and do not use element and connector attributes to capture the key architecture requirements of a software project. As a result there is big gap between a project's requirement specification and a concrete software architecture for its detailed design and implementation. Another weak point of traditional architecture design is that if the deployment environment changes, which is happening more often with the economy's globalization, the architecture design must start from scratch.

This book adopts an iterative, agile approach for developing software architectures that maximizes the reuse of architecture, design, and implementation investments. Given a project specification, an abstract high-level software architecture will first be proposed, and attributes will be identified for its elements and connectors. This abstract software architecture will generally be free of deployment considerations. The architecture will then go through multiple refinement processes to support particular deployment constraints. The unique features of this approach include the delayed binding of software connectors for more flexible implementation decisions and the seamless integration of multiple architecture styles in realizing different subsystems or levels of the same system.

In this section we incrementally extend an artificial system into a complex software architecture integrating multiple architecture styles. The resulting system is very similar to current web architecture. This example will illustrate how specification attributes can be used to refine an existing design recursively, to achieve the design objectives. This example also applies the most important software architecture styles, thus serving as a preview before their formal treatment in the following chapters.

Let us start with the design of an architecture for presenting data in a database to a client. This is a stand-alone application for serving data to a single user. Figure 2.5 shows a possible design, in which the *client GUI* module receives data retrieval criteria from the client and presents the selected data to the client in a graphical user interface. The *data retrieval & processing* module retrieves data from the database following client criteria and pre-processes the retrieved data. These two modules are supposed to run in different threads of the same process.

Now suppose the requirement specification changes and the application needs to run on a server to present the data over the Internet to multiple clients with matching client software. The connector between the *client GUI* module and the *data retrieval & processing* module now has a new *networked* attribute, as shown in Figure 2.6. Because all the clients will use the same client software to access the data server, the modules can be implemented in the same programming language using remote method invocation technology. If both of the modules are implemented in Java, then Java RMI can be used to implement the networked connector. If both modules are implemented in Windows, then Microsoft .NET remote invocation can be used to implement the networked connector.

In both of these examples, the connector between the *client GUI* module and the *data retrieval & processing* module is one-initiator, networked, and signature-based.

Now suppose we decide to support *client GUI* devices from third parties and present data in formats customizable on the server. Because we don't have control over the implementation technologies of the *client GUI* module, a message- and protocol-based connector can provide the needed flex-

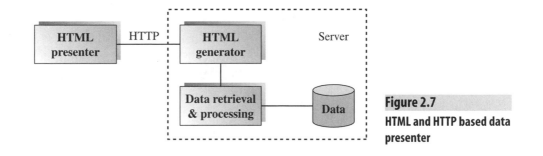

Figure 2.7
HTML and HTTP based data presenter

ibility. We use HTTP as the application-level protocol on top of the TCP/IP network connection between the client-side *client GUI* module and the server-side modules. For flexible data presentation that is modifiable on the server, we adopt the HTML markup language to specify how to present data to the client and submit client requests to the server through the HTTP protocol. As a result we introduce two tiers for data presentation: the server-side data presentation tier, implemented by the *HTML generator* module on the server, for dynamically generating HTML files; and the client-side data presentation tier, implemented by the *HTML presenter* module on the client side, for rendering data to the user according to the HTML markups. This is shown in Figure 2.7.

Now suppose we need to support significant data processing capability on the server. We apply the divide-and-conquer approach to the software architecture and divide the server-side software into three tiers: the presentation tier for generating HTML files, the business logic tier for serious data processing, and the data source tier for documents and data persistency. If we use the layered architecture style to design and implement the *HTML generator* and the *Data retrieval & processing* modules, our server-side presentation tier and business logic tier will be very similar to the web server and the application server of a typical web architecture. See Figure 2.8.

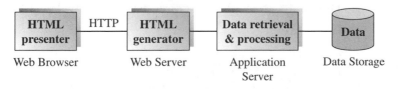

Figure 2.8
Web architecture

2.6   Summary

Software architecture determines the overall structure of a software system and greatly impacts its quality. The architecture can be viewed from multiple perspectives including the code structure (or static structure), runtime structure (or dynamic structure), and management structure (or deployment structure). Each type of structure consists of elements and connectors and their constraint attributes, which are derived from the requirements specification. To minimize the impact of changing project requirements and to maximize the ability to reuse design and implementation, an architect should adopt an iterative process during the design phase. Initial architecture designs should focus on the core functional and non-functional requirements; the resulting complex elements can then be refined into subsystems with their own architecture designs. A good architecture solution is typically based on multiple architecture styles for different subsystems or for different system abstraction levels.

2.7   Self-Review Questions

1. Which of the following structures describe the static properties of software architecture?

   a.   Software code structure

   b.   Software runtime structure

   c.   Software deployment structure

   d.   Software management structure

2. Which of the following structures describe the dynamic properties of software architecture?

   a.   Software code structure

   b.   Software runtime structure

   c.   Software deployment structure

   d.   Software management structure

3. Different architecture structures have different element and connector types.

   a.   True

   b.   False

4. Element and connector attributes are derived from the project requirements.

   a.   True

   b.   False

5. Architecture design is about choosing the right single architecture style for a project.

   a.   True

   b.   False

6. Divide-and-conquer is not a suitable methodology for architecture design.

   a.   True

   b.   False

7. Deployment decisions should be reflected in early architecture designs.

   a.   True

   b.   False

Answers to the Self-Review Questions

1. a, c, d   2. b   3. a   4. a   5. b   6. b   7. b

2.8   Exercises

1. Name at least one technology that can implement universally invocable connectors.

2. What types of connectors are used in standard four-tiered web architecture?

3. Name at least one technology that can implement self-descriptive connectors.

4. Is class inheritance a type of software architecture connector?

5. What are the main approaches to agile software architecture design?

6. What are the major types of connectors used in a university's online registration system?

2.9   Design Exercises

1. Design a high-level software architecture for a typical web-based business, and identify its major elements and connectors.

2. Design a high-level software architecture for a university's online registration system, and identify its major elements and connectors.

Suggested Reading

Bass, Len, Paul Clements, and Rick Kazman. *Software Architecture in Practice.* 2nd ed. SEI Series in Software Engineering, vol. 21, no. 26. Addison-Wesley, 2003.

CHAPTER 3

Models for Software Architecture

Objectives of this Chapter

- Introduce concepts of software architecture view models
- Discuss the UML notations as modeling tools for software architecture specification
- Discuss ADL as a modeling tool for software architecture specification

3.1   Overview

Software architecture specifies a high level of software system abstraction by employing decomposition, composition, architecture styles, and quality attributes. Every software architecture must describe its collection of components and the connections and interactions among these components. It must also specify the deployment configuration of all components and connections. Additionally, a software architecture design must conform to the project's functional and nonfunctional requirements.

There are many ways to describe software architecture. Box-and-line diagrams are often used to describe the business concepts and processes during the analysis phase of the software development lifecycle. These diagrams come with descriptions of components and connectors, as well as other descriptions that provide common intuitive interpretations. Box-and-line diagrams will be used throughout this book for specification purposes.

Figure 3.1 presents a box-and-line diagram for an online shopping business where customers browse the catalog and put their selected items in a shopping cart. After a customer checks out, the system examines the customer's

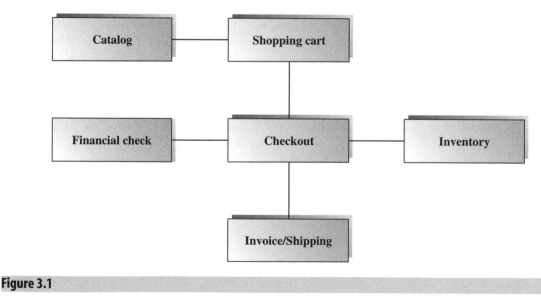

Figure 3.1

Box-and-line diagram

credit record, updates the inventory, and notifies the shipping department to process the order.

Lines in the box-and-line diagrams indicate the relationship among components. Notice that, unlike UML, the semantics of lines may vary—they may refer to dependency, control flow, data flow, etc. Lines may be associated with arrows to indicate the process direction and sequence.

A box-and-line diagram can be used as a business concept diagram describing its application domain and process concepts. This type of diagram helps us to understand the business concepts and to derive other software modeling and design diagrams such as UML. UML is one of the object-oriented solutions used in software modeling and design. We discuss this further in Section 3.2.

The 4+1 view model is another way to show the functional and nonfunctional requirements of a software project. There are five views in the model: the logical view, the process view, the development view, the physical view, and the user interface view. The logical view is used to identify software modules and their boundaries, interfaces, external environment, usage scenarios, etc. The process view addresses nonfunctional requirements such as module communication styles and performance issues at runtime. The development view organizes the software units in well-defined ways according to the actual file or directory structure. The physical view specifies the deployment infrastructure in terms of software, hardware, networking configurations, and installation for delivery purposes. All of these views work with, and are validated by, the scenarios view. The user interface view provides the look and feel of the system, and it may also impact other views. We explore the details of the 4+1 view model in Section 3.3.

The Architecture Description Language (ADL) is another way to describe software architecture formally and semantically. A simple software architecture specification example is demonstrated in Section 3.4.

3.2   UML for Software Architecture

The Unified Modeling Language (UML) is a graphical language for visualizing, specifying, constructing, and documenting the artifacts of a software-intensive system. UML offers a standard way to draw a system's blueprints including conceptual notions such as business processes and system functions as well as concrete designs such as programming language statements, database schemas, and reusable software components. UML is a typical object-oriented analysis and design notation tool that provides many useful analysis diagrams and even generates code skeleton.

UML is widely used as a guideline for software requirement analysis and design documents, which are the basis for software development. Typically, UML can be used to model the problem domain; describe the user requirements; identify significant architecture elements during software design, such as classes and objects; describe behavior and interactions among these elements; and organize the software structure, specify its constraints, describe the necessary attributes, and more.

UML provides several modeling diagrams that can be grouped into two major categories: structural (static) and behavioral (dynamic). Structural software architecture describes the static structure of all software elements in a system: class hierarchy, class library structure, and relationships between classes such as inheritance (is a), aggregation (has a), association (uses a), and messaging (method invocation). Static structural UML diagrams depict the control flow between system elements, and are time-independent. These can be class diagrams, component diagrams, deployment diagrams, etc.

A dynamic software architecture describes the behavior of objects (i.e., instances of classes) in the system such as object collaboration, interaction, activity, and concurrency. The related UML diagrams are sequence diagrams, collaboration diagrams, activity diagrams, etc.

They are many UML IDE (Interactive Development Environment) tools available; some of them are open source. The most popular UML tools are Rational Rose, Boland Together, and Microsoft Visio. Many of these are capable of mapping from UML diagrams directly to coding framework in popular programming languages such as C++, C#, and Java.

The following table summarizes the 13 UML 2.0 diagrams in the structural and behavioral categories:

1. Structural (Static) Diagrams

Diagram	Description
Class	An overview of classes for modeling and design. It shows how classes are statically related, but not how classes dynamically interact with each other.
Object	Objects and their relationship at runtime. An overview of particular instances of a class diagram at a point of time for a specific case. It is based on the class diagram.
Composite structure	Describes the inner structure of a component including all classes within the component, interface of the component, etc.
Component	Describes all components in a system, their interrelationships, interactions, and the interface of the system. It is an outline of the composition structure of components or modules.
Package	Describes the package structure and organization. It covers classes in the package and packages within another package.
Deployment	Describes system hardware, software, and network connections for distributed computing. It covers server configuration and network connections between server nodes in real-world setting.

2. Behavioral (Dynamic) Diagrams

Diagram	Description
Use case	Derived from use-case study scenarios. It is an overview of use cases, actors, and their communication relationships to demonstrate how the system reacts to requests from external users. It is used to capture system requirements.
Activity	Outline of activity's data and control flow among related objects. An activity is an action for a system operation or a business process, such as those outlined in the use-case diagram. It also covers decision points and threads of complex operation processes. It describes how activities are orchestrated to achieve the required functionality.
State machine	Describes the life cycle of objects using a finite state machine. The diagram consists of states and the transitions between states. Transitions are usually caused by external stimuli or events. They can also represent internal moves by the object.
Sequence	Describes time sequence of messages passed among objects in a timeline.
Interaction overview	Combines activity and sequence diagrams to provide control flow overview of the system and business process.
Communication	Describes the sequence of message passing among objects in the system. Equivalent to sequence diagram, except that it focuses on the object's role. Each communication link is associated with a sequence order number plus the passed messages.
Time sequence	Describes the changes by messages in state, condition, and events.

In the following section, we provide details of the aforementioned diagrams.

3.2.1   Structural Diagrams

The structural description diagrams comprise class and object diagrams; component, structure, and package diagrams; and deployment diagrams. We discuss each in turn.

3.2.1.1 Class Diagram

The class diagram provides a static view of the system. It captures the vocabulary of the designed system. It is the foundation diagram of the system design and the most frequently used UML diagram as well.

Class diagrams can be derived from use-case diagrams or from text analysis of the given problem domain. A class diagram is generated by system analysts and designers and will be iteratively refined in the subsequent phases during the software development life cycle.

Class diagrams describe each individual class with its type, interface, properties, and methods. The accessibility (visibility) of each attribute and operation can also be specified. Popular accessibility modifiers include *private, public, protected*, and *default.*

One important part of a class diagram is the interface of each class. A class interface provides the behavioral contracts that the class must support.

There are three main relationships among classes: inheritance, aggregation, and association. These relationships can be represented graphically in a class diagram. For each relationship, multiplicities among classes can also be denoted. Typical multiplicity types include one-to-one, one-to-many, and many-to-many mappings. In UML multiplicity notations, 1 stands for one instance, 0 stands for no instance, 0..1 stands for zero or one instance, and 1..* stands for at least one instance.

Figure 3.2 shows a class diagram for an online purchase order processing system. Here we see all kinds of relationships among classes such as inheritance (represented using hollow triangle arrows), aggregation (represented using hollow diamond arrows), and association (lines without arrows). The multiplicity indicators are also shown. Generally, the diagram describes the logical structure of a purchase order system that consists of six classes. The customer class is the base class of new and existing. A customer can place zero or more orders. Each order consists of multiple itemlines, which in turn, contain items.

A class diagram may be refined from time to time during the software development life cycle. Object diagrams and component structure diagrams can be derived directly from a class diagram. Other dynamic behavioral diagrams such as sequence diagrams and communication (collaboration) diagrams are also based on the class diagram.

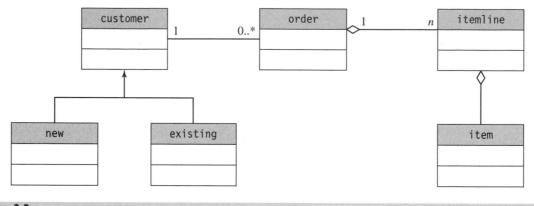

Figure 3.2

Class diagram

We will revisit class diagrams in Chapter 4 when we discuss the methodology of object-oriented design in detail. We will explore many issues related to specifying relationships among classes (e.g., inheritance, dependency, association, aggregation, and composition) in establishing the logical model of a system.

3.2.1.2 Object Diagram

Objects are the instances of classes. The object diagram is used to describe a sample subset of objects in the system at a specific point in time. This diagram shows a snapshot of class instance connection and interaction. It is derived from the preceding class diagram and is a concrete example of the class diagram at runtime. Many other behavioral diagrams (sequence diagrams, communication diagrams, and interaction diagrams) may make reference to the object diagram.

Figure 3.3 shows an object diagram based on the class diagram in Figure 3.2. Each rectangular box in the diagram represents an object that is an instance of some class. The diagram tells us that the customer with identification #1234 has ordered two items: book and gift.

3.2.1.3 Composite Structure Diagram

The composite structure diagram is used to describe the composition of interconnected elements or the collaboration of runtime instances. There are two basic notations in a composite structure diagram: collaboration (represented using a dashed eclipse) and structured class (represented

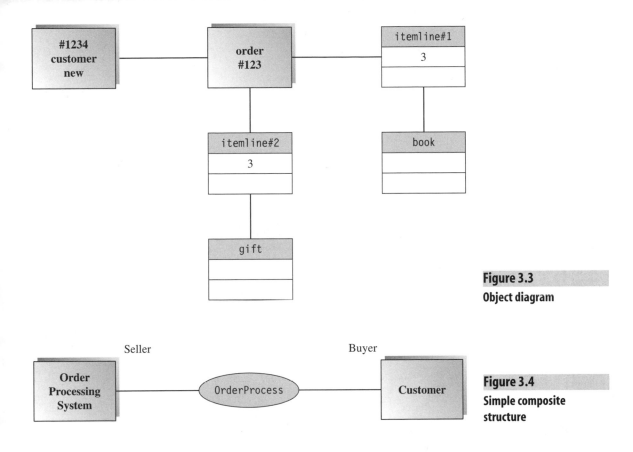

Figure 3.3
Object diagram

Figure 3.4
Simple composite structure

using a rectangular box). Each structure class may have an annotation that indicates its role in the collaboration. For example, Figure 3.4 describes two classes involved in an OrderProcess collaboration. The Customer class plays the role of "buyer" and the Order Processing System plays the role of "seller." Notice that OrderProcess is neither a class nor an object, it is a collaboration.

3.2.1.4 Component Diagram

A component is neither a class nor an object. A component is a deployable, reusable building block used in software design and development. For example, a JavaBean component is deployed in a jar file, an EJB component is deployed in an ear file, and a .NET component is deployed in a .dll file. Each component has an interface to expose its services and hide its implementations. The interface is the contract between a reusable component and its clients.

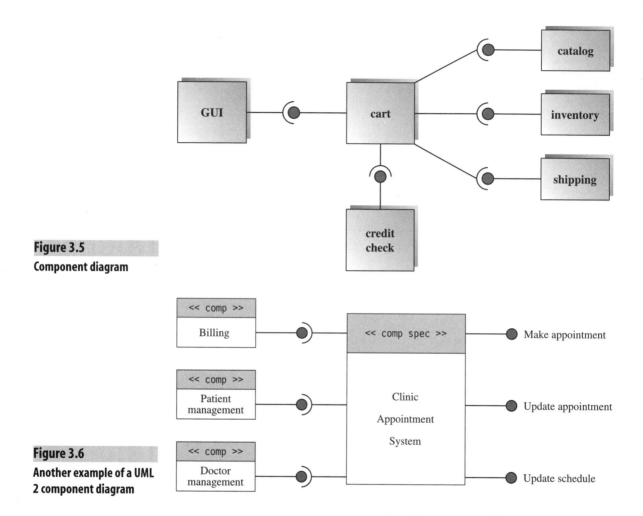

Figure 3.5

Component diagram

Figure 3.6

Another example of a UML 2 component diagram

UML 2.0 introduced a new notation for components and their connections. A lollipop shape of a component represents an implemented interface. A cup shape represents the required interface, and the required interface must be provided by some other components. In a component diagram, some of the components may exist and be available in-house or on the market. Other components are designed and developed by those working on the project.

Figure 3.5 shows a component diagram for a shopping cart application. The *cart* component provides services to front-end GUI interfaces such as ASP, JSP, or PHP web pages. The *cart* component itself may need services from other components: *catalog*, *inventory*, *shipping*, and *credit-check*.

The component diagram in Figure 3.6 shows four components: the *clinic* component, the *billing* component, the *patient* component, and the *doctor* component. The *clinic* component provides the following services (in the form of interface): *make appointment* by *patient,* *update appointment* by *patient,* and *update schedule* by *doctor.* The *clinic* component also needs services from the *billing* component, *patient* component, and *doctor* component.

3.2.1.5 Package Diagram

A package is represented by a tabbed folder that indicates where all included classes and subpackages reside. Packages play a similar role as a directory for grouping files in a file system; they allow the organization of all closely related classes in one "container."

For example, namespaces in .NET and packages in Java provide well-formed structures for class accessibility and class correlations. We can organize functionally related classes in the same package so that these classes can access each other within a default accessibility or visibility. We can also organize related packages in a same parent package to build a class and package hierarchy just like .NET class library and Java API. Another reason for using the package organization is namespace sharing; in this way, all classes in the same package have a unique name but they may have the same name in different packages (namespaces).

A package diagram shows the dependency relationship between packages in which a change of one package may result in changes in other packages. The package diagram may also specify the contents of a package, i.e., the classes that constitute a package and their relationships. The use of package diagrams to represent system structures can help reduce the dependency complexity and simplify relationships among groups of classes.

Figure 3.7 shows a simple package diagram in which the *checkout* package, containing all *checkout*-related classes, depends on classes grouped in the *shopping cart* package. Same with the user *interface* package which has all GUI presentation classes to render the *catalog* and *shopping cart.* The package diagram also describes the dependency relationship of the package units. This diagram is often used for component-based software architecture design.

3.2.1.6 Deployment Diagram

A deployment diagram depicts the physical configuration of the software system deployed on hardware server nodes and the network between the nodes (defined as protocols). This diagram is generated in the later phase of the software development life cycle. All components in the system must be

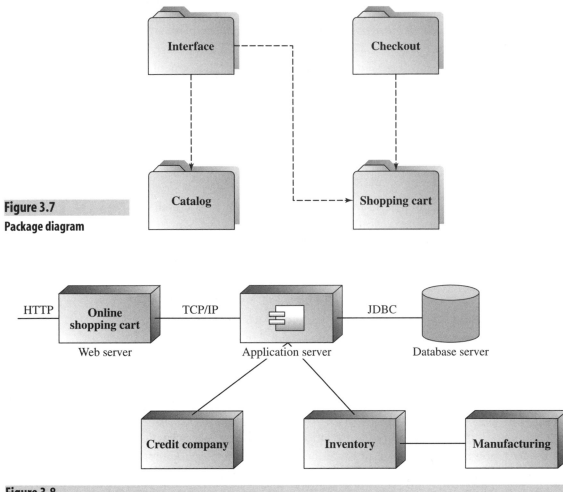

Figure 3.7

Package diagram

Figure 3.8

Deployment diagram

deployed on servers to provide services via network protocols. Component diagrams are the basis for deployment diagrams.

UML uses a cube symbol to represent a computing resource node; such a resource can be a hardware device or a deployed software subsystem. For example, data servers, web servers, and application servers can be nodes and are described by cubes in a deployment diagram. The link between nodes is the network connection depicted by the network protocol. The deployment diagram is used widely to model and design distributed software systems.

Figure 3.8 shows a deployment diagram in which a shopping cart is deployed in a web server, the business transaction component is deployed in a separate application server, and the database is available in a data server. The other services are available from three components deployed by the corresponding service providers.

3.2.2   Behavioral Diagrams

The behavior description diagrams comprise use case diagrams, activity diagrams, state machines, interaction diagrams, sequence diagrams, collaboration diagrams, and timing diagrams. We discuss each in turn.

3.2.2.1 Use Case Diagram

Use case diagrams describe user requirements in terms of system functionality as a contract between the users (actors) and the software system. This diagram consists of actors, use cases, and the links between them. An example of a use case is shown in Figure 3.9.

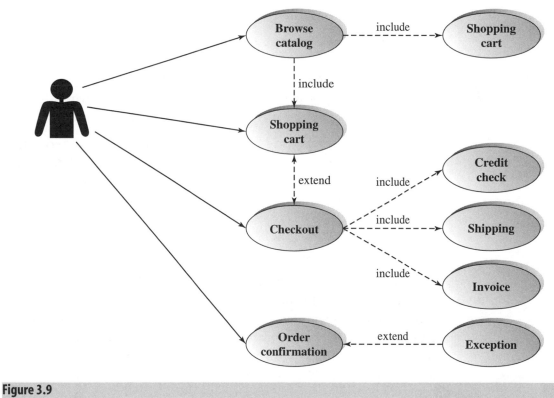

Figure 3.9

Use case diagram

An *actor* in a use case diagram is an external "user"; this may be a human end user, an application, an external device, or another system.

Each use case is a meaningful operational work scenario. That is, use cases are scenario-oriented in the sense that each is a sequence of working steps to be carried out by classes in order to provide the required system functionality. The detailed steps are specified in a separate note including the pre- and post-conditions of the action in the sequence.

The (simple) connection link from actor to use case shows the direction of actors using the use case. An <<include>> link, a special kind of link, from one use case to another, indicates that the first use case reuses or includes the second use case and is needed to complete the work necessary to fulfill the requirement. The <<include>> link is a dashed line with an arrow pointing to the reused use case. An <<extend>> link, another special link, shows a newly created optional use case from an existing use case. It covers alternative cases that may or may not necessarily take place. An <<extend>> link is also a dashed directed line with an arrow pointing toward the extended use case; these special links are labeled accordingly.

A complete use case diagram describes a set of scenarios; scenarios may have a set of subordinate, or lower-level, use cases. Use case diagrams are used in the early stages of the software development life cycle, such as analysis and design. These diagrams are one of the most frequently used UML diagrams for object-oriented system analysis and design.

System analysts employ use case diagrams to capture and verify user requirements. Architects and designers use these diagrams to derive structural diagrams (e.g., class diagrams) and behavioral diagrams (e.g., sequence diagrams and communication diagrams).

3.2.2.2 Activity Diagram

An activity diagram is used to describe complex business processes. This diagram typically involves complex workflow, decision making, concurrent executions, exception handling, process termination, etc. An activity diagram is a workflow-oriented diagram describing the steps in a single process. One activity diagram corresponds to one business process. There are many activities in a business process, and this diagram explores their dependency within the process.

UML activity diagrams use a rounded rectangle to represent an activity. Each activity diagram has a starting point and one or more finishing points. A small diamond represents a decision point in the diagram. Activity diagrams support parallel processing using a pair of black horizontal bars to indicate the corresponding fork/join actions in such pathways. UML activity diagrams also support communication between two concurrent flows by sending signals from one path to another. (This is called an event and is noted as a pair of convex polygons.)

An activity diagram gives a detailed dynamic view of a specific task or process within a system so that the software developer can easily recognize the implementation requirements. This diagram is a basis for a communication diagram and other dynamic interaction diagrams.

Figure 3.10 shows a partial set of activities in a purchase-order-processing system. The first black bar splits (forks) two concurrent activities that can

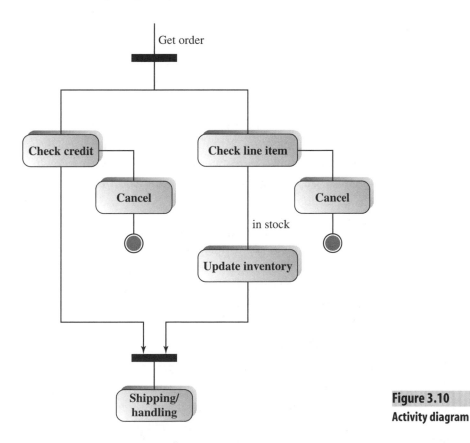

Figure 3.10
Activity diagram

be executed in parallel. The shipping/handling activity will not start until both of them complete and join together (indicated by the second bar at the bottom).

3.2.2.3 State Machine Diagram

A state machine diagram, called a state chart in UML 1.x, is widely used for embedded systems and device software analysis and design. It is an event-oriented diagram in which the system's elements change their states in response to external or internal stimuli (such as time events or other system events). These diagrams are ideal for specifying the internal behavior of objects.

In a state machine diagram, a state is a rounded rectangle with three subdivisions: state name, state variables, and state activities. A state is a situation in which an object meets conditions, takes actions, and waits for a new event. When a new event takes place in the current state, the machine will perform specified actions and then will enter a new state (the next state).

A complex composite state may have a subordinate state diagram. The substates in a composite state may be transited from one to the next, sequentially or concurrently.

Each state machine diagram has one starting point in a solid black circle and has one or more endpoints, the latter indicated by eye-circles. The transition links between states are solid lines with arrowheads to indicate direction. State diagrams help software developers understand how a system responds and handles external events and the corresponding event-triggering condition.

Figure 3.11 shows a state machine diagram that depicts a login process. Initially, the state machine executes a busy loop to wait for user login, and then the username/password pair is verified. If the pair matches the system records, the login is confirmed; otherwise the login is rejected.

3.2.2.4 Interaction Overview Diagram

An interaction overview diagram describes the control flow of the interactions rather than the message. It is a variant of the activity diagram. The nodes in an interaction overview diagram represent either a reference to an

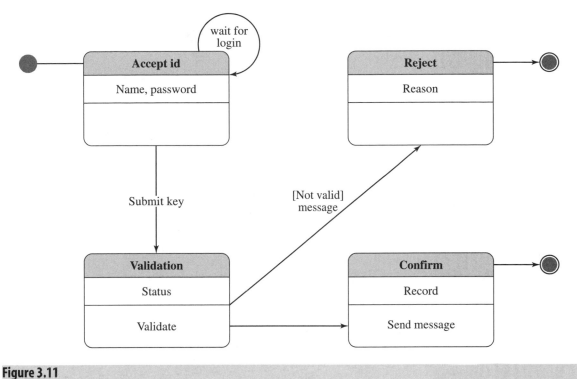

Figure 3.11

State machine diagram

existing diagram (ref), a basic interaction element [activity diagram(ad)], or a sequence diagram(sd)].

Each node (or frame) can be an interaction diagram such as a sequence diagram, communication diagram, activity diagram, or nested interaction overview diagram. A reference node, indicated by "ref" in the upper left-hand corner of the frame, points to an existing diagram, while the basic element displays the frame's dynamic interaction diagram. A basic element is indicated by an "ad" label for an activity diagram, an "sd" label for a sequence diagram, or a "cd" label for a communication diagram, and so on. The interaction overview diagram is a high-level abstraction of an interaction overview description.

Figure 3.12 presents an example interaction overview diagram showing reference diagrams that point to other UML diagrams and one "ad" diagram displaying a detailed activity diagram.

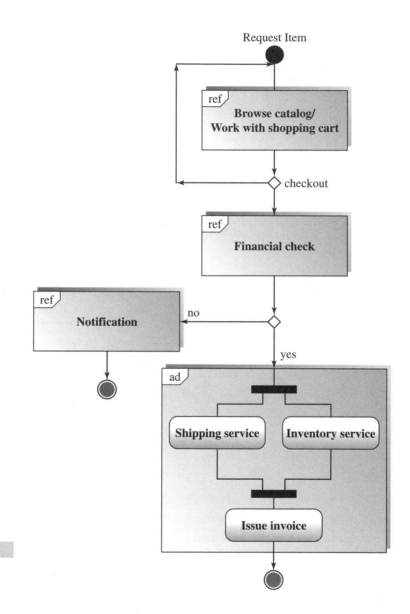

Figure 3.12

Interaction overview
diagram

3.2.2.5 Sequence Diagram

A sequence diagram is one of the most important and widely used UML
diagrams for software system analysis and design. It is a time-oriented interaction diagram showing the chronological sequence of messages between
objects. Usually, one sequence diagram corresponds to one use case.

Each participant object in this diagram has a vertical timeline for its life
cycle. Time goes forward along with the downward timeline. Each vertical

timeline has a number of narrow rectangular boxes (called activations) representing the object-activated state in which it receives or sends out messages. Each activation box may also have a self-recursive directed link pointed back to itself, indicating that the object passes messages to itself. An activation may also branch or fork many separate lifelines for the if-selection scenario conditions; eventually all forked lines will join together.

Passing messages between objects is represented by a horizontal arrow link from the source to the destination. A simple transfer message line, represented by a solid line with an arrowhead, transfers control from one object to the other. An object can send a synchronous message to another object by a line with a full arrowhead. A synchronous message means that the sender must wait for a reply from the target object before it can move forward in the timeline. An object can also send an asynchronous message to another object, which is indicated by a line with a half arrowhead. The sender of an asynchronous message can continue its work down the time-line without waiting for a return message from the target object.

Figure 3.13 shows a simplified sequence diagram for online shopping. The sequence of message exchanges starts from the *cart* object. After a *browse* message, the *cart* object sends a message to *checkcart* to check out. *Checkcart*

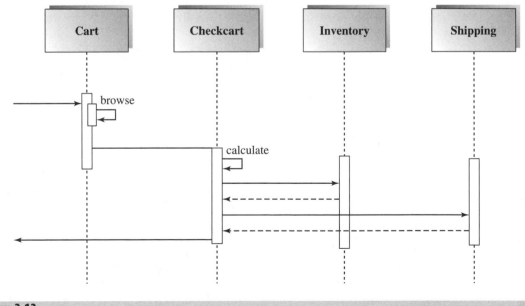

Figure 3.13

Sequence diagram

does a calculation (i.e., via self-message *calc*) and then sends a message to *inventory*. The message from *heckcart* to *inventory* is a synchronous one, because *checkcart* has to wait for the *response* message (represented using a dotted arrow line). Then *checkcart* contacts *shipping* and finally sends back a message to the actor that initiated the use case.

3.2.2.6 Communication or Collaboration Diagram

The UML communication diagram, known as the collaboration diagram in UML 1.x, is a message-oriented diagram that describes all message passing sequences, flow control, object coordination, etc., among the objects that participate in certain use cases. It summarizes how objects in the system receive and send messages. It is an extension of the static object diagram in which the links between objects represent association relationships. Above the links in a communication diagram are the numbered messages, indicating the order in which they are sent or received. The messages tell the receiver to perform an operation with specified arguments. Every communication diagram is equivalent to a sequence diagram, i.e., a communication diagram can be converted to an equivalent sequence diagram and vice versa. These two types of diagrams provide a message-oriented and time-oriented view, respectively.

Figure 3.14 shows an example of a communication diagram. It is equivalent to the sequence diagram shown in Figure 3.13 except that message names are given.

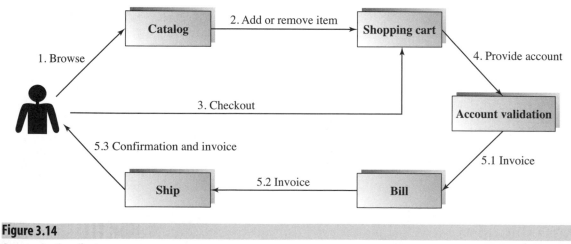

Figure 3.14

Communication diagram

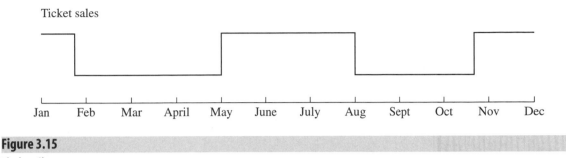

Ticket sales

Jan   Feb   Mar   April   May   June   July   Aug   Sept   Oct   Nov   Dec

Figure 3.15
Timing diagram

3.2.2.7 Timing Diagram

The timing diagram is a new diagram in UML 2.0. It combines the state diagram and time sequences to show the dynamic view of state change caused by external events over time. It is often used in time-critical systems such as real-time operating systems, embedded system designs, etc. Figure 3.15 shows a timing diagram for seasonal discount air ticket prices.

3.3   Architecture View Models

A model is a complete, simplified description of a system from a particular perspective or viewpoint. There is no single view that can present all aspects of complex software to stakeholders. View models provide partial representations of the software architecture to specific stakeholders such as the system users, the analyst/designer, the developer/programmer, the system integrator, and the system engineer. Software designers can organize the description of their architecture decisions in different views. Stakeholders can use a view to find what they need in the software architecture.

The 4+1 view model was originally introduced by Philippe Kruchten (Kruchten, 1995). The model provides four essential views: the logical view, the process view, the physical view, and the development view. The logical view describes, for example, objects and their interactions; the process view describes system activities, their concurrency and synchronization; the physical view describes the mapping of the software onto the hardware, the server, and the network configuration; and the development view describes the software's static structure within a given development environment.

There is also another view called the scenario view; this view describes the scenarios that capture the most important aspects of the functional requirements, drive the system design, and validate the system. The 4+1 view

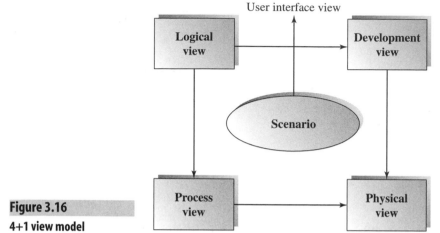

Figure 3.16

4+1 view model

model is a multiple-view model that addresses different aspects and concerns of the system. The 4+1 view model standardizes the software design documents and makes the design easy to understand by all stakeholders.

We extend the 4+1 view model with one more view, the user interface (UI) view. The UI view, for end users of the software system, describes the graphical user interface to verify and validate the user interface requirements; these significantly impact the system usability and other quality attributes.

Figure 3.16 shows the 4+1 view model extended with our fifth view, the user interface view. The scenario view is coherent with the other four views, whereas the user interface view complies with the scenario view and is supported by the other four views.

3.3.1   The Scenario View

The scenario view describes the functionality of the system, i.e., how the user employs the system and how the system provides services to the users. This view provides a foundation for the other four views and lets them work together seamlessly and coherently. It helps designers to discover architecture elements during the design process and to validate the architecture design afterward. So, the scenario view helps to make the software architecture consistent with functional and nonfunctional requirements.

The UML use case diagram and other verbal documents are used to describe this view. The stakeholders of this view are end-users, architects, developers, and all users of the other four views. Figure 3.9 on page 49 describes a use case diagram for online shopping.

The scenario view is used to drive architecture design in the earlier phases of software development and is also used for software validation at later phases of the development cycle.

3.3.2 The Logical or Conceptual View

The logical view is based on application domain entities necessary to implement the functional requirements. It focuses on functional requirements, the main building blocks, and key abstractions of the system. The logical view is an abstraction of the system's functional requirements. It is typically used for object-oriented (OO) modeling from which the static and dynamic system structures emerge. The logical view specifies system decomposition into conceptual entities (such as objects) and connections between them (such as associations). This view helps to understand the interactions between entities in the problem space domain of the application and their potential variation. In an object-oriented system, the architecture elements may be classes and objects.

The logical view is typically supported by UML static diagrams including class/object diagrams and UML dynamic diagrams such as the interaction overall diagram, sequence diagram, communication diagram, state diagram, and activity diagram. The class diagram is used to describe the conceptual or logical view. A class diagram defines classes and their attributes, methods, and associations to other classes in the system. A class diagram is static in the sense that it does not describe any user interaction nor any sequence of module interaction in the system.

A block diagram can also be used to provide an overview of the whole system. A sequence diagram shows how objects in the system interact. A communication diagram shows system objects and the message passing between them in time order.

In summary, the logical view points out all major tasks the system must complete, and presents the major components and their static relationships. The stakeholders of the logical view are the end-users, analysts, and designers. We can apply an object-oriented design methodology in the logical view because the view itself is object-oriented.

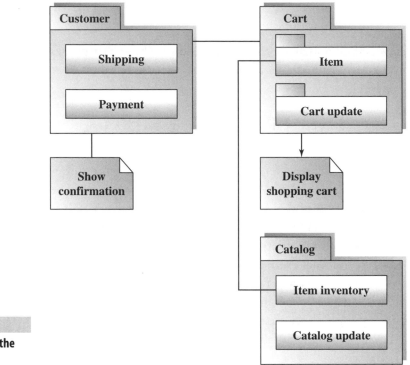

Figure 3.17

Package diagram in the development view

3.3.3   The Development or Module View

The development view derives from the logical view and describes the static organization of the system modules. Modules such as namespaces, class library, subsystem, or packages are building blocks that group classes for further development and implementation. This view addresses the subsystem decomposition and organizational issue. The software is packaged and partitioned into small units such as program libraries or subsystems created by many teams of developers. Each package has its own visibility and accessibility as package or default scope visibility (see static structure discussion on page 42).

The development view maps software component elements to actual physical directories and files. UML diagrams such as package diagrams and component diagrams are often used to support this view. The stakeholders of this view can be programmers and software project managers.

Figure 3.17 shows a simple development view using a package diagram.

3.3.4   The Process View

The process view focuses on the dynamic aspects of the system, i.e., its execution time behavior. This view also derives from the logical view. It is an abstraction of processes or threads dealing with process synchronization and concurrency. It contributes to many nonfunctional requirements and quality attributes such as scalability and performance requirements.

The process view looks at the system's processes and the communications among them. A software system can be decomposed into many runtime execution units. How to organize all execution units at runtime is presented in this view. The quality attributes such as performance, scalability, concurrency, synchronization, distribution, and system throughput are all addressed in the process view. This view maps functions, activities, and interactions onto runtime implementation with a focus on nonfunctional requirements as well as the implementation of the functional requirements.

The process view takes care of the concurrency and synchronization issues between subsystems. It can be described at several levels of abstraction, from independently executing logical networks of communicating programs to basic tasks running within the same processing node. The process view must also address nonfunctional requirements such as multithreading and synchronous/asynchronous communications for performance and availability. The UML activity diagram and interaction overview diagram support this view.

Figure 3.18 presents an activity diagram that documents the process view. Notice that after the *check credit* step, two processes are spawned to run concurrently.

The stakeholders of this view are the developers and integrators. Many architecture styles such as pipe and filter, multi-tier, and others can be applied in the process view.

3.3.5   The Physical View

The physical view describes installation, configuration, and deployment of the software application. It concerns itself with how to deliver the deployable system. The physical view shows the mapping of software onto hardware. It is particularly of interest in distributed or parallel systems. The

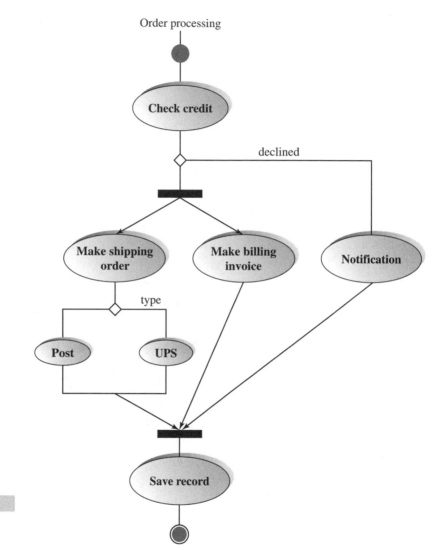

Figure 3.18
Activity diagram in the process view

components are hardware entities (processors), and the links are communication pathways; together these specify how the various elements such as communication protocols and middleware servers found in the logical, process, and development views are mapped onto the various nodes in the runtime environment.

A physical view also takes into account the system's nonfunctional requirements such as system availability, reliability (fault-tolerance), throughput

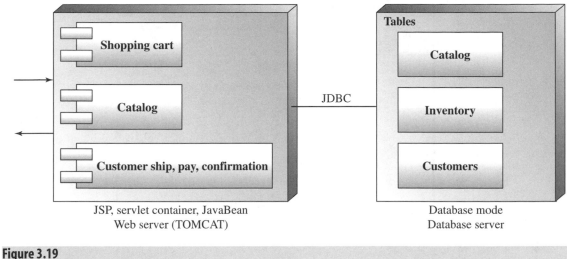

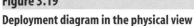

Figure 3.19
Deployment diagram in the physical view

performance, scalability performance, and security. For example, software can be delivered in different hardware and networking layouts, which will result in significant differences in these quality attributes.

The system topology in terms of hardware, network, and other infrastructure is all part of this view. This view explains the nonfunctional requirements and quality attributes such as performance, availability, reliability, and scalability. The physical view must address network connections and communication protocols such as server nodes and multi-tier distributed environment configurations. The UML deployment diagrams and other documentation are often used to support this view.

The stakeholders of this view are system installers, system administrators, system engineers, and operators. Figure 3.19 presents an example of a deployment diagram showing that the order processing system is deployed on two servers.

3.3.6   The User Interface View

The User Interface (UI) view is an extended view that provides a clear user-computer interface view and hides implementation details. This view may be provided as a series of screen snapshots or a dynamic, interactive prototype demo. Any modification on this view will have direct impact on the scenarios view. The screenshot in Figure 3.20 shows a GUI user interface for an online shopping cart.

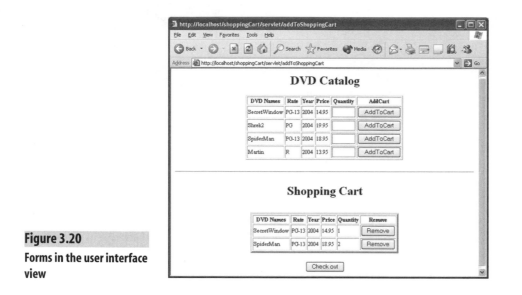

Figure 3.20

Forms in the user interface view

In summary, the 4+1 view is an architecture verification technique for studying and documenting software architecture design. Each view provides a window into the different aspects of the system. The 4+1 view covers all aspects of a software architecture for all stakeholders. The views are interconnected; thus, based on the scenarios view, we can start with the logical view, move to the development or process view, and finally go to the physical view. The user interface view is also established during this process.

The 4+1 view architecture model is available in the Rational Rose IDE kit.

3.4 Architecture Description Language (ADL)

An ADL is a notation specification providing syntax and semantics for defining software architecture. It also provides designers with the ability to decompose components, combine components, and define interfaces of components. An ADL is a formal specification language with well-defined syntax and semantics used to describe architecture components and their connections, interfaces, and configurations.

Garlan and Shaw (1996) list the following requirements for an ADL:

- *Composition:* "It should be possible to describe a system as a composition of independent components and connections." Large systems should be built from constituent elements, and it should be possible to consider each element independently of the system.

- *Abstraction:* "It should be possible to describe the components and their interactions in a way that describes their abstract roles in a system." It should not be necessary to consider implementation issues while specifying the architecture.

- *Reuse:* Reusability should be built-in at the component and connection level. The derivation of architecture patterns should also be supported to facilitate the reuse of architecture descriptions.

- *Configuration:* Architecture descriptions should enable comprehension and modification of an architecture without examination of each component and connector.

- *Heterogeneity:* "It should be possible to combine multiple, heterogeneous architectural descriptions."

- *Analysis:* The use of an ADL should facilitate the analysis of an architecture design. Analysis might include consideration of throughput, deadlock, input/output behavior, and scheduling.

A number of ADLs have been proposed over the last few years. These include UniCon and Wright, both from CMU; C2sadel from UC Irvine and USC; Rapide from Stanford; and Darwin from Imperial College, London. Acme is another ADL available in the research community. UML can also provide many of the artifacts needed for architecture descriptions, but is not a complete or sufficient ADL.

Let's take a close look at one of the ADLs listed earlier. Acme provides a formal and semiformal way to describe a software architecture as a static structure in a high-level of abstraction. This ADL provides many building block elements for architecture design description. Three of these basic elements are components, connectors, and systems; additional elements include ports, roles, representations, and rep-maps. Component elements can be any computing or data store units. Connectors represent interactions among components. The connector elements implement the communication and interactions among components in a system, such as synchronous or asynchronous communications.

Components and connectors in Acme play the same roles as boxes and lines in the block (box-and-line) diagram. However, they have a more specific purpose. For example, components have interfaces that are defined by a set of ports. Each port identifies a contact point between the component and its clients. A component may provide multiple interfaces by using different types of ports. A simple port may represent only a single procedure signature.

Connectors also have interfaces defined by a set of roles. Each role represents an interaction participant of the connector. A simple binary connector has two roles, such as the *caller* and *callee* roles of an RPC connector, the *reading* and *writing* roles of a pipe, or the *sender* and *receiver* roles of a message passing connector. Multiple role connectors may serve multiple roles; for example an event broadcast connector might have a single *event-publisher* role and multiple *event-receiver* roles.

Here, we present several examples showing how the Acme ADL and the AcmeStudio tool work together.

As shown in the following screenshot, a user can conveniently construct an architecture design using the AcmeStudio tool. The simple design consists of two components, a client and a server, connected by a connector. This architecture style is the client/server model. We can define the name and properties of each component and the connector in the diagram. The diagram can be translated by AcmeStudio to a specification in the Acme language. Any constraints preset by designers in the specification can be examined by AcmeStudio. The AcmeStudio also has plug-ins for many other checks, such as portability analysis. The Acme specification can also be used to construct a code framework in popular programming languages such as C++.

The next screenshot shows the architecture description (in Acme) generated automatically by AcmeStudio.

The architecture description generated by AcmeStudio may be translated into C++ or Java implementation as illustrated here.

```
System event-listener  =
{
     Component Client = { Port send-request; };
     Component server = { Port receive-request; };
     Connector broadcast = {
       Roels {event-announcer, event-receiver}
     };
     Attachments {
       Server.receive-request to broadcast.event-anouncer;
       Client.send-request to broadcast.event-receiver;
     }
}
```

The next screenshot shows an example of multiple users with a single-server architecture design.

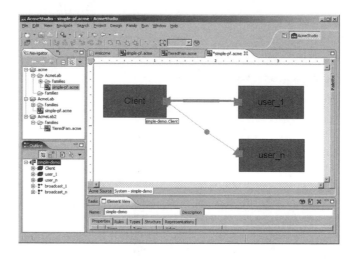

There are multiple event-receivers for a single event-announcer in this simple architecture. The following is the ADL architecture description generated by AcmeStudio.

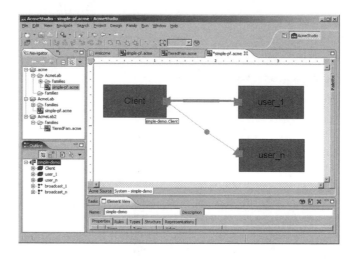

From the AcmeStudio demo we see that an ADL can be used to describe an architecture design using a description language with its own syntax and grammar. A software architecture specified by an ADL can be used to generate the implementation code, which makes the developer's job much easier.

3.5   Summary

Decomposition is the most important step in software design. The separation of software architecture into multiple views helps by reducing complexity; it also allows for the optimization of design guidelines such as low coupling and high cohesion within and between elements of a system. Multiple architecture views can also help with design trade-offs between software quality attributes.

An architecture design is based on the software requirement specification and generated in the design phase of the software engineering life cycle. The software architecture must satisfy the functional requirements as well as the nonfunctional requirements.

UML is a common modeling language for specifying complex software systems. It is widely accepted in the software industry for software analysis and design. This chapter discussed how to use UML to specify software architectures, to simplify the OO design, and to improve software design quality. UML notations are useful tools in describing software architectures. UML is also used in the 4+1 view model. This view model describes not only the functional requirements but deals with nonfunctional requirements as well. The 4+1 view model is a blueprint for the next phase of software development.

This model derives the software architecture's description from several viewpoints. Different views represent different aspects of the software; all views are based on use cases or the scenario view. The user interface view (added by the authors) is an end-user external view supported by all the other views, including the scenario view.

In this chapter, we also introduced Architecture Description Languages (ADLs); these are formal or semi-formal notations to describe software architecture.

In the next part of this book, we will discuss all the architecture styles in detail and you will find a case study chapter showing different styles applied to the same problem, which results in different quality attributes.

3.6   Self-Review Questions

1. Which of the following notations is used to support the logical view?

   a.   Sequence diagram

   b.   Collaboration diagram

   c. State diagram

   d. All of the above

2. Which of the following notations is used to support the physical view?

   a. Sequence diagram

   b. Collaboration diagram

   c. State diagram

   d. None of the above

3. Activity diagrams are used to support the process view.

   a. True   **b.** False

4. Deployment diagrams are used to support the physical view.

   a. True   **b.** False

5. Component diagrams are used to support the development view.

   a. True   **b.** False

6. The software submodules and their interfaces are described in the logical view.

   a. True   **b.** False

7. Concurrency control activity is part of the process view.

   a. True   **b.** False

8. System and network configuration decisions are part of the physical view.

   a. True   **b.** False

9. Software architecture is concerned only with functional requirements.

   a. True   **b.** False

10. Prototyping can be used to support UI design.

   a. True   **b.** False

11. ADL is a programming language.

   a. True   **b.** False

12. ADL can produce target code.

    a. True   **b.** False

13. ADL is used only for software architecture specification.

    a. True   **b.** False

14. UML diagrams are used for system analysis and design.

    a. True   **b.** False

15. Use case diagrams are generated in the early stages of the SDLC, whereas deployment diagrams are generated in the later stages of the SDLC.

    a. True   **b.** False

16. Composite structure diagrams are based on object diagrams.

    a. True   **b.** False

17. Component diagrams are based on object diagrams.

    a. True   **b.** False

18. A UML diagram must provide a complete view of the entire software system.

    a. True   **b.** False

19. A component is a class or an object.

    a. True   **b.** False

20. Asynchronous message invocation can be expressed in sequence diagrams.

    a. True   **b.** False

21. Conditional branching can be represented in sequence diagrams.

    a. True   **b.** False

22. An activation in an object lifeline may have its own cycle message pointed back to itself in a sequence diagram.

    a. True   **b.** False

23. An interaction overview diagram is based on all low-level interaction diagrams.

    a. True   **b.** False

Answers to the Self-Review Questions

1. d 2. d 3. a 4. a 5. a 6. a 7. a 8. a 9. b 10. a 11. b 12. a 13. b 14. a 15. a 16. a 17. a 18. a 19. b 20. a 21. a 22. a 23. a

3.7　Exercises

1. List all interaction UML diagrams.

2. List all structural UML diagrams.

3. List all early phase SDLC UML diagrams.

4. List all late phase SDLC UML diagrams.

5. Describe the relationship between sequence diagrams, communication diagrams, and interaction diagrams.

6. Enumerate the problem domains suitable to state machine diagrams.

7. List problem domains suitable to time diagrams.

8. In what case is the activity diagram a good choice?

9. What is ADL?

10. What is the 4+1 view model?

11. Describe the logical view in the 4+1 view model.

12. Does the 4+1 model work only with object-oriented design methodology?

13. Can ADL support a non-object-oriented model system?

14. Which diagrams are the static UML diagrams?

15. Which diagrams are the dynamic UML diagrams?

16. Is the component diagram used only for component-based design?

17. Is a 4+1 view model changed once it is released?

18. Is an ADL specification changed once it is released?

3.8　Design Exercises

1. Draw a use case diagram for an ATM machine transaction application software.

2. Draw a class diagram and object diagram for an ATM machine transaction application software.

3. Draw a state machine diagram and a sequence diagram for an ATM transaction application software.

4. Draw a use case diagram for a student online registration software system.

5. Draw a class diagram and an object diagram for a student online registration software system.

6. Draw a sequence diagram and a communication diagram for a student online registration software system.

7. Draw package and deployment diagrams for a student online registration software system.

8. Draw a component diagram for a hotel reservation system. Assume there are four components: customer, reservation, hotel, and billing. The billing component is available for reuse.

9. Use the 4+1 view model to describe an online bookstore software architecture.

10. Use the 4+1 view model to describe an inventory control software architecture.

11. Make the inventory control system part of the online bookstore system.

12. Use ADL to describe an online camping registration system for a national park.

3.9   Challenge Exercises

1. Use UML to model the software architecture of an online trusted payment system. The system users are buyer, seller, payer, and security trustee. There are many e-payment selections available. The buyers may be consumers, corporations, or organizations. The sellers may be merchants, service providers, and others. The payers may be banks, financial services, credit card companies, etc. The trustee may be a security service, transaction auditing company, etc.

   The system supports payment selection, security services, transaction protection, and process flow management. The system administrator is also a special system user.

2. Use UML to model the nationwide chain motel online reservation system. The system provides the reservation request service for room selection, date selection, reservation deposit handling, reservation cancellation, and reservation confirmation. The system also provides online information about location, direction, facility, motel photos, etc.

References

Garlan, David and Mary Shaw. *Software Architecture: Perspectives on an Emerging Discipline.* Upper Saddle River, NJ: Prentice Hall, 1996, 39–40.

Kruchten, Philippe. "Architectural Bluprint—The '4+1' View Model of Software Architecture." *IEEE Software,* vol. 12, no. 6. (1995): 42–50.

Suggested Reading

AcmeWEB. "The Acme Project." ABLE Project, Carnegie Mellon University, 2006, http://www.cs.cmu.edu/~acme/ (accessed in 2007).

The Object Management Group. "Unified Modeling Language." *Catalog of OMG Modeling and Metadata Specifications,* http://www.omg.org/technology/documents/modeling_spec_catalog.htm#UML (accessed in 2007).

The Object Management Group. "UML 2.0 Specification." Unified Modeling Language (UML), 2004, http://www.omg.org/technology/documents/formal/uml.htm.

Sparx Systems Pty Ltd. "UML Tutorial." 2005, http://www.sparxsystems.com.au/UML_Tutorial.htm.

CHAPTER 4

Object-Oriented Paradigm

Objectives of this Chapter

- Introduce concepts of object-oriented software architecture
- Describe a complete object-oriented analysis and design process
- Discuss general design principles in the context of object-oriented design

4.1   Overview

This chapter introduces you to the object-oriented (OO) analysis and design paradigm. A very popular design approach, object orientation applies to many of the software architecture styles introduced in later chapters. You may choose to skip this chapter if you are already familiar with the OO paradigm.

The popularity of the OO analysis and design paradigm is the logical result of the wide adoption of OO programming languages. OO programming languages did not become popular until the early 1980s. However, their history dates back to 1960s when high-level programming languages were still in their infancy. Simula 67 is probably the first programming language that introduced OO concepts such as objects, classes, inheritance, and virtual procedures. From the 1980s on, many programming languages were designed as pure OO languages or enhanced to include OO features. Typical examples include SmallTalk, Eiffel, C++, Ada, and CLOS.

OO software engineering is a much broader concept than OO programming. It refers to the whole process of analysis, design, and programming following the object-oriented paradigm. The output of OO analysis is a model of the requirements. OO design transforms this model into an architecture object design (or blueprint) to guide the next phase in software engineering—code development. Finally, OO programming produces code by using OO programming languages or tools. There are generally three main OO principles that are applied throughout the whole OO software engineering process: *encapsulation*, *inheritance*, and *polymorphism*.

- *Encapsulation:* Often called information hiding, the purpose of encapsulation is to separate interface from implementation. By hiding the implementation details that are likely to change, encapsulation allows for flexibility in design. For example, a *stack* interface can define two public operations, *push* and *pop*, that are available to other parts of the program. However, its internal data organization, e.g., whether to use a linked list or an array for storing stack elements, can be hidden.

- *Inheritance:* Developers can define new classes that derive from existing base classes, thus inheriting the base classes' interface elements (attributes and operations) and implementation of operations. Inheritance allows software reuse, hence improving the effectiveness of software development.

- *Polymorphism:* Polymorphism refers to the ability of an object to behave differently and assume different forms based on its inheritance hierarchy. Polymorphism includes vertical *override* operations between parent classes and derived classes, and horizontal *overloading* operations within the same class.

The object-oriented paradigm is a very important methodology in software development. Many of the architecture patterns (e.g., component-based, pipe and filter, data repository, etc.) can be implemented using the OO paradigm. Therefore, understanding the OO concepts will be important for understanding later chapters.

4.2   Introducing the Object-Oriented Paradigm

This section starts with the review of classes and objects, which are the building blocks of an OO design. Then you will investigate various relationships that exist among classes.

4.2.1   Classes and Objects

A class groups together related data and their operations. An object is an instance of a class. A class defines the attributes and behaviors shared by all of its objects. Although the syntactic description of a class may vary in different languages, it generally consists of three elements: a class name, a list of attributes, and a list of operations.

4.2.2   Relationships

In the OO paradigm, the blueprint of a design usually is represented using a class diagram. To describe a system, both dynamic and static descriptions must be provided. The dynamic (behavioral) specification describes the relationships among objects, e.g., how objects of the system accomplish the required functionalities via message exchanging. At the static (logical) level, the relationships among classes are described. Classes may be derived from other classes by composition and by inheritance. Classes may have other consistency requirements that are similar to those in relational database theory. Next you will have a brief review of the various static relationships among classes: composition, aggregation, association, and inheritance.

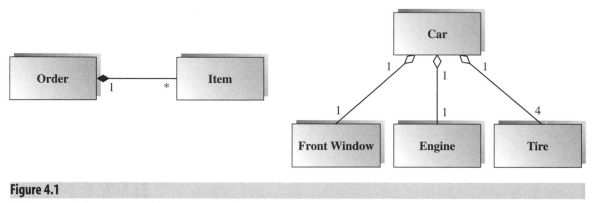

Figure 4.1

UML representation of composition and aggregation

4.2.2.1 Composition

Composition represents the whole/part relationship between classes. For example, an online order may consist of multiple items. Such a relationship is called "composition." In composition, the parts of a class have the same lifespan as their owner, and the parts cannot be involved in another composition. This restriction usually is enforced by the constructor and destructor operations of a class. For example, when an online order instance is destructed, all of its items are destructed. In UML, a composition relationship is represented using a solid diamond arrowhead. The diagram on the left of Figure 4.1 is an example of composition.

4.2.2.2 Aggregation

A similar but more relaxed compositional relationship is called aggregation. In UML, aggregation is represented using a hollow diamond arrowhead. Parts involved in an aggregation relationship do not have to share the same lifespan as the owner. In addition, they may be involved in more than one aggregation relationship. For example, a faculty member can serve as a committee member of multiple academic conferences at the same time. Or, to use the example of the windshield of a car, it exhibits an aggregation relationship as shown on the right side of Figure 4.1. Whereas in a composition relationship, the description of an object means that all of its attributes must be de-allocated from memory. In an aggregation relationship these attributes may instead be reused by other objects.

4.2.2.3 Association

Association represents the logical relationship among classes. Composition is one specific type of association. In UML, an association is represented by a solid line and it has the following parts: name of the association, end type at each end of the association link, and multiplicity at each end. For example, the upper portion of Figure 4.2 describes the relationship between a Customer class and an Order class. The name of the association is *place-order*. The solid triangle next to the name indicates the direction of the association, and the association reads as *Customer place-order on Order*. The type on the left end is composition, which, together with the multiplicities "*1*" and "***" at both ends, indicates that one Customer can place multiple Orders, and that each Order is associated to exactly one Customer. The right end arrow indicates the navigation relation. It means that from an instance of Customer it is possible to reference all Order instances that are associated with that Customer. In coding, navigation usually is accomplished by including a collection of references to the destination class as attributes of the source class.

A dependency relation can be regarded as a special type of binary association in which class X depends on class Y, if changes to the elements of Y lead to the changes of X. Usually class X depends on Y if X invokes Y's operation or accesses Y's attributes. For example, if the Shipping Dept class needs to access the list of products in an Order to estimate the shipping cost, then the Shipping Dept class depends on the Order class. If the Order class is recompiled, the Shipping Dept class may need to be re-compiled. In UML, the dependency relationship is denoted by a dotted arrow line. The bottom part of Figure 4.2 is one example of dependency. In OO design, it is desirable to minimize the number of dependency relationships. This not only expedites compiling, but also reduces the possibility of cascading modifications in design.

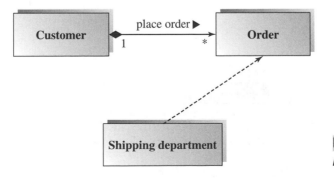

Figure 4.2
An example of association

4.2.2.4 Inheritance

In an OO design, very often two or more classes may have a large set of attributes and operations in common. To prevent repeatedly writing the same code for similar classes, OO provides the inheritance mechanism. When class A is derived from class B, class A inherits all attributes and operations of class B unless otherwise specified (e.g., private attributes are not to be inherited by derived classes). One special case of the inheritance association is polymorphism. Operations of base classes can be overridden by derived classes so that a base class reference (which points to an instance of a derived class) can exhibit different behaviors at runtime.

In UML, the inheritance relationship is represented using a line with a closed arrowhead. If the line is dashed, it is a *realization* relationship. In a realization relationship, the base class is an abstract class, i.e., a class that does not provide implementation for each of its operations, and the derived classes have to implement all their inherited operations. Figure 4.3 presents the inheritance relationship among three classes. The Regular and Member classes derive from the Customer class. Both of these classes inherit attributes such as custID and totalSpending from the Customer class. However, the two derived classes also use two different ways to track customers. For a Regular customer, a cookie number is used to track the user's browser. For a registered Member, user name and password are used for identification. Registered Members receive discounts according to their shopping history.

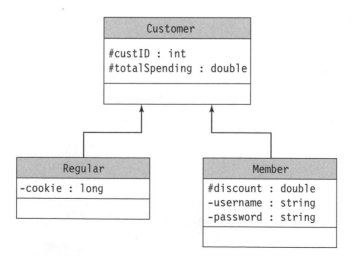

Figure 4.3

An example of inheritance

4.2.2.5 Composition vs. Inheritance

The OO paradigm provides two different approaches for reusing a design: composition (aggregation) and inheritance. In practice, how designers choose between the two depends on a number of principles. For example, suppose that you have two base classes: Person and House. How do you model a house owner? Do you model the HouseOwner class as a derived class of both Person and House? Or would you model it as a class that has two attributes referencing Person and House, respectively? Or would you rather model HouseOwner as a derived class of Person but with an attribute of House? Here are three general principles to follow to make the right decision:

- Use the inheritance relationship only when the derived class "is-a" base class. For example, a HouseOwner is a Person; however, a House-Owner is not a House. Thus, the HouseOwner class should not inherit from the House class.

- Composition (or aggregation) can be used to model the "has-a" relationship among classes. For example, it is natural to include an attribute referencing to House in the HouseOwner class, because a HouseOwner has a House.

- Be careful when using inheritance. Inheritance could possibly weaken the encapsulation of an OO design (Venners, 1998).

Consider the following scenario in Figure 4.4(a). An AmericanCitizen has to pay federal tax each year, the amount of which is based on the yearly income. The calculation of tax rate is a very complicated process, and fortunately it is encapsulated in the ReportTax() operation of the AmericanCitizen class. American-Lawyer and AmericanProfessor are derived from AmericanCitizen and inherit its attributes. Notice that, in the current design, ReportTax() returns an integer. A fourth class IRS is implemented by another group of designers, and it invokes the ReportTax() function of each derived class to collect tax. Now suppose that the system designer of AmericanCitizen decides to increase the accuracy of tax reports, and changes the return type of ReportTax() to a floating point number. What happens? The implementation of IRS has to change, because ReportTax() does not return an integer anymore.

Clearly, one weakness of inheritance is that changes to the design of a base class may lead to cascading changes to derived classes and the users of derived classes. This problem can be solved by using a delegation mechanism provided by the aggregation approach. Consider the classes shown in

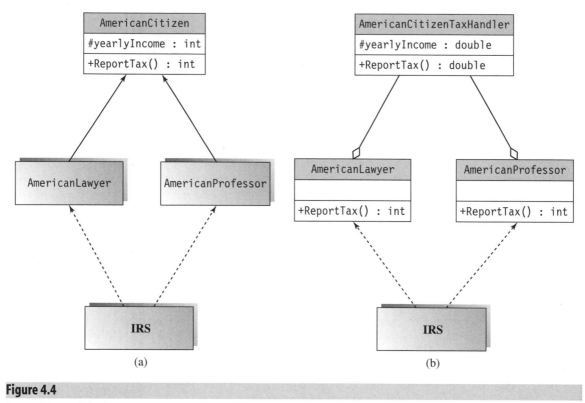

Figure 4.4

Composition vs. inheritance

Figure 4.4(b). To handle tax related affairs, an AmericanCitizenTaxHandler class is created. Each of the AmericanLawyer and AmericanProfessor class has an attribute referencing an instance of AmericanCitizenTaxHandler. Both AmericanLawyer and AmericanProfessor provide the operation ReportTax(), which invokes the ReportTax() operation provided by AmericanCitizen-TaxHandler, rounds the double number to an integer, and returns the result. Such delegation mechanisms allow great flexibility—while the invocation interface provided to IRS can remain intact, the implementation of ReportTax() can be changed by replacing the tax handler classes at any time.

You might wonder, what about polymorphism? In Figure 4.4(a), if IRS needs to invoke the ReportTax() of a list of American citizens, programmers can simply use an AmericanCitizen reference to iterate through the list and invoke the operation. However, it is not able to do so in Figure 4.4(b) because AmericanLawyer and AmericanProfessor are two separate classes.

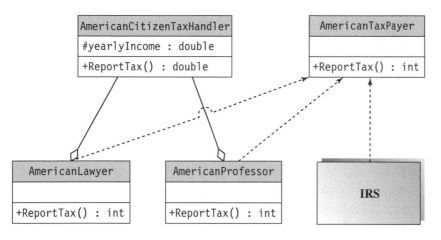

Figure 4.5
Refined design of Figure 4.4 (b)

In Figure 4.5 an improved design of Figure 4.4(b) is provided. Both American-Lawyer and AmericanProfessor realize an interface called AmericanTaxPayer. AmericanTaxPayer defines a public operation ReportTax(), which has to be implemented by both the AmericanLawyer and AmericanProfessor classes. On the other hand, the actual processing work of ReportTax() is done by the AmericanCitizenTaxHandler class—the ReportTax() operation of AmericanLawyer and AmericanProfessor simply rounds and returns the result generated by AmericanCitizenTaxHandler. Thus the design in Figure 4.5 enjoys the benefits provided by both inheritance and aggregation.

4.3 OO Analysis

The next two sections guide you through the complete process of OO software development. Generally an OO development process has three stages: OO analysis, OO design, and OO implementation. The first stage, OO analysis, is concerned with initial domain and problem requirement analysis. As a result, it establishes an object-oriented abstract model of the system to be built. The results produced by OO analysis are then utilized during the design phase. In the design process, responsibilities are assigned to each class that constitutes the system. The attributes and operations of each class also are determined in the design stage. Finally, the OO design is implemented using an OO programming language. This is followed by testing, deployment, and product maintenance. For a more thorough discussion of OO analysis and design, you can consult *UML 2 and the Unified Process: Practical Object-Oriented Analysis and Design* (Arlow and Neustadt, 2005).

Throughout the chapter, a case study is used to illustrate the main concept of OO analysis and design. You will design a web application for this case study. (However, notice that, OO analysis and design can be used in many other application domains.) Assume that you are going to construct an Order Processing System (OPS). OPS is an important part of an online store. The online store has the following subsystems: an online product catalog for user browsing; the order processing system for user orders; the financial department, which contacts credit card companies for financial charges; and the shipping department, which is responsible for packaging products and shipping. OPS must interact with other components and provide the following service to customers:

- Each customer has an online shopping cart, which allows him to add and remove items to be purchased.

- A customer is able to check out using a credit card. A transaction is approved only when the financial department has verified the credit card.

- Before the transaction is completed, a customer should be able to learn about his order's estimated arrival date, which is determined by the order processing time of the shipping department.

- A customer can choose to cancel the transaction by clearing all items in the shopping cart.

- OPS must be available as a web accessible system. Customers can use popular Internet browsers to interact with OPS.

Next you will proceed with OO analysis of the OPS system. The purpose of OO analysis is to understand the application domain and specific requirements of the system. The outcome of the analysis stage is a requirement specification and an initial analysis of the logical structure and feasibility of the system. Different from the traditional software analysis process, OO analysis relies on two UML tools: use case diagram and analysis-class diagram. The UML use case diagram captures user requirements. The analysis-class diagram describes the conceptual abstractions in the system and breaks down the system into components so that the complex design process can be divided and conquered.

4.3.1   Step 1: Design of a UML Use Case Diagram

An effective approach to understanding a system is to build use case diagrams to describe the functionality of a system. A use case diagram consists of multiple actors and use cases. Here an actor is a role played by a user—a user might be a real person, an organization, a computer system, or a component of the whole software system. A use case may be a concrete use case, or an abstract one. A use case is composed of other use cases, and can be extended by other use cases. Figure 4.6 shows the use case diagram of *OPS*. To come up with the details of such a diagram, developers must go through a time-consuming interview process with all stakeholders of the system.

As shown in Figure 4.6, OPS has three actors: the customer, the financial department, and the shipping department. A customer can register an account as a new user. A customer can also interact with the system in a session to conduct a number of operations. These operations include logging in, logging out, adding an item into the shopping cart, deleting an item from the shopping cart, clearing the shopping cart, and checking out the shopping cart.

Each use case (represented using an oval in Figure 4.6) is accompanied by a brief text description, which specifies the flow of events associated with the use case. Based on the flow of events, sequence diagrams can be developed

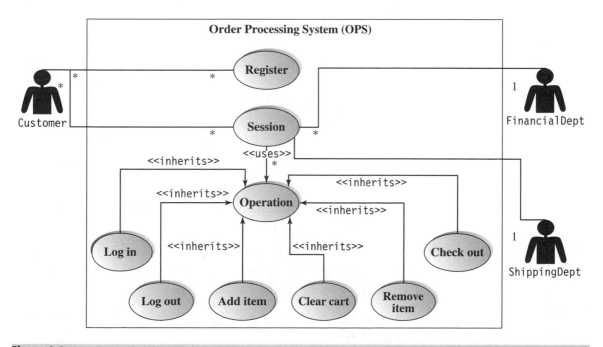

Figure 4.6

Use case diagram of the OPS system

in the detailed-level design stage. In the following, a number of use cases in Figure 4.6 are described.

- *Register:* A customer visits the registration page and specifies the desired user name and password. If there is already an existing user name/password pair, the system reports error; otherwise, it reports success. When registration is completed, the user name, password, real name, and the billing address are stored in a database system.

- *Session:* When a customer logs in using the correct user name and password, the customer starts a session. During the session, the system maintains a shopping cart for the user, which records the list of items the customer wants to purchase. The session is terminated when the user checks out the shopping cart, logs out of the system, or times out. A session consists of a list of operations.

- *Operation:* The operation use case is an abstract use case. It is extended by more specific operations such as log in, log out, adding an item, removing item, clearing the cart, and checking out.

- *Log in:* This is always the first operation of any session. When the supplied user name and password are correct, a session starts. A maximum number of three trials is allowed for each user to submit the correct user name and password. The account is locked if a user fails to log in after three times.

- *Log out:* When the customer has not checked out all items in the shopping cart, the shopping cart is saved in the database so that when the customer logs in again, his shopping cart is loaded with those items.

- *Add item:* Before an item is added to the shopping cart, the catalog and inventory database should be checked to verify availability, cost, and price of the item.

- *Remove item:* By removing an item from the shopping cart, the item is put back into the inventory database.

- *Clear shopping cart:* This use case removes all items from the shopping chart.

- *Checkout:* The user is asked to input credit card information, which is then sent to the financial department for verification. If the transaction is approved, the credit card is charged; otherwise, the system prompts the user that the checkout process has failed. When the transaction is successful, instructions are sent to the shipping department.

Usually in an OO design, each use case is monitored by a `controller` class, especially when the use case has a complex event flow. Sometimes a use case can be modeled as an operation, if its logic is simple. Next, you will proceed to the development of an analysis class diagram.

4.3.2   Step 2: Develop an Analysis Class Diagram via Noun Extraction

Another useful tool for describing a system in its entirety is the analysis class diagram (also called a conceptual class diagram). An analysis class diagram describes the key classes of a system and their interrelationships but is not the design of the system. An analysis class diagram describes the functionality of the system in terms of abstractions (classes) of the concepts found in the problem and the domain. It captures the functionalities and logical relationships among the different elements of the system. It is a model of the system, abstracting design details so that people can better understand the system's overall architecture. In the design stage, the class diagram will be further refined; the relationships among the classes might be changed or fine-tuned to trade for speed, economy, or other system requirements.

Because the details of each class will be furnished in the design stage, a set of simpler graphical notations can be used in an analysis class diagram. Many UML editors (such as Visio) provide UML stereotypes, or extensions, that include the three graphical notations shown in Figure 4.7: `boundary` class, `entity` class, and `controller` class. Boundary classes are those classes that

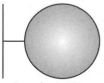
Boundary Class

Entity Class

Controller Class

Figure 4.7

Three types of classes in an analysis class diagram

serve as the interface between a system and the outside world. These are usually in the form of graphic user interface classes (e.g., web forms, windows dialogs, browser plug-in widgets, etc.) or wrapper classes of other systems (e.g., middle-ware wrappers of remote procedures). Entity classes are used to represent the information stored and exchanged among elements of the system. For example, the product information in OPS should be modeled as an entity class. Controller classes control and coordinate the activities of other classes. Usually a controller class is associated with one specific use case or a set of closely related use cases. A controller class coordinates the interactions that are required to accomplish the use case. For example, it is appropriate to model the session of the OPS system as a controller class. The session class must maintain and keep track of all related information, such as shopping cart and customer identity information. It has to interact with other components of the system, such as the financial and shipping departments, to ensure that each operation in the session is executed. The session class handles exceptions thrown out by any of its operations.

- To construct an analysis class diagram, developers must first identify the classes that constitute the system. One simple approach is to extract nouns and verbs from the use case descriptions. Nouns are candidates of classes and verbs are candidates of their functions and relations. For example, take a look at the registration use case shown in the following (where nouns are in italics):

- *Register:* A *customer* visits the *registration page* and specifies the desired *user name* and *password.* If there is already such a *user name/password pair,* the *system* reports *error;* otherwise, it reports *success.* When the *registration* is completed, the *user name, password, real name,* and the *billing address* are stored in a *database system.*

The following nouns are extracted from the register use case description. (Notice that not all of the nouns will be represented as classes.)

- *customer:* actors (which are outside of the system) need not be represented. Consequently, customer should not be a class of the system.

- *registration page:* modeled as a boundary class.

- *user name:* an attribute, not a class. It is modeled as an attribute of the CustomerIdentity class.

- *password:* similarly, this is an attribute of `CustomerIdentity`.

- *username/password pair:* attributes of `CustomerIdentity`.

- *system:* the phrase "system reports error" in the initial description of the use case is not accurate enough. It should be rephrased as "errors are reported in a `RegistrationErrorPage`." Thus a `RegistrationErrorPage` should be created as a `boundary` class.

- *error:* it should not be modeled as a class, following the same argument for system.

- *success:* following the same argument for system, `RegistrationSuccessPage` is created as a `boundary` class.

- *registration:* refers to the registration process. You have to create a `controller` class named `RegistrationController` for this use case.

- *real name:* part of the `CustomerInformation` class.

- *billing address:* part of `CustomerInformation` class.

- *database system:* the catalog and inventory database systems are out of the scope of OPS. However, a `wrapper` class (i.e., `boundary` class) called `CustomerInfoDB` is created to interact with the database.

After the analysis on the `Registration` use case, the following classes are now included in the analysis class diagram:

- `RegistrationPage`: a `boundary` class for registration.

- `RegistrationErrorPage`: a `boundary` class for reporting registration error.

- `RegistrationSuccessPage`: a `boundary` class for concluding the registration process.

- `CustomerIdentity`: an `entity` class that records the user name and password of a customer.

- `CustomerInfomation`: an `entity` class that records the information of a customer, including `CustomerIdentity`, real name, and billing address.

- `CustomerInfoDB`: a `boundary` class that manipulates the customer information database.

- `RegistrationController`: a `controller` class which coordinates the registration process.

By examining other use cases, the following classes are identified:

- `SessionController`: a `controller` class for coordinating a session. This class provides various operations for logging in, logging off, adding items, deleting items, clearing the shopping cart, and checking out.

- `BrowserPage`: a `boundary` class for browsing the product catalog.

- `LoginPage`: a `boundary` class for logging in.

- `LogoutPage`: a `boundary` class for logging off.

- `CheckoutPage`: a `boundary` class for accepting user credit card information and checking out.

- `CheckoutSuccessPage`: a `boundary` class for presenting success information and a receipt.

- `CheckoutFailurePage`: a `boundary` class for presenting failure information.

- `ShoppingCartPage`: a `boundary` class for displaying the contents of a shopping cart and allowing the customer to add/remove items.

- `FinancialDeptWrapper`: a `boundary` class for interacting with the financial department.

- `ShippingDeptWrapper`: a `boundary` class for interacting with the shipping department.

- `InventoryDB`: a `boundary` class for interacting with the inventory database.

All user operations (such as adding and deleting items) are included as operations of the `SessionController` class. An alternative way is to map directly from the use case diagram—declare an abstract class called `operation`, and then make each related use case a derived class of the `operation` class. The first solution is chosen because of its simplicity.

Shown in Figure 4.8 is the analysis class diagram that is developed as the result of the preceding analysis. Notice that `boundary` classes account for the majority of the design. This is normal for most web portal systems. Most of the relations shown in Figure 4.8 are association with navigation. For example, from each web page you can navigate to the corresponding `controller` object (either `RegistrationController` or `SessionController`), and

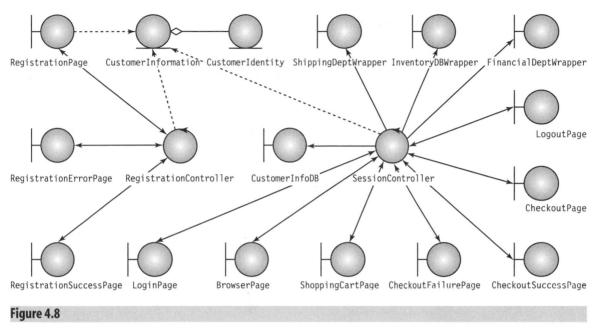

Figure 4.8
Analysis class diagram of OPS

from the controller you can navigate to all pages. Such associations are natural because each web page needs a controller object for handling events, and the controller object needs access to every page so that it can coordinate the entire customer service process by redirection of web pages. Usually navigation is accomplished by including a reference attribute in a class design, for example, each registration-related web page should have a reference to the RegistrationController object. Notice that both the RegistrationController and SessionController classes depend on the CustomerInformation class because they pass CustomerInformation objects as parameters when invoking operations provided by CustomerInfoDB.

With the domain and requirement analyses complete, you can now proceed to the design stage. Notice that the UML use-case diagram and analysis class diagram are very useful in the OO design process. For example, from use-case descriptions designers are able to derive interaction diagrams such as sequence diagrams and communication diagrams. From the use case diagram and analysis class diagram, Class-Responsibility-Collaborator (CRC) card analysis can be applied to discover more classes needed for detailed design. These techniques will be covered in the next section.

4.4   OO Design

The goal of design is to develop the structural architecture of a system. There are numerous design approaches, including structured design, data-driven design, event-driven design, real-time design, and others. All of these approaches break down the problem into manageable pieces. A unique feature of OO design is that a system is decomposed into logical components called classes. For each class, its interface, consisting of public attributes and public operations, is clearly specified in the design stage. Then, in the implementation stage, the interface of each class is translated into code using an OO language.

Generally, OO design can be split into two stages: high-level (conceptual) design and low-level (detailed) design. In high-level design, all classes needed for building the system are identified and each class is assigned a certain responsibility. Then a class diagram is constructed to further clarify the relations among the classes. Based on the analysis of use cases, interaction diagrams also are drawn to depict the flow of events. In low-level design, attributes and operations are assigned to each class based on the interaction diagrams. Then state machine diagrams are developed to describe further design details.

4.4.1   Step 1: Identify Classes—CRC Card

An analysis class diagram presents an abstract logical structure of the system. The classes included in this diagram may be only a subset of the classes that are needed by the system. In the following, you will use the CRC modeling approach to identify classes and assign them responsibilities. Originally proposed by Kent Beck and Ward Cunningham, CRC card modeling has been used widely for OO analysis (Beck and Cunningham, 1989).

CRC card modeling is a team-based approach. To play the cards, a team (usually six people at most) needs a collection of 4″ × 6″ cards. Each card is used to define the responsibilities of one class. As shown in Figure 4.9, a CRC card consists of three sections: class name, responsibility, and collaborator.

In CRC modeling, a *responsibility* of a class is a task that must be performed by the class or the knowledge that is known by the class. For example, one responsibility of the `SessionController` class in OPS might be to perform the adding item operation. `SessionController` also has to know how to nav-

Class Name	
Responsibility	**Collaborators**

Figure 4.9
CRC card template

igate to the wrapper object of the CustomerInfoDB database. This can also be regarded as a responsibility.

A collaborator is a class that is involved in accomplishing the responsibility of a class. For example, to add an item to the shopping cart, the InventoryDB object is contacted to save the contents of the shopping cart to the database. Hence, InventoryDB is a collaborator for the adding_item responsibility of the SessionController class.

Three types of participants play CRC cards: (1) domain users, (2) OO design analysts, and (3) facilitators. Domain users are the experts in the business model. They know the business logic well and should have good communication skills for explaining the business needs to OO design analysts. OO design analysts are the ones who know OO modeling well and are responsible for filling out the contents of the cards. The facilitator is in charge of explaining the session rules and moving the discussion session forward.

The facilitator begins by explaining the objective and rules of the CRC session. A set of initial classes is created. These classes may come from the analysis class diagram, or they may be existing design classes that are obviously needed and hence identified by system architects. Each OO design analyst is assigned one or more cards and plays the role of the cards. The team examines the use cases one by one, simulating the interaction and flow of events that are used to accomplish each use case. When a class is involved in the execution of some interaction, the responsibility is recorded for that class, and the class role player has to enumerate the actions performed by the class and the other classes' collaborators that are involved. The session continues until all details of each use case are examined and all details of each responsibility of each class are clear. In the following exercise you will start from the *register* use case and create a series of CRC cards.

Register: A customer visits the registration page and specifies the desired user name and password. If there is already such a username/password pair, the system reports error; otherwise, it reports success. When the registration is completed, the user name, password, full name, and the billing address are stored in a database system.

From the analysis class diagram, a class named RegistrationPage is included in the initial set of CRC cards. An instance of RegistrationPage is created whenever a customer uses an Internet browser to visit the registration page. When the user clicks the *Submit* button, the RegistrationPage needs to know the user name and password entered by the user. Hence, two responsibilities are defined to denote the fact (as seen Figure 4.10). For these two responsibilities, there are no collaborators needed. Now when the *Submit* button is clicked, a request should be sent to RegistrationController to register the user. Therefore, the RegistrationPage must be able to navigate to the RegistrationController. It should also handle the button-click event of the *Submit* button. Hence the RegistrationPage has two other responsibilities: "Knows RegistrationController" and "Handles button-click event of *Submit* button." The collaborator of the last responsibility is RegistrationController.

Now think about the details of how to handle the button-click event by RegistrationPage. The event handler is essentially a delegate that forwards the registration request to RegistrationController. Now turn to the CRC design

RegistrationPage	
Responsibility	**Collaborators**
Know user name	
Know password	
Know RegistrationController	
Handle button-click event of *Submit* button	RegistrationController

Figure 4.10

CRC card of RegistrationPage

of RegistrationController (in Figure 4.11). To accomplish the responsibility of handling a registration request, RegistrationController needs to interact with CustomerInfoDB to verify whether the user name/password pair already exists. When CustomerInfoDB verifies the nonexistence of the desired user name/password pair, RegistrationController issues a request to CustomerInfoDB to create an account for the user name/password pair. The collaborator for this responsibility is the wrapper class CustomerInfoDB. When the registration is successful, RegistrationController creates an instance of RegistrationSuccessPage. A similar process is carried out when the user name/password pair does exist; in this case, an instance of RegistrationFailurePage is created.

Now, this is the moment when the expertise and experience of designers are needed. Consider the CRC card design of CustomerInfoDB (Figure 4.12). From the earlier discussion, it seems that CustomerInfoDB has two responsibilities: (1) to check the existence of the user name/password pair, and (2) to create a new account with the specified user name/password pair.

The theory of operating systems has shown that special care is needed when dealing with *concurrent* systems. What if two customers happen to

RegistrationController	
Responsibility	**Collaborators**
Handle the registration request (creates a user account with the desired user name/password)	CustomerInfoDB, RegistrationSuccessPage, RegistrationFailurePage
Know RegistrationPage	
Know (or create) RegistrationSuccessPage	
Know (or create) RegistrationFailurePage	

Figure 4.11
CRC card of Registration-Controller

CustomerInfoDB	
Responsibility	**Collaborators**
Accomplish the following two tasks in one atomic step: (1) verify the nonexistence of a user name/password pair, and (2) if successful, insert that pair into database.	

Figure 4.12
CRC card of CustomerInfoDB

SessionController	
Responsibility	**Collaborators**
Handle login request	CustomerInfoDB
Handle logout request	CustomerInfoDB
Add an item into shopping cart	InventoryDB, ProductInfo
Delete an item into shopping cart	InventoryDB, ProductInfo
Clear shopping cart	InventoryDB, ProductInfo
Check out shopping cart	InventoryDB, ProductInfo, FinancialDeptWrapper, ShippingDeptWrapper
Know shopping cart contents	
Know customer information (real name, billing address, etc.)	
Know LoginPage, LogoutPage, BrowserPage, etc.	

Figure 4.13
CRC card of
SessionController

request the same user name and password pair simultaneously? It is possible that both of them will get their user name/password approved. To prevent such *racing conditions*, designers have to combine the aforementioned two responsibilities into one atomic step, that is, one that cannot be interrupted by concurrent requests. Therefore, only one responsibility is written on the CRC card of CustomerInfoDB. Following a similar procedure, you get the CRC card design of the SessionController class shown in Figure 4.13.

4.4.2   Step 2: Construct an Interaction Diagram

Based on the design of CRC cards, you can now construct the interaction diagram for each use case. An interaction diagram describes how the objects that compose the system interact with one another to accomplish a use case. UML provides two popular forms of interaction diagrams: sequence diagrams and communication diagrams. They are semantically equivalent. In the following, a sequence diagram is used to model OPS.

In a sequence diagram (e.g., Figure 4.14), the boxes on the top of the diagram denote objects, classes, or actors (e.g., the ":RegistrationPage" in Figure

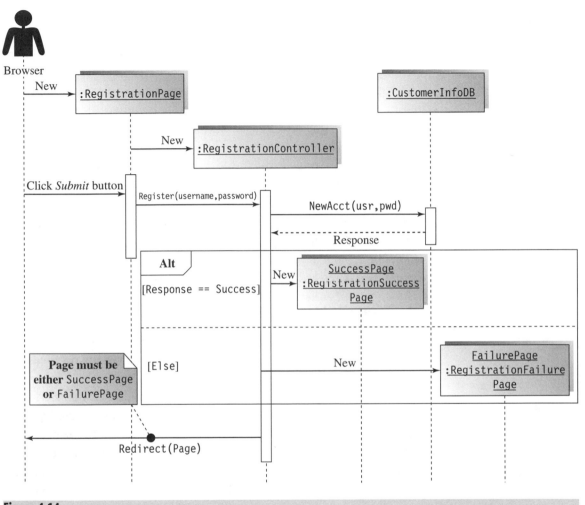

Figure 4.14

Sequence diagram of the Registration use case

4.14). To the left of the colon (:) is the optional object name; to the right is the class name. If the object name is anonymous, the left part is left empty.

To build a sequence diagram you follow the flow of events description for each use case. Each action or step mentioned in the use case description is modeled as a message sent from one object to another, which translates into an invocation of an operation on the target object. The translation procedure is natural.

Figure 4.14 presents the sequence diagram for the Registration use case. First, the customer browser (an actor) visits the registration page and instantiates a new instance of RegistrationPage. Once created, the RegistrationPage object creates one RegistrationController object that monitors the whole registration process. When the customer fills out the desired user name and password information and clicks the *Submit* button on the RegistrationPage, a request to register the new user is sent to the RegistrationController. The RegistrationController attempts to register the new account by interacting with the CustomerInfoDB object. Based on its response, the RegistrationController object creates an instance of either the RegistrationSuccessPage or the RegistrationFailurePage and redirects the customer browser to the corresponding page. Notice that both of the objects SuccessPage:RegistrationSuccessPage and FailurePage:RegistrationFailurePage are named objects, because their names are passed by the RegistrationController to redirect the customer's browser.

4.4.3   Step 3: Build a State Machine Diagram

When the analysis class diagram, interaction diagrams for each use case, and CRC card designs are completed, you can proceed to the detailed level design. The objective of the detailed level design is to specify the interface of each class and make decisions about implementation. The interface is the public interconnection border of the class that is accessible by other components of the system. Implementation means to realize the behaviors specified by the interface. The outcome of the detailed design process is a detailed class design diagram, where for each class a list of attributes and operations are listed. For classes with complex behaviors, state machine diagrams are usually defined to clarify the design.

This section introduces the state machine diagram design. A state machine diagram (e.g., Figure 4.15) consists of two types of basic elements: (1) *state*, which is represented using a rounded rectangle, and (2) *transition*, which is a directed arc between states. There are two cases of building a state machine diagram:

1. When a class is responsible for a single use case, designers simply look into the flow of events and corresponding interaction diagram to identify the different states that an object of this class goes through and the corresponding transitions.

2. When a class is involved in multiple use cases, designers have to combine all the information and consider the environment and the change of internal data values to identify the states. Sometimes, when a state machine diagram is too complex, you can take advantage of the substate utility included in UML 2.

Figure 4.15 presents the state machine diagram for the SessionController class. The SessionController is triggered by the logon event. When the logon

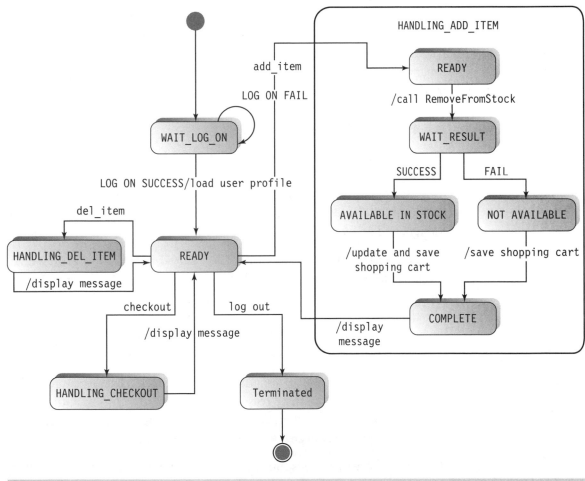

Figure 4.15

State machine diagram of SessionController **class**

is successful, the session class enters a READY state that waits for user interactions. When a user invokes an operation, the system enters in a corresponding state to process that call (e.g., HANDLING_DEL_ITEM, HANDLING_CHECKOUT, HANDLING_ADD_ITEM, etc). Finally, when the LogoutPage is visited, the session enters a final state. Notice that a complex state machine diagram design can be simplified using "divide and conquer" strategy. A state in a high-level diagram can be represented using another low-level state diagram (the idea is similar to the encapsulation provided by procedural call). Such a state is called composite-state and the states that are nested within the composite-state are called substates. For example, the HANDLING_ADD_ITEM is a composite-state that handles the invocation from BrowserPage when its "*add to shopping cart*" button is clicked. The composite-state itself is essentially one state machine, which starts from the READY state, invokes a RemoveFromStock() operation provided by InventoryDB, updates and saves the shopping cart, and finally displays results to the user using boundary web forms.

4.4.4   Step 4: Class Specification

The first step in a detailed class specification is to identify the public interface of the class. While the implementation of a class can change over the time, the public interface is nailed down after the design phase. Any changes to the public interface might damage the work already done by other designers. Therefore, the public interface should be complete and stable.

Public interface design starts with CRC cards. By examining the class's responsibilities and interaction diagram, you can list the attributes and operations that must be declared in the class. Note that, if it is too complex, the class can be split into more classes in the detailed design. A class should be split if it cannot be described using a simple sentence. When a class is split, the CRC model should be reorganized accordingly.

In general, unless designers are pursuing for speed, declaring public attributes for information security reasons is discouraged. (One exception is for declaring class-wide constant values.) The following discussion of the public interface will be concentrated on public operations.

Generally, a class provides four categories of operations in its public interface: (1) constructor operations, (2) destructor operations, (3) accessor operations, and (4) mutator operations.

A constructor operation is used to initialize the data members of an object when it is created. A class can have a number of constructors for different scenarios.

A destructor operation is used to clean up memory and free system resources when an object is no longer in use. Notice that even if the implementation environment provides garbage collection (i.e., the runtime system automatically reclaims the memory occupied by unused objects), destructors are useful in many situations. For example, when a process object is destroyed in an operating system, all the files opened by that process should be closed. Such clean-up actions can be defined in a destructor.

An accessor operation retrieves information from the object—it can retrieve the value of a data member, or finish some computation based on the state of the object. An accessor operation does not change the state of an object.

A mutator operation resets the value of one or more object attributes. Invocation of a mutator operation usually causes the transition between object states.

Once the public operations are identified, you can define the implementation details of the class, i.e., the private attributes and additional operations. The implementation design process goes through a similar procedure identifying the needed attributes and operations. Usually designers start from the state machine diagram of the class, if one exists, examine each of the public operations, and then nail down what attributes are needed. Designers continue this process until no more attributes and operations are needed.

You must consider the following when identifying private attributes.

1. According to the CRC cards, what must be known by the class?

2. Based on the state machine diagram, what states does the object go through? (States will be defined as constant attributes.)

3. What association factors (especially dependency and navigation) should be modeled?

4. What other data members might be needed for the implementation of operations?

Breaking down the implementation of public operations can help you identify private operations. For example, suppose that when implementing the SaveShoppingCart() operation of CustomerInfoDB, a hash is generated for the shopping cart contents to facilitate product search. The hashing algorithm is system specific. In this case, it is desirable to define a separate private operation called computeHash(). In the following, the SessionController class is taken as an example for class design.

Examining the CRC card of SessionController (Figure 4.13), you can identify the following two attributes: refCustomerInformation (an instance of CustomerInfomation) and refShoppingCart (a list of ProductInfo).

You can also examine the analysis class diagram to ensure that the detailed design is complete. For example, all associations in the analysis class diagram need to be modeled. Because the SessionController class navigates to Customer-InfoDB, InventoryDB, FinancialDeptWrapper, and ShippingDeptWrapper, you must include a reference for each of these wrapper classes. All of these attributes should be private because they are for the internal use of SessionController.

Another place you can look for attributes is the state machine diagram (Figure 4.15). It is desirable to define an attribute for recording the state of the object, and correspondingly, you need several predefined constants for state names (e.g., READY, WAIT_LOG_ON, HANDLING_ADD_ITEM, etc.). All of them can be declared as private attributes because they are for internal use only.

Are there any more operations to be included in the detailed design? A good place to start is the interaction diagram. Each incoming solid arrow is modeled as a public operation of the class. Operations such as add_item, delete_item, clear_cart, log_in, log_out, and check_out are included in the class design; all of these operations should be public. Combining the earlier analysis results, a sample design of SessionController is shown in Figure 4.16.

The next step is to refine the design of operations. Two important problems must be addressed for each operation: (1) What parameters are needed to invoke the operation?, and (2) What should be the return value? Given all the alternatives, you should consider the pros and cons of each and make the best decision based on the project requirements.

After you repeat the same design process for each class, the final outcome is a detailed design class diagram containing documentation of each class in the system (specification of public interface, attributes, and operations,

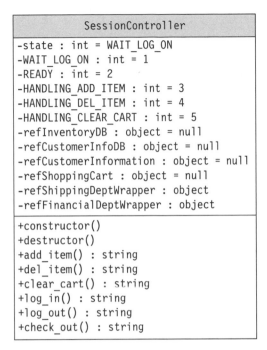

```
                  SessionController
-state : int = WAIT_LOG_ON
-WAIT_LOG_ON : int = 1
-READY : int = 2
-HANDLING_ADD_ITEM : int = 3
-HANDLING_DEL_ITEM : int = 4
-HANDLING_CLEAR_CART : int = 5
-refInventoryDB : object = null
-refCustomerInfoDB : object = null
-refCustomerInformation : object = null
-refShoppingCart : object = null
-refShippingDeptWrapper : object
-refFinancialDeptWrapper : object
+constructor()
+destructor()
+add_item() : string
+del_item() : string
+clear_cart() : string
+log_in() : string
+log_out() : string
+check_out() : string
```

Figure 4.16
Detailed design of
SessionController class

including the parameters, return type, pre-/post-conditions, and brief algorithm descriptions of each operation).

4.5   Design Principles

The design process does not simply identify one solution for a problem and then furnish the solution's details. Instead, a good designer has to identify several alternative design solutions and select the one that fits the project requirements best. This section introduces several design principles in the context of OO analysis and design. Note that the principles discussed in this section can be applied to other architecture styles as well, with slight modification.

4.5.1   Principle of Decoupling

A system with a set of highly interdependent classes is very hard to maintain because a change in one class may result in cascading updates of other classes. In an OO design, tight coupling may be removed by introducing new classes or inheritance.

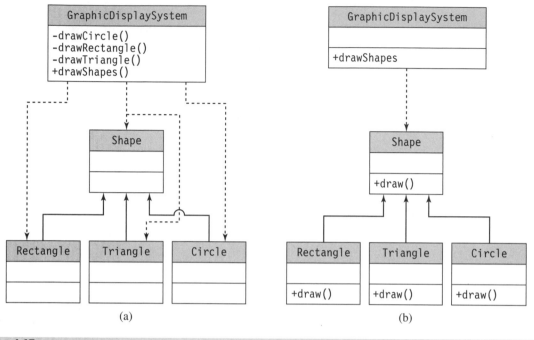

Figure 4.17

An example of the decoupling principle

Consider the example shown in Figure 4.17. Assume that you are to design a GraphicDisplaySystem (GDS). The system needs to display a list of shapes (e.g., rectangle, triangle, and circle) every 0.05 second. To accomplish this task, the GDS class provides an operation called drawShapes() whose parameter is a list of Shape objects. There are two possible designs of GDS, as shown in Figure 4.17(a) and 4.17(b), respectively.

In Figure 4.17(a), the solution is to provide a series of operations, e.g., draw_circle(Circle), draw_triangle(Triangle), etc., where each operation handles one specific shape.

In Figure 4.17(b), each shape is a derived class of the Shape class, and has to implement a polymorphic operation called draw(). This way, when the GDS tries to display the list of shapes, a shape reference can be used to iterate through the list and call the draw() operation. Thanks to the polymorphism of OO, correct behaviors will be exhibited when the draw() operation is invoked.

Which design is better? Obviously, it is the design in Figure 4.17(b). This solution has the following benefits:

- *Less interdependency:* In Figure 4.17(a), the GDS class depends on all Shape classes, including Shape, Rectangle, Triangle, and Circle. Any changes of these classes will lead to ripple effects in the GDS implementation. In Figure 4.17(b), the GDS class depends on only the Shape class. Changes in Rectangle will not affect the GDS class.

- *Easy extension:* The design in Figure 4.17(b) is much easier to extend when new shapes, e.g., trapezium, are added into GDS. In the solution offered in Figure 4.17(a), programmers would have to modify the code of GDS, add a function called draw_trapezium(), and then recompile the class file of GDS. In the second solution, programmers need to create only one new class for trapezium and realize the draw() operation; none of the other classes are affected.

- *Simplicity and elegance in implementation:* Think about the implementation of the drawShapes() operation in Figure 4.17(a). Inside its function body, programmers need a loop to iterate through the list of shapes. During each iteration, the code must go through a big switch case statement which, depending on the type of the Shape instance, selects the corresponding draw_shape() operation. The implementation of the second design, due to the polymorphism provided by OO, requires much less code.

Notice that tight coupling is not always bad. Sometimes it is necessary given the requirements or the nature of the problem. One typical example is the callback invocation between two objects.

4.5.2 Ensuring Cohesion

Coupling and cohesion are two well-known design concepts (DeMarco, 1979). While coupling involves two or more classes, cohesion is about the design of a single class. A cohesive class is one that performs a set of closely related operations. If a class performs unrelated operations, it is said to lack cohesion. Although lack of cohesion does not affect the functionality of the whole system, it makes the overall structure of the software hard to manage, expand, maintain, and modify. As operations of a less-cohesive system are not logically grouped together, any modification over the existing design may involve more than the necessary classes.

Consider the example shown in Figure 4.18. A Professor class provides services to both students and the registrar's office. Students can invoke

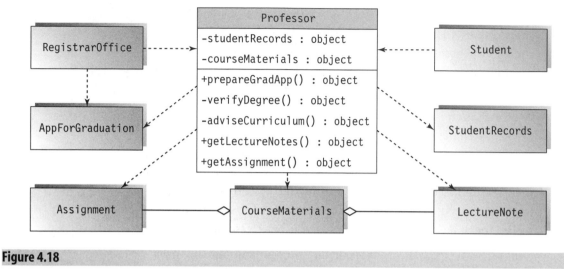

Figure 4.18

Initial design of Professor class

operations such as getLectureNotes(), and getAssignment() to retrieve course materials. The registrar's office can invoke an operation called prepareGradApp() to ask the professor to prepare a graduation application for one of his/her advisees. To prepare a graduation application, a professor needs to verify whether the student's current transcript satisfies the degree requirements by invoking private operations such as verifyDegree() and adviseCurriculum(). As shown in Figure 4.18, both the Student and RegistrarOffice classes depend on the Professor class.

One problem with the design in Figure 4.18 is that the Professor class has to bear two unrelated responsibilities: (1) to prepare a graduation application as an advisor, and (2) to distribute course materials as an instructor. While there is nothing wrong with the functionality of the system, the design is not cohesive.

One solution to improve the design in Figure 4.18 is simply to split the Professor class into two subclasses: an Advisor class and an Instructor class. The corresponding attributes and operations can be moved down to those classes, leaving the shared attributes and operations up in the root Professor class.

If the Professor class cannot be split, the use of inheritance and public interface can help improve cohesion. One sample solution is shown in Figure 4.19. Two new interfaces are defined in the improved design: Advisor

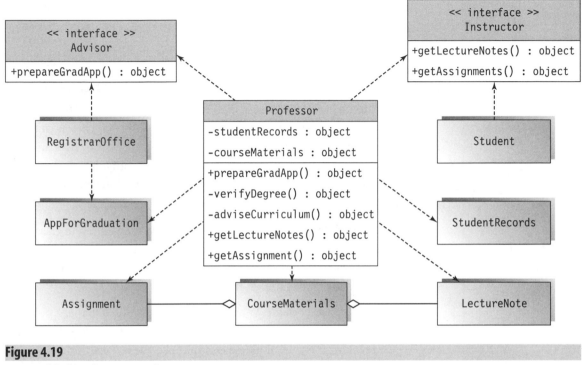

Figure 4.19

Improved design of Professor class

and Instructor. These interfaces declare the operations that must be realized by the derived classes, e.g., prepareGradApp() and getLectureNotes(). The Professor class realizes these two interfaces. In addition, when the Student and the RegistrarOffice need to access the corresponding functions provided by the Professor class, they do not directly refer to the Professor class. Instead, they depend on the Advisor and Instructor interfaces. Such minor changes in class relationships can greatly improve the cohesion of the overall design.

4.5.3 Open-Closed Principle

The open-closed principle was first proposed by Bertrand Meyer in his book *Object-Oriented Software Construction* (Meyer, 1997). The principle encourages OO designers to practice the following two guidelines:

1. *Open to extension:* the system should have the ability to be extended to meet new requirements.

2. *Closed to modification:* the existing implementation and code of the system should not be modified as a result of system expansion.

One technical approach to achieve the open-closed principle is abstraction via inheritance and polymorphism. A typical example may be seen in Figure 4.17(b). When a new shape, e.g., trapezium, is added into the system, the code of the Shape class and its derived classes do not need modification. Another example may be seen in Figure 4.19. The Professor class is made to realize two interfaces: Advisor and Instructor. The users of the Professor class do not depend on the Professor class. Such arrangement allows for great flexibility. The open-closed principle has many interesting implications that also serve as the thumb of rules during OO design:

- *Separate interface and implementation:* For each concrete class (i.e., a class that has implementations of its operations), it will be beneficial to abstract out its functionality in one or more interfaces and let the class realize the interface(s).

- *Keep attributes private:* When a class has attributes that are publicly visible to other classes, any change of these public attributes leads to reexaminination of all classes that use them. In a multithreaded environment, exposing public attributes is more dangerous—racing conditions in attempts to access public attributes might cause bizarre and hard-to-debug errors.

- *Minimize the use of global variables:* It is hard to trace uses of global variables. Changes in the definition of such global variables can easily lead to their misuse, which causes other modules to crash. The same rule applies to class variables (e.g., static class attributes in the Java language).

4.6   Summary

The OO paradigm is probably the most popular design methodology in use since the 1990s. One advantage of OO is to bundle data and its related operations together in one unit. Inheritance and polymorphism not only allow for reuse of code and implementation, but also provide vital mechanisms for abstraction and encapsulation. With the invention of UML, the OO-based software engineering process has matured. Use cases and class diagrams are used in the analysis stage to help further designers' understanding of a system's requirements and overall structure. In addition, these diagrams can be integrated into the design stage. Using CRC cards, interaction diagrams, state machine diagrams, and design class diagrams, OO designs can be refined, verified, and documented.

The key to design is not to create only one solution for a problem, but to choose among several possible solutions and make the best decision. Given the same problem, there are numerous possible designs, at different costs and with different qualities. The responsibility of a system analyst or a designer is to follow the general principles of OO design and to make the design sustainable, reusable, expandable, and easily maintainable. The trade-offs of various design alternatives—e.g., composition vs. inheritance, loose coupling vs. tight coupling, public vs. private visibility, etc.—must be evaluated against the problem setting.

In general, the OO paradigm is a design methodology that is both easy and difficult to use. The "easy" part is its natural modeling capability that allows designers to describe and abstract the real world in a way much easier to understand than the structured programming paradigm. The "hard" part is the numerous design principles that a designer must follow. There may be many designs that work for a problem; however, it is very likely that only a few of them are really good.

4.7 Self-Review Questions

1. Which of the following are benefits of OO design?

    a. Ease of code reuse

    b. Well-supported by programming tools

    c. Information hiding

    d. Real-world problems mapping

    e. All of the above

2. Which of the following are features of OO methodology?

    a. Concurrency

    b. Interactivity

    c. Inheritance

    d. Exchangeability

3. C is a popular OO programming language.

   a. True

   b. False

4. The set of classes in a design is nailed down when the analysis class diagram is finished.

   a. True

   b. False

5. The CRC card method is used to identify the responsibilities of each class.

   a. True

   b. False

6. Sequence diagrams do not describe loops in a message exchange process.

   a. True

   b. False

7. A class is said to be cohesive if it supports as many associated responsibilities as possible.

   a. True

   b. False

8. Abstraction via inheritance is one effective way to achieve the open-closed principle.

   a. True

   b. False

9. A part involved in an aggregation relationship should be born and terminate at the same moment as its owner.

   a. True

   b. False

10. To conform to the open-closed principle the use of global variables should be minimized.

    a. True

    b. False

Answers to the Self-Review Questions

1. e   2. c   3. b   4. b   5. a   6. b   7. b   8. a   9. b   10. a

4.8   Exercises

1. Explain how encapsulation is achieved in Java.

2. Compare C++ and Java, from the perspective of their support of inheritance.

3. Using one example, explain the difference between coupling and cohesion.

4. Give one example that shows composition is more appropriate than aggregation for modeling the relationship between two classes.

5. Give one example that shows aggregation is more appropriate than composition for modeling the relationship between two classes.

6. Give one scenario that shows inheritance is more appropriate than composition in design reuse.

7. Give one scenario that shows composition is more appropriate than inheritance in design reuse.

8. Give one example that shows tight coupling is not always bad.

4.9   Design Exercises

1. Use the noun extraction method to extract the set of classes involved in the *check-out* use case.

2. Develop the CRC card for the InventoryDB class.

3. Design the sequence diagram for the *check-out* use case.

4. Design the state machine diagram for the RegistrationController class.

5. Develop the public interface of the InventoryDB class.

4.10   Challenge Exercises

1. Follow and complete the design of OPS in this chapter. Your design should include: (1) the complete use case diagram, accompanied by the event flow description for each use case; (2) analysis class diagram; (3) design of CRC cards; (4) sequence diagrams for

each use case; (5) state machine diagrams for all the controller classes in the design; and (6) specification and design of each class. The specification of each class should include: (1) the class name, (2) a list of public operations and public attributes if there are any, and (3) a list of private/protected attributes and operations.

For each operation, the specification should include: (1) a list of parameters and the return type, (2) pre- and post-conditions, and (3) a brief explanation or pseudocode of the operation.

2. Implement your design of Challenge Exercise 1 using a popular OO language.

3. If there are multiple solutions to Challenge Exercise 1, select and compare two different designs, considering the following factors: (1) development cost, (2) extensibility, (3) modifiability, and (4) system performance.

References

Arlow, Jim and Ila Neustadt. *UML 2 and the Unified Process: Practical Object-Oriented Analysis and Design.* 2nd ed. Addison-Wesley Professional, 2005, 1–624.

Beck, Kent and Ward Cunningham. "A Laboratory for Teaching Object-Oriented Thinking." *OOPSLA'89, Object-oriented programming systems, languages and applications.* SIGPLAN: ACM Special Interest Group on Programming Languages. New Orleans, LA, October 1989, 1–6.

DeMarco, Tom. *Structured Analysis and System Specification.* Yourdon Press Computing Series. Upper Saddle River, NJ: Prentice Hall, 1979, 310–312.

Meyer, Bertrand. *Object-Oriented Software Construction.* 2nd ed. Upper Saddle River, NJ: Prentice Hall, 1997, 57–61.

Venners, Bill. "Inheritance versus composition: Which one should you choose? A Comparative Look at Two Fundamental Ways to Relate Classes." *JavaWorld.com* (November 1, 1998). Network World, Inc., http://www.javaworld.com/jw-11-1998/jw-11-techniques.html.

Suggested Reading

Gorman, Jason. "Object-Oriented Analysis & Design." (from "UML for Managers," ch. 3) 2005, http://www.parlezuml.com/e-books/umlformanagers/umlformanagers_ch3.pdf.

CHAPTER 5

Data Flow Architectures

Objectives of this Chapter

- Introduce the concepts of data flow architectures
- Describe the data flow architecture in UML
- Discuss the application domains of the data flow architecture approach
- Assess the benefits and limitations of the data flow architecture approach
- Demonstrate the batch sequential and pipe and filter architectures in OS and Java scripts

5.1   Overview

The data flow software architecture style views the entire software system as a series of transformations on successive sets of data, where data and operations on it are independent of each other. The software system is decomposed into data processing elements where data directs and controls the order of data computation processing. Each component in this architecture transforms its input data into corresponding output data. The connection between the subsystem components may be implemented as I/O streams, I/O files, buffers, piped streams, or other types of connections. Data can flow in a graph topology with cycles or in a linear structure without cycles, or even in a tree type structure. A sample block diagram for data flow architecture is shown in Figure 5.1. Regardless of the type of topology, the data moves from one subsystem to another. In general, there is no interaction between the modules except for the output and the input data connections between subsystems. In other words, the subsystems are independent of each other in such a way that one subsystem can be substituted by another without affecting the rest of the system, as long as the new subsystem is compatible with the corresponding input and output data format. Since each subsystem does not need to know the identity of any other subsystem, modifiability and reusability are important property attributes of the data flow architecture.

There are many different ways to connect the output data of a module to the input of other modules which result in a range of data flow patterns. There are two categories of execution sequences between modules: batch

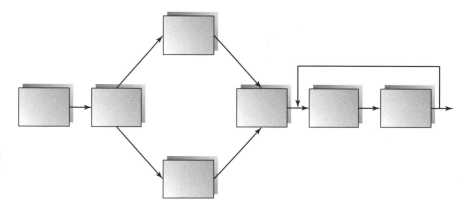

Figure 5.1

Block diagram of data flow architecture

sequential and pipe and filter (nonsequential pipeline mode). The close-loop process control is a typical data flow architecture style where data also drives the sequence of the program executions. From the standpoint of design orientation philosophy, we can choose either a traditional procedure-oriented design or an object-oriented design.

The data flow architecture is applicable in certain problem domains. This architecture can be used in any application involving a well-defined series of independent data transformations or computations with an orderly defined input and output, such as data streams. Typical examples are compilers and business batch data processing; neither of these require user interactions.

Next we discuss in detail the three subcategories in the data flow architecture styles. These are:

- Batch sequential
- Pipe and filter
- Process control

5.2   Batch Sequential

The batch sequential architecture style represents a traditional data processing model that was widely used from 1950 to 1970. RPG and COBOL are two typical programming languages working on this model.

In batch sequential architecture, each data transformation subsystem or module cannot start its process until its previous subsystem completes its computation. Data flow carries a batch of data as a whole from one subsystem to another. Figure 5.2 shows a typical example of batch sequential style.

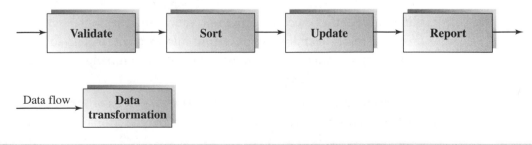

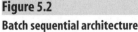

Figure 5.2

Batch sequential architecture

In this example, the first subsystem *validates* the transaction requests (insert, delete, and update) in their totality. Next, the second subsystem *sorts* all transaction records in an ascending order on the primary key of data records to speed up the update on the master file since the master file is sorted by the primary key. The transaction *update* module updates the master file with the sorted transaction requests, and then the report module generates a new list. The architecture is in a linear data flow order.

All communications (connection link arrows) between subsystem modules are conducted through transient intermediate files which can be removed by successive subsystems. Business data processing such as banking and utility billing are typical applications of this architecture. Figure 5.3 depicts a similar example of this architecture. A script is often used to make the batch sequence of the subsystems in the system.

Figure 5.3 is a detailed example of the previous block diagram of Figure 5.2. It shows that the data files are the driving force for processing forward.

We can run a Unix Shell script as follows in batch sequential mode:

`myShell.sh`

```
(exec) searching kwd < inputFile > matchedFile
(exec) counting < matchedFile > countedFile
(exec) sorting    < countedFile > myReportFile
```

Where (exec) may be required by some Unix shell.

In this Unix shell script, each executable program takes its input from `stdin` and outputs the results to `stdout`, *the Unix default input/output*. The redirect operators ("<" and ">") are used to make `stdin` and `stdout` point to specific files. The first executable program, *searching*, reads in the text file `inputFile` and sends its output into file `matchedFile`. The second command line runs another executable program called *counting*, which takes its input from `matchedFile` and places its output into `countedFile`, and so on. We can easily replace any one of these executable commands as long as the input/output formats are the same.

For example, taking advantage of the search methods of `String` class in Java API, we can substitute a Java program performing similar functions:

`exec java searching kwd inputFile matchedFile`

Here, `searching` is a Java bytecode class file instead of a Unix executable file. This example shows that a change of one executable module will not affect

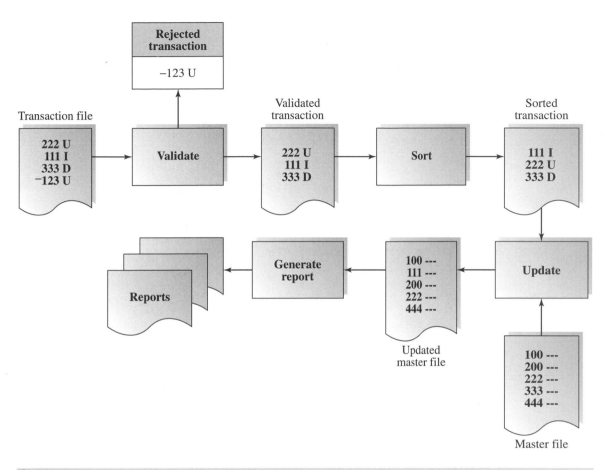

Figure 5.3

Batch sequential in business data processing

the others as long as it produces identical formatted data to be used by the subsequent executable module. This is very similar in a DOS environment, for example, in making a batch file called *myBatch.bat* with the following:

```
searching  kwd  inputFile matchedFile
counting  matchedFile  countedFile
sorting  countedFile
```

We can also implement the batch sequential software architecture at the programming language level. Here is a Java sketch template:

```
public class batch_sequential
{
. . .
```

```java
public static void main() {
    searching(kwd, inputFile, matchedFile);
    counting(matchedFile, countedFile);
    sorting (countedFile, reportFile);
 }

public static void searching(String kwd, String
 inFile, String outFile)
  { . . . }

public static void counting(String inFile,
String outFile)
{ . . . }

public static void sorting(String inFile, String
outFile)
{ . . . }
}
```

This is a sample skeleton of the batch sequential architecture in Java. Notice that there is no single instance (object). This is because we used static methods, and these do not belong to any individual object; rather, they belong to the class where they are defined.

Applicable domains of batch sequential architecture:

- Data are batched.
- Intermediate file is a sequential access file.
- Each subsystem reads related input files and writes output files.

Benefits:

- Simple divisions on subsystems.
- Each subsystem can be a stand-alone program working on input data and producing output data.

Limitations:

- Implementation requires external control.
- It does not provide interactive interface.
- Concurrency is not supported and hence throughput remains low
- High latency.

5.3　Pipe and Filter Architecture

Pipe and filter architecture is another type of data flow architecture where the flow is driven by data.

This architecture decomposes the whole system into components of data source, filters, pipes, and data sinks. The connections between components are data streams. The particular property attribute of the pipe and filter architecture is its concurrent and incremented execution.

A data stream is a first-in/first-out buffer which can be a stream of bytes, characters, or even records of XML or any other type. Most operating systems and programming languages provide a data stream mechanism; thus it is also an important tool for marshaling and unmarshaling in any distributed system.

Each filter is an independent data stream transformer; it reads data from its input data stream, transforms and processes it, and then writes the transformed data stream over a pipe for the next filter to process. A filter does not need to wait for batched data as a whole. As soon as the data arrives through the connected pipe, the filter can start working right away. A filter does not even know the identity of data upstream or data downstream. A filter is just working in a local incremental mode.

A pipe moves a data stream from one filter to another. A pipe can carry binary or character streams. An object-type data must be serialized to be able to go over a stream. A pipe is placed between two filters; these filters can run in separate threads of the same process as Java I/O streams.

There are three ways to make the data flow:

- Push only (Write only)

  A data source may push data in a downstream.

  A filter may push data in a downstream.

- Pull only (Read only)

  A data sink may pull data from an upstream.

  A filter may pull data from an upstream.

- Pull/Push (Read/Write)

  A filter may pull data from an upstream and push transformed data in a downstream.

There are two types of filters: active and passive.

- An *active filter* pulls in data and pushes out the transformed data (pull/push); it works with a passive pipe that provides read/write mechanisms for pulling and pushing. The pipe and filter mechanism in Unix adopts this mode. The `PipedWriter` and `PipedReader` pipe classes in Java are also passive pipes that active filters must work with to drive the data stream forward.

- A *passive filter* lets connected pipes push data in and pull data out. It works with active pipes that pull data out from a filter and push data into the next filter. The filter must provide the read/write mechanisms in this case. This is very similar to data flow architecture.

The Java `PipedWriter` and `PipedReader` classes work together to synchronize the data stream pulling and the data stream pushing between active filters.

In the following class diagram for pipe and filter architecture in Figure 5.4, the solid lines indicate the class connections, the data source provides the read mechanism, the data sink provides the write mechanism, and the pipe provides both read and write mechanisms for filters to use. So, this class diagram covers active filter and passive pipe. Both the data source and the data sink are also passive. The dashed lines indicate an alternative configuration for pipes that connects the data source and data sink with filter.

As we can see in the UML class diagram in Figure 5.4, one pipe class may connect to three other classes. They are data source, filter, and data sink. In a pipe and filter system there may be many pipe instances and filter instances. This class diagram focuses only on active filters which push data into pipe and pull data from a pipe.

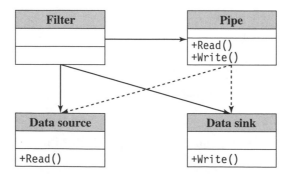

Figure 5.4

Pipe and filter class diagram

The UML sequence diagram Figure 5.5 shows one pipe connecting to two filters. One filter connects to a data source and the other connects to a data sink.
We can tell from the diagram that Filter1 reads data from the data source by
the read function of the data source and writes data to the pipe using the write
function of the pipe. Filter2 reads data from the pipe using the function of the
pipe and writes data to the data sink by the write function of the data sink.

Figure 5.6 illustrates a detailed example of a pipelined pipe and filter architecture. The conversion filter converts all characters from lowercase to

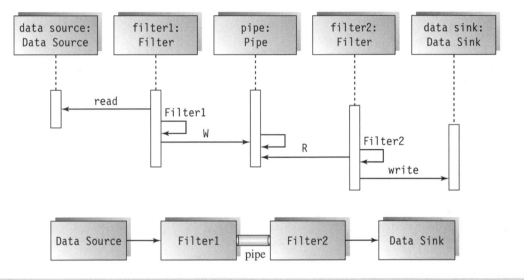

Figure 5.5

Pipe and filter block and sequence diagram

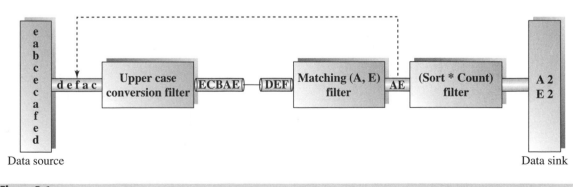

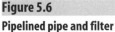

Figure 5.6

Pipelined pipe and filter

uppercase, and the matching filter selects characters "A" and "E" in the stream. The conversion filter and matching filter are working concurrently; the matching filter can start its job before conversion completes its transformation of the whole input stream. The sort and count filter counts the number of occurrences of "A" and "E" and sorts them in alphabetical order. It can take its input before the matching filter finishes the job but cannot output data until it gets all data in.

Figure 5.7 shows that there are two types of reading: no-blocking reading and blocking reading. The reading operation is blocked out in the blocking

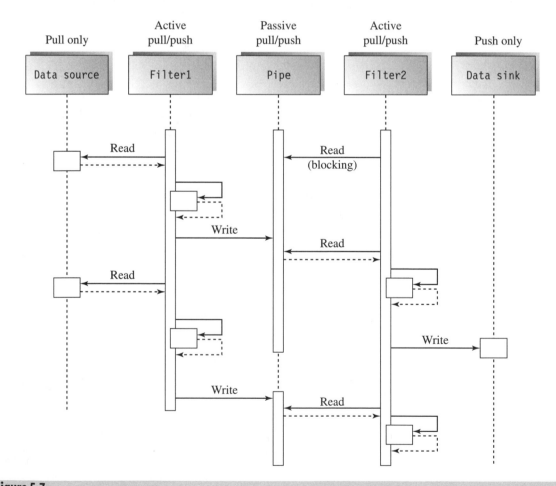

Figure 5.7
Pipe and filter sequence diagram

reading if data is not available for reading. This case is shown in Filter2's first reading.

Pipe and Filter in Unix

The pipe operator "|" moves the stdout from its predecessor to the stdin of its successor. The successor can start data transformation over the data stream before the predecessor completes its transformation or processing. For example, the pipeline of Unix commands reports the number of users who are currently logged onto the system.

who | wc −1

The who command sends the current users to its output stream; the wc command takes its input stream from the pipe and counts the number of lines (i.e., the number of the current users). The wc command starts its counting before the who command completes its output.

Unix also supports named pipes to connect the filters. A named pipe may be placed between two processes as a Unix stream pipe.

The following example, illustrated in Figure 5.8, shows two Unix processes, one running in the background and the other running in the foreground. Both of these processes have their data pipe streams, one is a Unix implicit pipeline and other consists of pipeA and pipeB. The cat command sends the contents of the infile to the pipe, and the tee command sends the same data to two pipelines. The background process with named pipeline

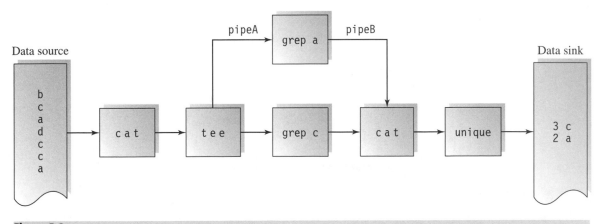

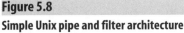

Figure 5.8

Simple Unix pipe and filter architecture

searches for 'a' and the foreground one searches for 'c'; the two processes are joined together at the second cat command with "-" (current process) and pipeB; the last filter reports the counts of each character matched.

The filter used above can be replaced by any other Unix command or application program as long as they take input from stdin and outputs data to stdout. Here is such a situation:

```
$ mkfifo pipeA
$ mkfifo pipeB
$ grep a < pipeA >pipeB &
$ cat infile | tee pipeA | grep c |cat - pipeB | uniq -c
```

Pipe and Filter in Java

The Java API provides the PipedWriter and PipedReader classes in the java.io package; this allows for filters to push data into downstream or to pull data from the upstream. Filters can run in separate threads, and they can be synchronized in a parallel manner by PipedWriter and PipedReader.

Here is a simple example to illustrate the use of Java pipe and filter facilities: The Filter1 runs in one thread and produces a data stream to a pipe which is consumed by Filter2 in another thread.

Filter1.java:

```java
package pf;
import java.io.*;
public class Filter1 extends Thread {
  PipedWriter myPw;

  public Filter1(PipedWriter pw) { myPw=pw; }

  public void run() {
    int j;
    try {
      for (int j = 1; j<100; j++) pw.write(j);
      pw.write(-1);
    }
    catch(Exception e){. . .}
  }
}
```

Filter2.java:

```
package pf;
import java.io.*;

class Filter2 extends Thread {
  PipedReader myPr;

  public Filter2(PipedReader pr) { myPr = pr; }

  public void run() {
    int j;
    try {
      while (myPr.read()!= -1){ . . . }
    }
    catch(Exception e){. . .}
  }
}

pipeFilter.java:

import pf.*;
import java.io.*;

public class pipeFilter {
  public static void main(String[] args) {
    try {
      PipedWriter pw = new PipedWriter();
      PipedReader pr = new PipedReader(pw);
      Filter1 f1 = new Filter1(pw);
      Filter2 f2 = new Filter2(pr);
      f2.start();
      f1.start();
    }
    catch(Exception e){ . . . }
  }
}
```

The pipeFilter Java program runs two threads in addition to itself: Filter1
and Filter2. They are connected by a synchronized pipe (PipedWriter and
PipedReader). Filter1 writes to the pipe and Filter2 reads from the pipe. It is
not necessary to start Filter1 before starting Filter2. The main program
actually starts Filter2 before Filter1. The order of filters in the sequence is
not important as long as the synchronization is set.

Applicable domains of pipe and filter architecture:

- The system can be broken into a series of processing steps over data streams, and at each step filters consume and move data incrementally.

- The data format on the data streams is simple, stable, and adaptable if necessary.

- Significant work can be pipelined to gain increased performance.

- Producer or consumer-related problems are being addressed.

Benefits:

- *Concurrency:* It provides high overall throughput for excessive data processing.

- *Reusability:* Encapsulation of filters makes it easy to plug and play, and to substitute.

- *Modifiability:* It features low coupling between filters, less impact from adding new filters, and modifying the implementation of any existing filters as long as the I/O interfaces are unchanged.

- *Simplicity:* It offers clear division between any two filters connected by a pipe.

- *Flexibility:* It supports both sequential and parallel execution.

Limitations:

- It is not suitable for dynamic interactions.

- A low common denominator is required for data transmission in the ASCII formats since filters may need to handle data streams in different formats, such as record type or XML type rather than character type.

- Overhead of data transformation among filters such as parsing is repeated in two consecutive filters.

- It can be difficult to configure a pipe and filter system dynamically.

5.4   Process Control Architecture

Process control software architecture is suitable for the embedded system software design where the system is manipulated by a process control variable data. Process control architecture decomposes the whole system into subsystems (modules) and connections between subsystems. There are two types of subsystems: an executor processing unit for changing process control variables and controller unit for calculating the amounts of the changes. Figure 5.9 shows the data flow of a feedback close-loop process control system. The connections between the subsystems are the data flow.

A process control system must have the following process control data:

- *Controlled variable:* a target controlled variable such as speed in a cruise control system or the temperature in an auto H/A system. It has a *set point* goal to reach. The controlled variable data should be measured by sensors as a feedback reference to recalculate manipulated variables.

- *Input variable:* a measured input data such as the temperature of return air in a temperature control system.

- *Manipulated variable:* can be adjusted by the controller.

The input variables and manipulated variables are applied to the execution processor which results in a controlled variable. The set point and controlled variables are the input data to the controller; the difference between the controlled variable value and the set point value is used to arrive at a new manipulated value. Car cruise-control and building temperature control systems are examples of this process control software architecture type of application.

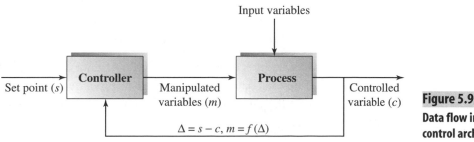

Figure 5.9

Data flow in the process control architecture

In a cruise control system there is an engine process unit that drives the wheels and a controller that sets the throttle based on the current wheel speed and set point value. The architecture is similar to the design shown in the preceding diagram.

Applicable domains of process control architecture:

- Embedded software systems involving continuing actions
- Systems that need to maintain an output data at a stable level
- The system can have a set point—the goal the system will reach at its operational level.

Benefits of close-loop feedback process control architecture over open forward architecture:

- It offers a better solution to the control system where no precise formula can be used to decide the manipulated variable.
- The software can be completely embedded in the devices.

5.5   Summary

The data flow architecture decomposes a system into a fixed sequence of transformations and computations. There is no direct interaction between any two consecutive subsystems except for the exchange of data through data flow links. No data sharing occurs among subsystems in data flow architecture. It is not suitable for interactive business processing. Three types of data flow architectures were discussed: batch sequential, pipe and filter, and process control. The pipe and filter is an incremental data transformation processing model and runs concurrently.

The data flow and the control flow in pipe and filter are implicit. Reading and writing I/O files drive the data flow in batch sequential architecture; its control flow is thus explicit. The batch sequential architecture may cause bottlenecks because it requires batched data as input and output.

The process control architecture is another type of data flow architecture where the data is neither batched sequential nor pipelined streamed. The mechanism to drive the data flow comes from a set of variables that controls the process execution.

The design guidelines for a data flow based software system are as follows:

- Decompose the system into a series of process steps; each step takes the output of its previous step.
- Define the output and input data formats for each step.
- Define the data transformation in each step.
- Design pipelines if concurrency is necessary.

5.6   Self-Review Questions

1. Which of the following are *not* benefits of pipe and filter?

   a. Concurrency

   b. Interactive

   c. Incremental

   d. Exchangeable

   e. None of the above

   f. All of the above

2. Which of the followings are *not* benefits of batch sequential?

   a. Concurrency

   b. Interactive

   c. Incremental

   d. Exchangeable

   e. None of the above

   f. All of the above

3. COBOL is widely used to implement batch sequential.

   a. True

   b. False

4. Two modules in a data flow system can change their order without any constraints.

   a. True

   b. False

5. Java can be used to implement a pipe and filter design system.

   a. True

   b. False

6. The control flow in pipe and filter is explicit.

   a. True

   b. False

7. The control flow in batch sequential is implicit.

   a. True

   b. False

8. There are data sharing (shared data) among all subsystems in a data flow system.

   a. True

   b. False

9. Sequential flow control can be predetermined in pipe and filter.

   a. True

   b. False

10. Sequential flow control can be predetermined in batch sequential.

   a. True

   b. False

Answers to the Self-Review Questions

1. b   2. b   3. a   4. b   5. a   6. a   7. a   8. b   9. a   10. a

5.7   Exercises

1. What is a pipe and filter architecture?

2. What is a data flow architecture?

3. What is a batch sequential architecture?

4. What is the domain for pipe and filter?

5. What is the domain for batch sequential?

6. What are the benefits and limitations of pipe and filter architecture?

7. In Unix is the pipe concept active?

8. Is the batch sequential architecture phased out?

9. Enumerate all possible ways to drive the data stream.

10. Enumerate all types of filters.

5.8 Design Exercises

1. Develop a batch sequential practice example in C++.

2. Develop a pipe and filter practice example in Unix.

3. Develop a pipe and filter practice example in Java.

4. In the Pipe and Filter in Java section in this chapter, modify the example so that Filter1 can read text line by line from a file, and Filter2 can read text line by line via pipe and convert all text into uppercase.

5. Design a bank transaction batch processing software based on batch sequential architecture.

5.9 Challenge Exercises

1. Apply the data flow architecture styles to the applicable domains in the Challenge Exercises of Chapter 3.

2. Apply the data flow architecture style to the applicable domains in the university admission processing system which covers application checking and validation per university-wide and department-wide requirements, finance requirements, additional information inquiry, decision notification, and other admission processing.

Suggested Reading

Garlan, David and Mary Shaw. *Software Architecture: Perspectives on an Emerging Discipline.* Upper Saddle River, NJ: Prentice Hall, 1996.

Pressman, Roger. *Software Engineering: A Practitioner's Approach.* 6th ed. New York: McGraw-Hill, 2005.

CHAPTER 6

Data-Centered Software Architecture

Objectives of this Chapter

- Introduce the concepts of data-centered software architecture
- Describe repository and blackboard architectures
- Discuss applicable domains for data-centered software architecture
- Evaluate the benefits and limitations of data-centered software architecture
- Examine data-centered architecture when incorporated with other architectures

6.1   Overview

Data-centered software architecture is characterized by a centralized data store that is shared by all surrounding software components. The software system is decomposed into two major partitions: data store and independent software component or agents. The connections between the data module and the software components are implemented either by explicit method invocation or by implicit method invocation. In pure data-centered software architecture, the software components don't communicate with each other directly; instead, all the communication is conducted via the data store. The shared data module provides all mechanisms for software components to access it, such as insertion, deletion, update, and retrieval.

There are two categories of data-centered architecture: *repository* and *blackboard*. These are differentiated by the flow control strategy. The data store in the repository architecture is passive, and clients of the data store are active; that is, clients (software components or agents) control the logic flow. Clients may access the repository interactively or by a batch transaction request. The repository style is widely used in database management systems, library information systems, the interface repository (IR) in CORBA, the UDDI registry for web services, compilers, and Computer Aided Software Engineering (CASE) environments. A well-known CASE tool is Rational Rose. It supports a graphic editor to draw UML diagrams, generates various programming code, and provides reverse engineering functionality to generate graphic diagrams from code. All Interactive Development Environments (IDE), and similar software development kits are good examples of application domains for the repository architecture. It is also widely used in complex information management systems where the most important issue is reliable data management.

The data store in the blackboard architecture option is active, and its clients are passive; thus, the flow of logic is determined by the current data status in the data store. The clients of a blackboard are called knowledge sources, listeners, or subscribers. A new data change may trigger events so that the knowledge sources take actions to respond to these events. These actions may result in new data, which may in turn change the logic flow; this could happen continuously until a goal is reached. Many applications designed in the blackboard architecture include knowledge-based AI systems, voice and

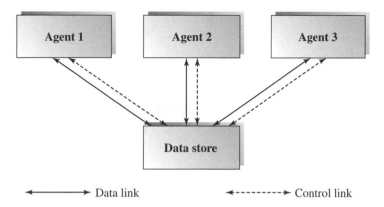

Figure 6.1
**Block diagram of typical
data-centered architecture**

image recognition systems, security systems, business resource management systems, etc.

Figure 6.1 shows an overall block diagram of a data-centered architecture. The solid lines in the diagram describe the bidirectional data link (get data and put data), while the dashed lines describe the bidirectional control flow links (control over the data or control over the agents).

6.2   Repository Architecture Style

The repository architecture style is a data-centered architecture that supports user interaction for data processing (as opposed to the batch sequential transaction processing discussed earlier). The software component agents of the data store control the computation and flow of logic of the system. Figure 6.2 gives a general picture of the repository architecture. The dashed lines pointing toward repository in Figure 6.2 indicate that repository clients have full control over the logic flow. Clients can get data from the data store and put data in the data store. Different clients may have different interfaces and different data access privileges.

Figure 6.3 shows a class diagram for a simple data store for student management. It describes the static relationships between data classes and their backup database tables, and between data classes and their collection classes. This diagram presents a programming-oriented view of the repository design architecture. A Students collection (Vector or ArrayList, or any other suitable collection type) has an aggregation relationship with Student class.

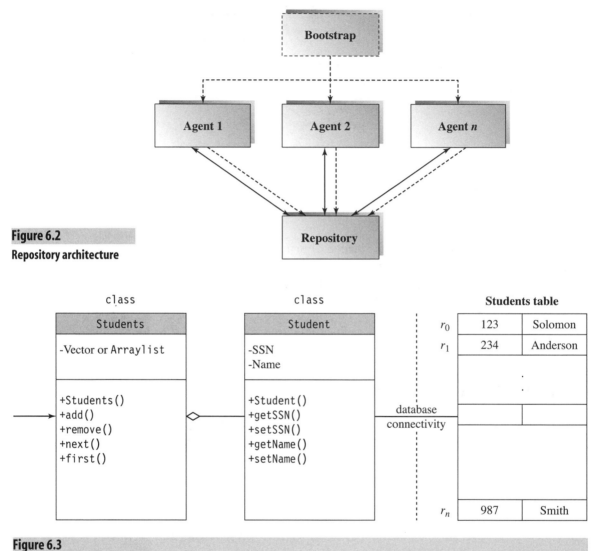

Figure 6.2
Repository architecture

Figure 6.3
Class diagram

Clients can add in or remove a student from the Students set that will also affect the *Students* table in the database via database connectivity technology.

We use a simple fragment of java code to explain the class diagram above.

```
public class Student implements Serializable {
    String SSN;
    String Name;
```

```
public Student() {
  SSN = "";
  Name = "";
}
public Student(String ssn, String name) {
  SSN = ssn;
  Name = name;
}
public void setSSN(String ssn) { SSN = ssn; }
public String getSSN() { return SSN; }
public void setName(String name) { Name=name; }
public String getName() { return Name; }
}
```

The Student class is a data bean backed up by a corresponding table in a database. The instance of this class represents one specific record in the database table (a table row) at a time. Assume that there is a table called *students* which has two columns: *ssn* and *name*. This class provides a default *constructor* and a customized *constructor*. It also provides getter and setter methods for each of its attributes.

The following fragment shows the connection between the data bean class and the database. The Java DataBase Connectivity (JDBC) driver makes a connection to an Oracle database table called *students* first, as follows.

```
. . .
  try {
  Class.forName("sun.jdbc.odbc.JdbcOdbcDriver");
Connection connection =
  DriverManager.getConnection(
    "jdbc:odbc:students");
  }
  catch(Exception e){...}
```

The Java code below creates a JDBC SQL statement to select all records from the *students* table and place them in the ResultSet. An instance of the data bean class is created by the *new* operator. The while loop iterates the ResultSet and adds every record into the studentList one at a time through the instance of the Student class.

```
. . .
ArrayList studentList = new ArrayList();
Statement statement = connection.createStatement();
ResultSet results =
```

```
  statement.executeQuery("SELECT * FROM students");
Student student = new Student();
while (results.next()) {
  student.setSsn(results.getSsn(1));
  student.setName(results.getName(2));
  studentList.add(student);
}
```

This code fragment may be a part of client application program. The clients iterate the JDBC ResultSet and put data in the object of the data bean class Student which then associates with a record in the corresponding table by JDBC and, in turn, adds the object to the studentList, an ArrayList collection type data structure.

Figure 6.4 depicts a dynamic view of this repository architecture. It indicates that one instance object can be shared and accessed by multiple clients with reading and writing for search, update, insertion, and deletion. The clients can access the same data with command line interface, GUI interface, program interface, Remote Procedure Call interfaces (RPC), or object-oriented Remote Method Invocation (RMI).

The relational database management system is a typical design domain for the repository architecture. The data store of the repository maintains all types of data including schema (metadata), data tables, and index files for

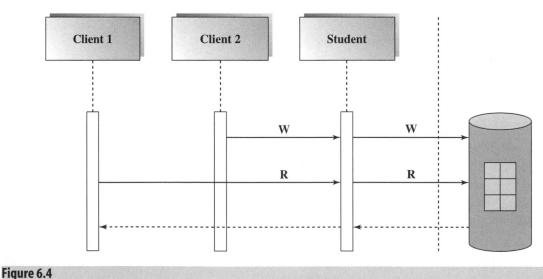

Figure 6.4

Sequence diagram of repository architecture

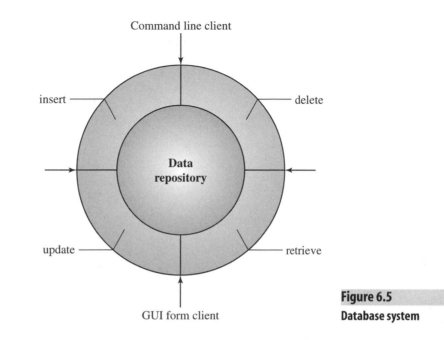

Figure 6.5
Database system

data tables. Many tools are available to develop applications on the database stored in the database management system. These include design, development, maintenance, and documentation tools. Oracle Designer, Oracle Developer (Form, Graphics, and Reporter), Oracle SQL and PL/SQL, Oracle Financials, Oracle e-Business, Oracle data warehouse, and many other software tools are available for Oracle database system. The diagram in Figure 6.5 shows a typical database system with its data repository.

A Computer Aided Software Engineering (CASE) system is another popular application domain for the repository software architecture. There are many CASE tools surrounding the data store in Figure 6.6. A user of CASE tools can draw a UML design diagram such as a class diagram, collaboration diagram, or sequence diagram by Booch method, Rumbaugh method, or Jacobson method, and store the design blueprints in the CASE data store. These UML diagrams can then be converted from one format to another. Java or C++ skeleton code can also be generated based on these UML diagrams. If there is code without the original design diagram, the UML diagram can still be regenerated by reverse engineering tool. There are many other input formats available for design and many output formats, as well.

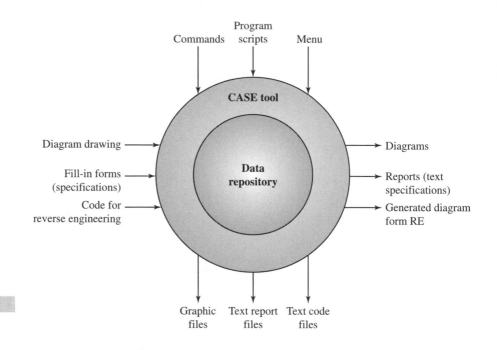

Figure 6.6

CASE system

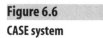

The biggest advantage of CASE tools is its centralized data with many supporting software tools which can generate different products for different purposes based on the same set of data.

Compiler construction is another good example of the repository architecture design. Every compiler system has its own reserved keyword table, identifier symbol table, constant table generated after lexical analysis, and syntax and semantics trees generated by syntax and semantics analysis. These tables' data structure in memory is shared by all phases of the compilation. Each phase will generate new data or update the existing data in the data repository. The flow control is controlled by a program which takes a source code as its input, then goes through each phase step by step, and finally produces the target binary code which is either executable or interpretable, such as Java bytecode. In other words, all agents in a repository system are not necessarily completely independent. There is a logical order in the executions of all compilation phases. There may still be some communication between individual agents. For example, the lexical analysis may find some unacceptable characters, so that the compilation must be abandoned and compile errors must be reported. Let's take a closer look at the simple compilation example shown in Figure 6.7.

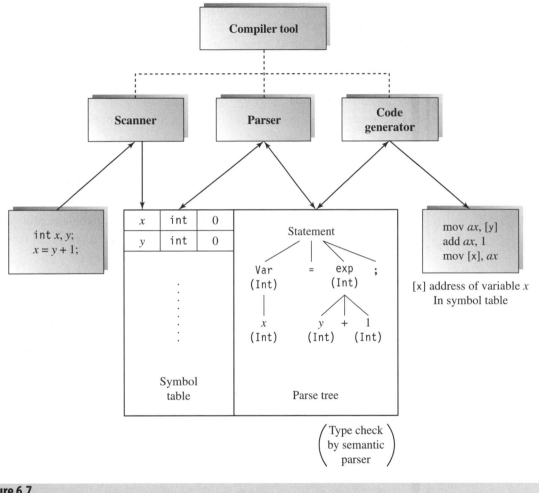

Figure 6.7

Compiler system

The scanner takes two lines of an `int` type variable declaration and an assignment statement. The lexical analyzer (scanner) tokenizes all input entities and puts them in the symbol table used by the syntax analyzer (parser) to build a syntax tree based on the grammar. This syntax tree is checked again by the semantics analyzer (not shown) and is also used by the code generator to produce the target code. We can see that the data in memory are shared by all agents and that the agents don't pass on data to each other directly.

There are variants of repository architecture such as virtual repository and decentralized (distributed) repository. The virtual repository is built up on the top of multiple physical repositories. Most database systems allow users or developers to create views that are virtual repositories since they do not exist physically. This approach can simplify the complexity of overall database structure; it can also provide security management of authority privileges in terms of scope of data and types of manipulations for different users or groups.

In a distributed repository system, also known as a distributed database system or an enterprise information system, all data are distributed over all sites linked by network. Data are replicated in order to improve reliability and local accessibility. But it brings up many other issues such as vertical or horizontal data partitions, synchronizations of duplicated data, and cost of data transmission on the network; collaboration in a distributed transaction is a complicated two-phase transaction commitment.

Applicable domains of repository architecture:

- Suitable for large, complex information systems where many software component clients need to access them in different ways

- Requires data transactions to drive the control flow of computation

Benefits:

- Data integrity: easy to back up and restore

- System scalability and reusability of agents: easy to add new software components because they do not have direct communication with each other

- Reduces the overhead of transient data between software components

Limitations:

- Data store reliability and availability are important issues. Centralized repository is vulnerable to failure compared to distributed repository with data replication.

- High dependency between data structure of data store and its agents. Changes in data structure have significant impacts on its agents. Data evolution is more difficult and expensive.

- Cost of moving data on network if data is distributed.

Related architecture:

- Layered, multi-tier, and MVC

6.3 Blackboard Architecture Style

The blackboard architecture was developed for speech recognition applications in the 1970s. Other applications for this architecture are image pattern recognition and weather broadcast systems. Typical examples of this architecture are the Hearsay-II speech recognition expert system and the CRYSTALIS molecular structure analysis system.

The word blackboard comes from classroom teaching and learning. Teachers and students can share data in solving classroom problems via a blackboard. Students and teachers play the role of agents to contribute to the problem solving. They can all work in parallel, and independently, trying to find the best solution.

The idea of blackboard architecture is similar to the classroom blackboard used in solving problems without deterministic outcome. It is a data-directed and a partially data-driven architecture. The entire system is decomposed into two major partitions. One partition, called the *black-board*, is used to store data (hypotheses and facts), while the other partition, called *knowledge sources*, stores domain-specific knowledge. There also may be a third partition, called the *controller*, that is used to initiate the blackboard and knowledge sources and that takes a bootstrap role and overall supervision control.

The connections between the blackboard subsystem and knowledge sources are basically implicit invocations from the blackboard to specific knowledge sources, which are registered with the blackboard in advance. Data changes in the blackboard trigger one or more matched knowledge source to continue processing. Data changes may be caused by new deduced information or hypotheses results by some knowledge sources. This connection can be implemented in *publish/subscribe* mode.

Figure 6.8 illustrates a block diagram of the blackboard architecture. The solid lines indicate data links, while dashed lines represent the flow logic control, which is controlled by any data changes in the data store. That is, the data in the blackboard store directs the flow of the computation.

Many domain-specific knowledge sources collaborate together to solve a complex problem such as pattern recognition or authentication in information security. Each knowledge source is relatively independent from the other knowledge sources. They don't need to interact with each other, which

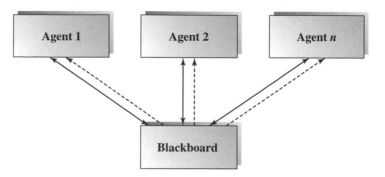

Figure 6.8

Blackboard architecture

is very similar to a repository system. They need only interact and respond to the blackboard subsystem. Each source works on a specific aspect of the problem and contributes a partial solution to the ultimate solution.

Figure 6.9 shows a UML class diagram of a rule-based blackboard software architecture. As we can see, one blackboard may have many knowledge sources associated with it, working on given data and deduced data available in the blackboard subsystem. Each knowledge source helps to solve problems in its expertise area. Knowledge can be stored in different knowledge representation formats depending on the reasoning strategy. For

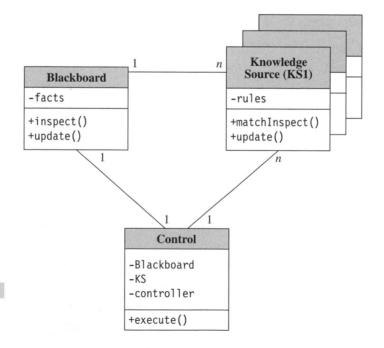

Figure 6.9

Class diagram of black-board architecture

example, a knowledge source stores all related rules and provides activation mechanisms for the blackboard to trigger in rule-based expert system. Of course, knowledge sources must register themselves with the blackboard so that if any change takes place in the blackboard, they will be notified to fire up actions in the corresponding knowledge sources, which can deduce new facts and update the blackboard. Each individual knowledge source may have its own problem solving strategy and use its own knowledge expertise to contribute to a partial solution which will lead to a final solution. The blackboard class holds the current data state, and the final problem solution will be placed in the blackboard for the controller to pick up and use to generate a final report. The rule-based strategy is one of many reasoning algorithms in use today. There are many other problem solving strategies that can be applied including Fuzzy set theory, probability and statistics, neural network, data mining, and heuristic searching.

Since the blackboard architecture is basically a self-activated system, the controller subsystem in the architecture only acts at the beginning of the process to initiate blackboard and all knowledge sources; it also periodically inspects the current state of the blackboard to determine whether to terminate the processing if the solution is acceptable or optimal enough.

Let's take a look at a well-known animal identification knowledge-based system (KBS). The knowledge is represented in the format of production rules with condition and action parts. For each rule, if the condition is true then the action is taken. The action is to put new conclusion data in the data store, which is the blackboard.

Here is a set of rules:

R1: IF animal gives milk *then* animal is mammal

R2: IF animal eats meat *then* animal is carnivore

R3: IF animal is mammal *and* animal is carnivore *and* animal has tawny color *and* animal has black stripes *then* animal is tiger

The set of facts is:

F1: animal eats meat

F2: animal gives milk

F3: animal has black stripes

F4: animal has tawny color

The goal is to recognize the animal. The problem may ask you to approve a statement or get a best recognition in the animal category.

All the facts are placed in the blackboard and all knowledge is placed in the knowledge sources by the controller. There may be many different reasoning models such as forward reasoning or backward reasoning.

The forward reasoning starts with the initial state of data and proceeds toward a goal. It may reach the given goal or it may fail to reach the goal. If the goal is not given, the reasoning will arrive at a point where no more new facts can be derived, indicating that the best result has been determined. The backward reasoning works in the opposite direction.

Let's follow the forward reasoning sequence. F1 matches the condition of R2, and "animal is carnivore" is derived and stored in the blackboard. If the algorithm checks the newest generated data first and the new fact does not match any rules, it then checks F2 which matches the condition of R1. Then, "animal is mammal" is derived and stored in the blackboard. After this point there is no single fact that matches any rule, and if combined data are used R3 is matched and "animal is tiger" is derived and put back in the data store. While this is a relatively simple example, it tells us how the knowledge is used in reasoning. In a more realistic blackboard system, there are many knowledge resources, each with its own knowledge representations and reasoning algorithms.

The sequence diagram in Figure 6.10 illustrates the dynamic interactions in a blackboard system. The controller initiates the blackboard and all knowledge sources first and then starts the processing by inspecting the blackboard and knowledge sources and activates the control flow. Any changes in the blackboard may satisfy the conditions of rules, and new actions will be taken against the blackboard and the blackboard updated. It will keep going until the controller determines to stop the processing after an optimal acceptable conclusion is produced or simply abandons the processing due to a failure.

The diagram in Figure 6.11 illustrates the *publish/subscribe* relationship between the blackboard and the knowledge sources in the blackboard system.

All knowledge sources register or subscribe specific facts and hypotheses stored in the blackboard store by the `addEventListener()` method of the blackboard. The registrations are stored in a vector **v**. If any data are added

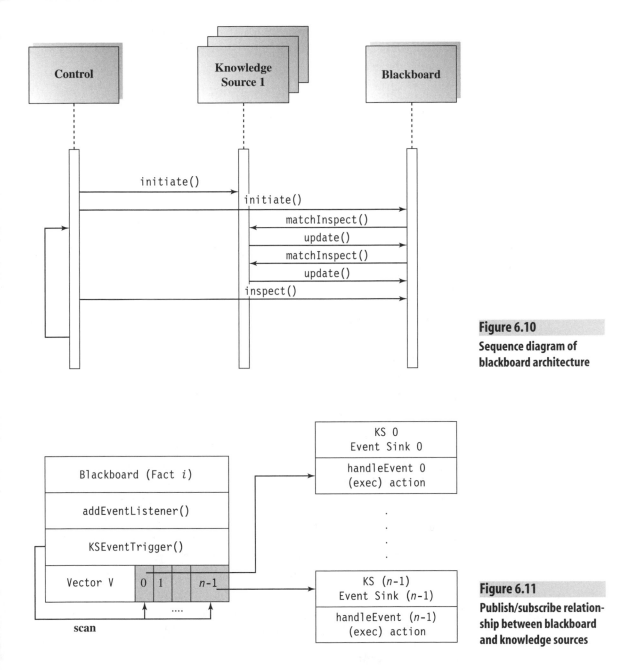

Figure 6.10

Sequence diagram of blackboard architecture

Figure 6.11

Publish/subscribe relationship between blackboard and knowledge sources

or changed, the blackboard will notify the registered knowledge sources by eventTrigger() so that the knowledge sources will take actions to respond or handle the events.

A simple example application from daily life illustrates the fundamentals of blackboard architecture. Think of a smart travel consulting system that could assist you to plan your travel efficiently in terms of time and cost. Clients just need to fill out a form and the system will respond with many optional plans from which to choose.

The blackboard architecture is a good fit because making a travel plan requires many near-at-hand agents such as airline, hotel reservation, auto rental, and attraction agents. It also involves a data store of budget, available time, and other facts to be shared by all agents. The system itself produces all plans without much additional interaction.

After a client submits a request, the system stores all these data in the data store and makes a request to air agents. Once air reservation data returns and is saved in the data store, the change will trigger hotel, auto rental, and attraction ticket agents to work together to produce an optimal plan within the given budget and timetable. After the client selects one of the plans, the system activates the billing process to finalize the plan.

Figure 6.12 shows the blackboard architecture for this travel consulting system. There may be many air travel agencies, hotel reservation systems, car rental companies, or attraction reservation systems to subscribe to or register with through this travel planning system. Once the system receives a client request, it publishes the request to all related agents and composes plan options for clients to choose from. The system also stores all necessary data in the database. After the system receives a confirmation from the client, it invokes the financial billing system to verify credit background and to issue invoices. The data in the data store plays an active role in this system. It does not require much user interaction after the system receives client requests since the request data will direct the computation and activate all related knowledge sources to solve the problem.

Applicable domain of blackboard architecture:

- Suitable for solving open-ended and complex problems such as artificial intelligence (AI) problems where no preset solutions exist.

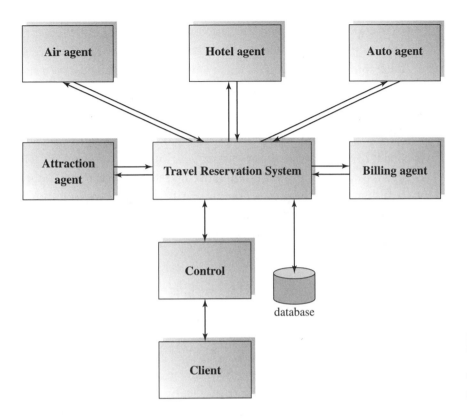

Figure 6.12
**Blackboard architecture
for a travel consulting
system**

- The problem spans multiple disciplines, and each problem involves completely different types of knowledge expertise and problem-solving paradigms that require cooperation.

- Partial or approximate solution is acceptable to the problems.

- Exhaustive searching is impossible and impractical since it may take forever because available knowledge and even data and hypotheses may not be complete or precisely accurate.

Benefits:

- *Scalability:* easy to add or update knowledge source.

- *Concurrency:* all knowledge sources can work in parallel since they are independent of each other.

- Supports experimentation for hypotheses.

- Reusability of knowledge source agents.

Limitations:

- Due to the close dependency between the blackboard and knowledge source, the structure change of the blackboard may have a significant impact on all of its agents.

- Since only partial or approximate solutions are expected, it can be difficult to decide when to terminate reasoning.

- Synchronization of multiple agents is an issue. Since multiple agents are working and updating the shared data in the blackboard simultaneously, the preference or priority of executions of multiple agents must be coordinated.

- Debugging and testing of the system is a challenge.

Related architecture:

- Implicit invocation architecture such as event-based, MVC architecture

6.4   Summary

Data centered repository architecture may be one of the most popular software architectures since most software applications require a data repository. Repositories are often used in layered architecture, client-server architecture, data tier in multi-tier architecture, and many other architecture designs. Agents of the data store in data-centered repository architecture control the logic flow. The data store is passive in the repository architecture, and agents control and trigger all operations on the data store. Data-centered blackboard architecture is a knowledge-based architecture where the status of the data in the data store controls and triggers most operations. The data store is active in the blackboard software architecture. The connection between the components in the blackboard architecture is implemented implicitly (instead of explicit invocation) in the repository systems. There are many expert systems for pattern recognition, voice or speech recognition, or other similar systems with this architecture.

6.5   Self-Review Questions

1. Which of the following is *not* a benefit of repository architecture?

   a.   Independent agents

   b.   Reusable agents

c. Concurrency

d. Loose coupling

2. Which of the following is a typical design domain of blackboard architecture?

a. AI system

b. Business information system

c. Compilers

d. Virtual machine

3. The Yellow Page of web service is an example of repository design.

a. True

b. False

4. Implicit notification is often used in blackboard architecture.

a. True

b. False

5. Repository architecture design must also be object-oriented design.

a. True

b. False

6. Agents in the repository architecture normally do not talk with each other directly, except though the data store.

a. True

b. False

7. Loose coupling is used between repository agents.

a. True

b. False

8. There is tight dependency of agents on the data store in the repository architecture.

a. True

b. False

9. Rule-based knowledge is installed in the blackboard component of the blackboard architecture.

   a. True

   b. False

10. The facts or hypotheses are stored in the knowledge source component of a blackboard system.

    a. True

    b. False

Answers to the Self-Review Questions

1. c 2. a 3. a 4. a 5. b 6. a 7. a 8. a 9. b 10. b

6.6 Exercises

1. What is data-centered architecture?

2. How many sub-architecture styles are there in this category?

3. What is the domain for repository architecture?

4. What is the domain for blackboard architecture?

5. What are the benefits of repository architecture and its limitation?

6. Is JVM an example of repository architecture?

7. Can a repository be decentralized?

8. Can repository architecture be a virtual repository?

9. Can the agents of a repository talk with each other?

6.7 Design Exercises

1. Design software architecture for a student record management system by repository architecture. The system provides privileges for the administrator to add or update student records and lets students check their own records.

2. Design software architecture for a weather broadcast system using blackboard architecture. Draw the block diagram and class diagram.

3. Design software architecture for an animal identification system using a rule-based blackboard architecture style. Draw the block diagram and class diagram.

6.8 Challenge Exercise

Design a security check-in system that provides face, fingerprint, voice, height, weight, and other document identification recognition means. The system has its recognition rules and preinstalled facts about trusted and target people. All KSS cooperate together to provide the authentication integrity.

Suggested Reading

Garlan, David and Mary Shaw. *Software Architecture: Perspectives on an Emerging Discipline.* Upper Saddle River, NJ: Prentice Hall, 1996.

CHAPTER 7

Hierarchical Architecture

Objectives of this Chapter

- Introduce the concepts of hierarchical software architecture
- Describe the main-subroutine, master-slave, and layered architectures
- Discuss the application domains of hierarchical software architecture
- Discuss the benefits and limitations of hierarchical software architecture
- Demonstrate the hierarchical software architecture in OS scripts and Java

7.1   Overview

The hierarchical software architecture is characterized by viewing the entire system as a hierarchy structure. The software system is decomposed into logical modules (subsystems) at different levels in the hierarchy. Modules at different levels are connected by explicit or implicit method invocations. In other words, a lower-level module provides services to its adjacent upper-level modules, which invokes the methods or procedures in the lower level. In procedural language, the function and procedures may be organized in a header file or in a library. In order to make use of services, an upper-level module must call the functions or procedures from these files or from library. In an object-orientation implementation of this architecture style, the services may be organized in a package of classes, this package is then imported by the upper-level modules to obtain the needed services by making calls to the corresponding class operations.

System software is typically designed using the hierarchical architecture style; examples include Microsoft .NET, Unix operating system, TCP/IP, etc. One thing these have in common is that services at lower levels provide more specific functionality down to fundamental utility services such as I/O services, transaction, scheduling, and security services, etc. Middle layers, in an application setting, provide more domain-dependent functions such as business logic or core processing services. Upper layers provide more abstract functionality in the form of user interfaces such as command line interpreters, GUIs, Shell programming facilities, etc. Each layer provides services to its immediate upper layer. Any changes to a specific layer may affect only its adjacent upper layer, but only when its interface is changed. Otherwise there are no ripple effects of changes.

This architecture category is characterized by the hierarchical structure and explicit method invocation (call-and-return) connection styles. It is also used in the organization of class libraries such as Java API in package hierarchy or .NET class library in name space hierarchy.

A variety of design types—procedure-oriented, object-oriented, component-oriented, domain-specific—can all implement the hierarchical software architecture.

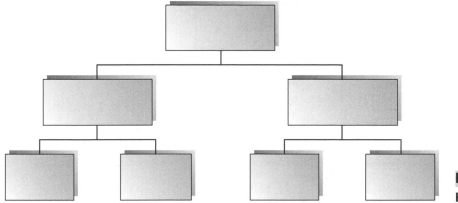

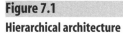

Figure 7.1
Hierarchical architecture

Additionally, as discussed earlier, an architecture style can work together with other styles. In fact, it is hard to find software designs that only use one architecture style. The hierarchical structure is one of the most popular styles that often combine with other styles.

There are four particular styles that are hierarchical: the main-subroutine, master-server, layered, and virtual machine.

Figure 7.1 shows the block diagram of typical hierarchical software architecture.

7.2   Main-Subroutine

The main-subroutine design architecture has dominated the software design methodologies for a very long time. The purpose of this architecture style is to reuse the subroutines and have individual subroutines developed independently. In the classical procedural paradigm, typically data are shared by related subroutines at the same level. With object orientation, the data is encapsulated in each individual object so that the information is protected. People often refer to the main-subroutine style as a traditional style rather than OO style.

Using this style, a software system is decomposed into subroutines hierarchically refined according to the desired functionality of the system. Refinements are conducted vertically until the decomposed subroutine is simple enough to have its sole independent responsibility, and whose functionality may be reused and shared by multiple callers in the upper layers.

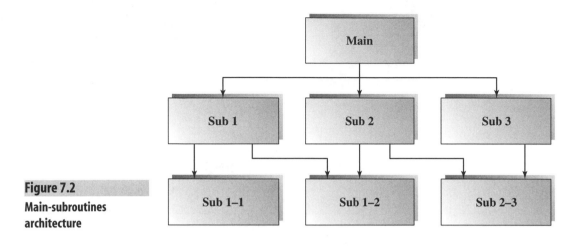

Figure 7.2

Main-subroutines architecture

Data is passed as parameters to subroutines from callers. Two ways to pass on parameter data are:

- Pass by reference where the subroutine may change the value of data referenced by the parameter; and

- Pass by value where the subroutine only uses the passed data but cannot change it.

Another less frequently used parameter passing is passing by name, depending on the implementation technology used. You can even pass in a reference to a procedure or function to implement callbacks (see next section).

Typically a "main" program drives the control over the sequencing of the subroutine calls by at least once looping over the invocations in some order. Figure 7.2 shows subroutine sharing in the main-subroutine hierarchy style.

The following describes how to map a requirement specification to the main-subroutine design style. A data flow diagram (DFD) is often used to model the software requirement in this case, where bubbles or circles represent processing or activities and arrows represent data flow. Figure 7.3 shows a DFD for the purchase order processing requirement. There may be two types of information flows: transform flow and transaction flow. In a DFD, the overall information flow is sequential. Both transform and transaction flows can occur in the same DFD.

In a transform flow, incoming flow feeds data in an external format, such as XML, which is transformed into another format; then the outgoing flow carries the data out.

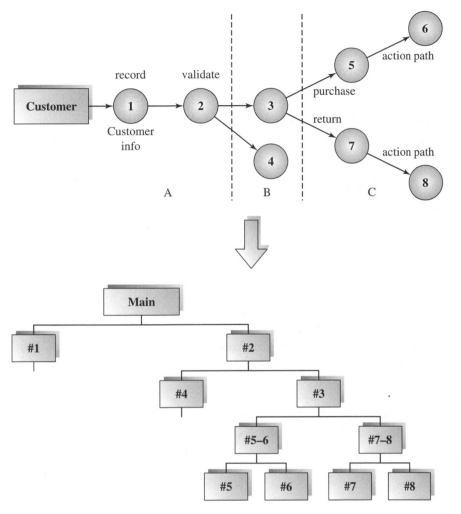

Figure 7.3
DFD mapped into main-subroutine structure

The transaction flow evaluates its incoming data and decides to follow one of many action paths.

During the mapping from DFD to the main-subroutine architecture, first we need to find the transform or transaction flows (Pressman, 2005). Separate the incoming path and all action paths, and classify each action path as transform or transaction flows. The resulting action modules themselves may be transaction centers too or may involve transform flows. This factoring analysis continues until each module in the software architecture has its sole responsibility.

In most cases an overall flow is a transform flow. The transform center can be easily isolated from the incoming and outgoing flows. A transform flow is mapped by a controlling module for incoming, transform, and outgoing information processing.

A transaction center can also be easily located in a DFD because the transaction centre is located at the fork origin of action paths. The transaction centre becomes a dispatcher control module that controls all subordinate action modules.

The DFD diagram in Figure 7.3 depicts a simple example of a purchase process requirement. The process circle #1 receives requests from the customer and records all related information. The data is forwarded to the next process (circle #2) which validates the request (either return or purchase), and if the request is invalid it is rejected and the customer is notified (circle #4).

To continue the transaction process #3 next selects one of the two different action paths; process #5 checks stock availability, while process #6 checks the customer credentials before making the invoice. On the alternate path, process #7 checks the return policy, while process #8 performs the refund transaction accordingly.

If procedure-oriented software architecture is adopted, the software architect or designer needs to map the DFD to a hierarchy structure with the mapping rules previously discussed. The result is shown at the bottom of Figure 7.3.

Benefits:

- It is easy to decompose the system based on the definition of the tasks in a top-down refinement manner.
- This architecture can still be used in a subsystem of OO design.

Limitations:

- Globally shared data in classical main-subroutines introduces vulnerabilities.
- Tight coupling may cause more ripple effects of changes as compared to OO design.

7.3   Master-Slave

The master-slave architecture is a variant of the main-subroutine architecture style that supports fault tolerance and system reliability. In this architecture, slaves provide replicated services to the master, and the master selects a particular result among slaves by certain selection strategies. The slaves may perform the same functional task by different algorithms and methods or by a totally different functionality.

Figure 7.4 shows a master-slave architecture where all slaves implement the same service. The master configures the invocations of the replicated services and receives the results back from all slaves. It then determines which of the returned results will be selected.

The diagram in Figure 7.5 shows a UML class diagram for the master-slave architecture where multiple slave classes implement the same interface in different ways.

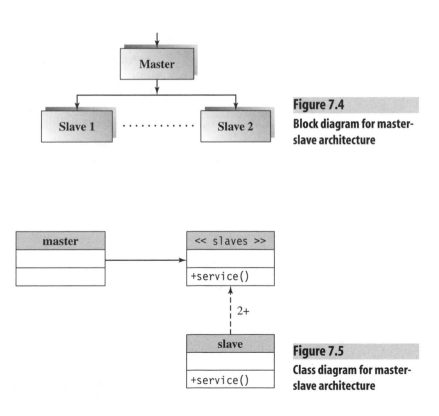

Figure 7.4

Block diagram for master-slave architecture

Figure 7.5

Class diagram for master-slave architecture

Other characteristics of this architecture include parallel computing and accuracy of computation. All slaves can be executed in parallel. Since the same task is delegated to several different implementations, inaccurate results can be ruled out easily with a majority vote strategy or other algorithms.

Applicable domains of master-slave architecture:

Master-slave architecture is used for the software system where reliability is critical. This is due to the replication (redundancy) of servers.

It should be noted that in database schema design, the terms master-slave or parent-child are employed to specify the dependency of one entity on another. If the master node is deleted then the slave node has reason to stay. This concept does not apply to the discussion here.

7.4   Layered

As its name suggests, in a layered architecture the system is decomposed into a number of higher and lower layers in a hierarchy; each layer consists of a group of related classes that are encapsulated in a package, in a deployed component, or as a group of subroutines in the format of method library or header file. Also, each layer has its own sole responsibility in the system.

A request to $layer_{i+1}$ invokes the services provided by the $layer_i$ via the interface of $layer_i$. The response may go back to the $layer_{i+1}$ if the task is completed; otherwise $layer_i$ continually invokes services from the $layer_{i-1}$ below. The interface of each layer encapsulates all detailed service implementations in the current layer and the interfaces of the layers below. A request from a higher layer to the layer below is made via method invocation and the response goes back up via the method return.

Each layer has two interfaces: the up interface provides services to its upper layer and the low interface requires services from its lower layer.

In a pure layered hierarchy, each layer only provides services to the adjacent upper layer and only requests services from the adjacent layer directly below. Special cases may employ a bridge type connection, where an upper layer get services from a layer more than one level down, and a breach connection where a lower layer gets services from its upper layer.

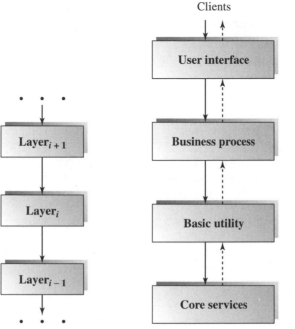

Clients

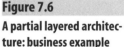

Figure 7.6
A partial layered architecture: business example

The higher layer provides more generic or application oriented services, which are more abstract; the lower layer provides more specific utility type services, which are less abstract, and common services which many upper layer components may need.

Figure 7.6 also depicts a typical layered architecture for business application software with user interaction. The solid lines indicate the service request direction path, while the dashed lines indicate the response path. The higher the layer, the more abstract the services are (in terms of the distance from the physical operating system layer). On the top level, users only see the user interfaces such as a GUI, but not any detailed implementations.

We can deploy each layer in a component format such as a jar file in Java. This is a compressed file deployed as a component of a package. A jar file includes all the service classes from lower levels plus other related classes provided in the same layer, and possibly those provided by Java API. As long as a jar file is on the `classpath` environment variable, you can access any classes in the jar file. Figure 7.7 shows an example of the logical package organization of the layered architecture. The UML notation for class package is used here. The top level deals with user interface, the next level is for utilities, and the one below utility provides core services. Each layer gets

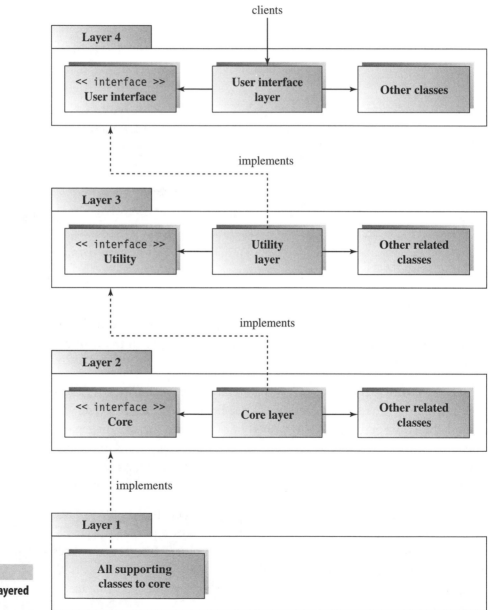

Figure 7.7

Component-based layered architecture

support from its lower adjacent layer by an interface implementation and from the related classes in the same layer.

A simple software system may consist of two layers: an interaction layer and a processing layer:

- The interaction layer provides user interfaces to clients, takes requests, validates and forwards requests to the processing layer for processing, and responds to clients.

- The processing layer receives the forwarded requests and performs the business logic process, accesses the database, returns the results to its upper layer, and lets the upper layer respond to clients since the upper layer has the GUI interface responsibility.

The diagram in Figure 7.7 shows the separate responsibilities for upper and lower layers and decoupling of business logic from presentation.

There are many good and widely known models designed using the layered architecture, such as ISO's OSI 7-layered model with layers of application, presentation, session, transport, network, data link, and physical. Another is the web services model with layers of SOAP, XML, HTML, TCP, and IP; other examples arc the Unix operating system design with layers of shell, core utility, device drivers, and the Microsoft .NET platform with CTS, JIT, and CLR sublayers.

The networks protocols are designed also as layered architecture, except that there are two layered stacks connected by a network link. A client makes a message or service request to the top layer of one stack. Then all subsequent layers perform their supporting services and pass on the data with the request all the way down to the bottom layer. The request with the data is sent to the server side and moves all the way up until it reaches the server application. The response will come in the reverse direction. This works in a request-response mode.

Figure 7.8 shows an example of the Simple Object Access Protocol (SOAP). The SOAP based web services technology supports cross-platform remote object, request-response Internet computing. A web service client sends a request in the SOAP message format to a web service housed at a web service engine and gets a SOAP formatted response message back from the web service via the pair of protocol stacks. SOAP needs XML and HTML

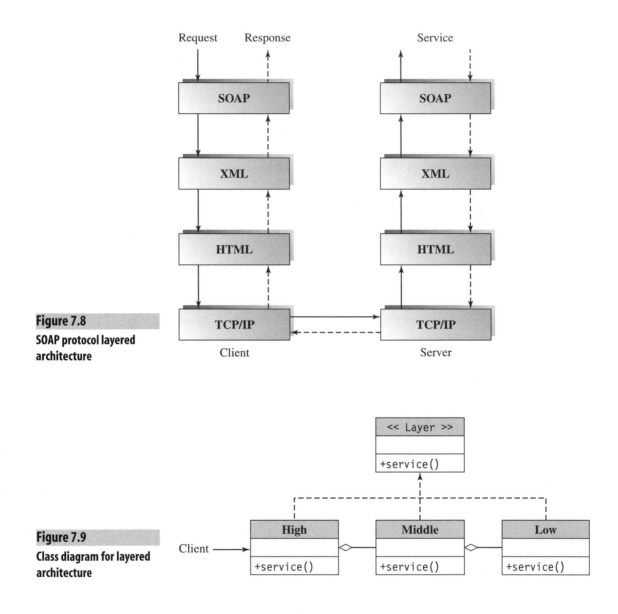

Figure 7.8
SOAP protocol layered architecture

Figure 7.9
Class diagram for layered architecture

protocols support; the XML and HTML get services from TCP/IP protocol, while TCP/IP takes care of communication over the Internet.

A simplified UML class diagram for layered architecture is shown in Figure 7.9. All layers implement a common layer interface thus making each layer easier to be replaced. A higher layer is linked to its immediate lower layer by an aggregation relationship.

Applicable domains of layered architecture:

- Any system that can be divided between the application-specific portions and platform-specific portions which provide generic services to the application of the system.

- Applications that have clean divisions between core services, critical services, user interface services, etc.

- Applications that have a number of classes that are closely related to each other so that they can be grouped together into a package to provide the services to others.

Benefits:

- Incremental software development based on increasing levels of abstraction.

- Enhanced independence of upper layer to lower layer since there is no impact from the changes of lower layer services as long as their interfaces remain unchanged.

- Enhanced flexibility: interchangeability and reusability are enhanced due to the separation of the standard interface and its implementation.

- Component-based technology is a suitable technology to implement layered architecture; this makes it much easier for the system to allow for plug-and-play of new components.

- Promotion of portability: each layer can be an abstract machine (see Section 7.5) deployed independently.

Limitations:

- Lower runtime performance since a client's request or a response to a client must go through potentially several layers. There are also performance concerns of overhead on the data marshaling and buffering by each layer.

- Many applications cannot fit this architecture design.

- Breach of interlayer communication may cause deadlocks, and "bridging" may cause tight coupling.

- Exceptions and error handling are issues in the layered architecture, since faults in one layer must propagate upward to all calling layers.

Related architecture:

- Virtual machine, repository, and client-server

7.5   Virtual Machine

A virtual machine is built up on an existing system and provides a virtual abstraction, a set of attributes, and operations. In most cases a virtual machine separates a programming language or application environment from an execution platform. A virtual machine may appear similar to emulation software.

The diagram in Figure 7.10 describes the Unix operating system as a virtual machine; one that provides multiple shells such as C shell, Korn shell, and Born shell on top of the Unix kernel. The Unix kernel provides all core capabilities and utility libraries, which make all shell system calls independent from the underlying device drivers and actual physical devices.

The common language runtime (CLR) of Microsoft .NET platform also plays the role of a virtual machine that uses a single intermediate language to unify several modules VB.NET, VC.NET, and C# (see Figure 7.11). This way, a VB.NET client can use a component written in C# or C++.

Another well-known example of virtual machine is the Java Virtual Machine (JVM). This is a runtime environment (RTE) that makes the Java programming language platform independent. In other words, the Java bytecode and other Java internal code generated by a compilation system (e.g., javac) can run on any operating system that supports JVM. JVM itself is platform dependent in that the RTE must be developed based on a specific platform. JVM makes Java programs portable, which is one of the most significant advantages over other executable programming languages such as C++. The early procedural language Pascal introduced the concept

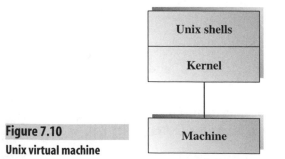

Figure 7.10

Unix virtual machine

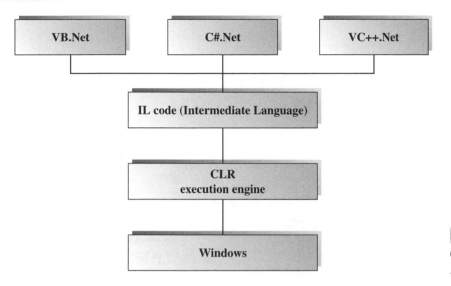

Figure 7.11
CLR virtual machine in
.NET platform

for the first time in the late 1970s (the P-machine and P-code). The Ada programming language specifies a standard runtime kernel, thus making it also similar to a virtual machine environment. In contrast, a C++ executable program can only run on the type of platform on which it was generated. If we want to run it on another machine we must get the original source code recompiled on that machine, and hence it is not portable, at least at the runtime level.

Figure 7.12 describes how the JVM separates the bytecode from the OS machine code. The bytecode is actually in a method format, and each op code can be interpreted by an interpreter. The virtual machine itself is thus implemented as an interpreter.

Any interpreter is like an execution engine which keeps track of the current state of the engine including the Program Counter (PC), data registers, program-wide data, parameter data, method local data, operation stacks, and the source code being interpreted. The interpreter system itself can be decomposed into code (class) loader and an executor. Let's look at a very simple java code and see how it is interpreted by its JVM.

```
public class simple{
public static void main(){
 for (int i=0; i<2; i++)
   System.out.println(i);
}
}
```

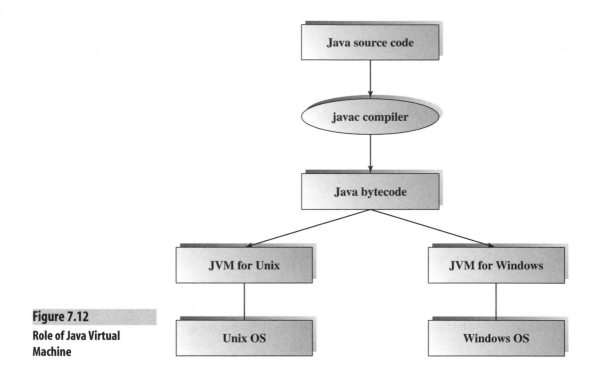

Figure 7.12
Role of Java Virtual
Machine

After compiling the bytecode into a class file, you can view it by issuing the command "javap −c simple". The bytecode class file consists of a series of method calls (similar to assembly code) that operate on an internal stack in memory.

```
C:\Java\JDK15~1.0\bin>javap −c simple
Compiled from "simple.java"
public class simple extends java.lang.Object{
public simple();
  Code:
   0:    aload_0
   1:    invokespecial    #1; //Method java/lang/Object."<init>":()V
   4:    return

public static void main();
  Code:
   0:    iconst_0
   1:    istore_0
   2:    iload_0
   3:    iconst_2
   4:    if_icmpge       20
   7:    getstatic       #2; //Field java/lang/System.out:Ljava/io/PrintStream;
   10:   iload_0
   11:   invokevirtual   #3; //Method java/io/PrintStream.println:(I)V
   14:   iinc      0, 1
   17:   goto      2
   20:   return
```

The following section describes the VM detailed interpretation.

The label n: at the beginning of each line tells the offset of the bytecode from the beginning address of the interpreted code. The character "i" at the beginning of the instruction indicates an integer operation.

The execution engine fetches the first bytecode instruction at location 0.

The iconst_0 instruction at location 0 is an in-line instruction pushing a constant 0 onto the stack.   Stack: 0

The istore_0 at location 1 pops the top of the stack to a register variable V0
                                                    Stack: ; V0: 0

The iload_0 at location 2 pushes the V0 onto the stack.   Stack: 0 ;   V0:0

The iconst_2 at location 3 pushes constant 2 onto the stack.
                                                    Stack:0,2;   V0:0

The is_icmpge at location 4 pops the top two values and compare 0 with 2, if 0 >= 2 is true go to 20. Because 0 < 2 the execution engine continues on to the next instruction at location 7.

(if_icmpge instruction itself takes 3 bytes)   Stack: ; V0:0

The getstatic #2 at location 7 pushes reference to the out field of the PrintStream class onto the stack.   Stack: ref; V0:0

The iload_0 at location 10 pushes the V0 onto the stack.   Stack: ref,0; V0:0

The invokevirtual at location #3 invokes the println() method after it pops out the ref and data 0. 0 is printed out at this time.   Stack: ; V0:0

The iinc 0, 1 increments the V0 by 1.   Stack: ;V0: 1

Goto location 2 to start a new iteration until i equals 2.

From the preceding discussion we can track the life cycle of an interpreter execution engine; its logic flow emulates a CPU operation. Figure 7.13 depicts the block diagram of a virtual machine for an interpreter.

An execution engine of a virtual machine can be described by the following pseudocode. Assume that the bytecode is loaded in memory already. It keeps running until it comes to the end of the interpreted code.

```
Void virtualMachine(...){
. . .
While(more bytecode)
{fetch next bytecode;
    fetch opcode;
    fetch parameters if any;
   switch(opcode)
```

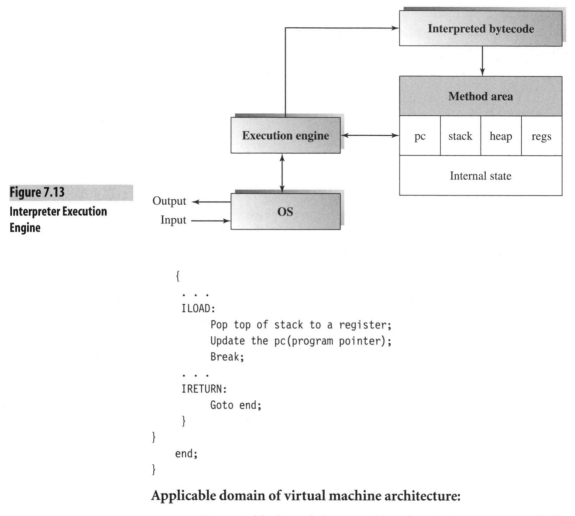

Figure 7.13
Interpreter Execution Engine

```
{
    . . .
    ILOAD:
        Pop top of stack to a register;
        Update the pc(program pointer);
        Break;
    . . .
    IRETURN:
        Goto end;
    }
}
    end;
}
```

Applicable domain of virtual machine architecture:

- It is suitable for solving a problem by simulation or translation if there is no direct solution.

- Sample applications include interpreters of microprogramming, XML processing, script command language execution, rule-based system execution, Smalltalk and Java interpreter type programming languages.

Benefits:

- Portability and machine platform independency

- Simplicity of software development

- Simulation for disaster working model

Limitations:

- Slow execution of the interpreter due to the interpreter nature
- Additional overhead due to the new layer

Related architecture:

- Interpreter, repository, and layered architecture

7.6   Summary

The hierarchy architecture style decomposes a system into a number of layers in a hierarchical manner. Upper layers get services from adjacent lower layers. The connection between two adjacent layers is made by explicit method invocations from the upper layer to the lower layer. The main-subroutines, master-slave, layered, and virtual machine styles are all sub-architecture styles of the hierarchical architecture model.

Hierarchical architecture style, although very popular for the design of system software, such as operating system design, networking protocol design, interpreters, and other business data processing, is also used in the design of application software. The style can be implemented using structural technology, as well as modern object-oriented and component-oriented approaches.

Here are some design guidelines for hierarchical architecture modeling.

- Define the decomposition criteria: a layer only depends on its lower layer; each layer has its clear and specific tasks.
- Determine the number of layers (≤ 7) based on the division criteria.
- Define the interface for each layer.
- Define each layer services.
- Define the connections between any two adjacent layers.
- Design error handling.

7.7   Self-Review Questions

1. Which of the following is *not* a benefit of hierarchical architecture?
   a. Concurrency
   b. Interactive
   c. Security
   d. Exchangeable

2. Which of the following is a disadvantage of hierarchical architecture?

    a. Overhead

    b. Interface separation

    c. Incremental

    d. Exchangeable

3. Web service is an example of hierarchy architecture design.

    a. True

    b. False

4. Hierarchical architecture is a procedure-oriented design paradigm only.

    a. True

    b. False

5. Hierarchical architecture can also be applied in any object-oriented software design.

    a. True

    b. False

6. Only directly adjacent layers can invoke each other's methods in a layered architecture.

    a. True

    b. False

7. Component deployment is a good practice in a layered architecture.

    a. True

    b. False

8. There is data sharing between all layers in a layered architecture.

    a. True

    b. False

9. The callback method is typically used in a main-subroutine architecture.

    a. True

    b. False

10. The master-slave architecture is a specialized form of main-subroutine architecture.

     a. True

     b. False

Answers to the Self-Review Questions

1. a   2. a   3. a   4. b   5. a   6. b   7. a   8. b   9. b   10. a

7.8   Exercises

1. What is a hierarchy architecture?

2. Enumerate all the sub-architecture styles in this category.

3. What is the application domain for layered architectures?

4. What is the application domain for master-slave architectures?

5. What are the benefits of hierarchy architecture and its limitations?

6. Is JVM an example of hierarchical architecture? Explain why or why not?

7. Can a hierarchical architecture be built in bottom-up mode?

8. Can a hierarchical architecture be built in a top-down mode?

9. Can a request-response process model be applied in a hierarchical architecture design?

7.9   Design Exercises

1. Design the software architecture for a student record management system using an OO layered architecture. The top layer is the GUI interface, the middle layer is the business process layer, and the bottom layer is for data access. Draw a block diagram, a UML class diagram, and a sequence diagram.

2. Implement the above system using Java according to the design architecture.

3. Design the software architecture for a device driver by a layered architecture.

4. Design an XML interpreter virtual machine that processes XML documents according to a DTD or an XML Schema that you define for the XML documents.

7.10 Challenge Exercises

1. Construct a layered architecture using the application presentation layer, application domain layer, library service layer, and third party layer to group all software components in the online payment system and motel reservation system at the end of Chapter 3.

2. Analyze the .NET framework class library and sketch the .NET framework in a layered architecture.

3. Analyze the Java 2 Enterprise Edition framework API and sketch the Java 2 EE framework in a layered architecture.

References

Pressman, Roger. *Software Engineering: A Practitioner's Approach*. 6th ed. New York: McGraw-Hill, 2005, 255–291.

Suggested Reading

Garlan, David and Mary Shaw. *Software Architecture: Perspectives on an Emerging Discipline*. Upper Saddle River, NJ: Prentice Hall, 1996.

CHAPTER 8

Implicit Asynchronous Communication Software Architecture

Objectives of this Chapter

- Introduce concepts of the asynchronous communication software architecture
- Describe the nonbuffered event-based and buffered message-based architectures
- Discuss applicable domains
- Discuss the benefits and limitations of the asynchronous software architecture
- Discuss other related architectures

8.1   Overview

This chapter discusses software designs with asynchronous implicit invocation communications used in blackboard architecture in Chapter 6. An asynchronous implicit invocation communication can be specified in two different modes: nonbuffered and buffered. We have seen some architectures that apply the publisher-subscriber or producer-consumer patterns where the subscribers/consumers are interested in some events or messages issued by a publisher/producer. Subscribers register themselves with the event source. The subscriber is actually an event listener that, after registration, is notified of such occurrences. Once an event is fired off by an event source, all corresponding subscribers are notified, which then take corresponding actions. It is up to the subscribers to decide on the actions to execute. The *Observer* pattern is another name used for this type of architecture.

The message queue and message topic are typical buffered asynchronous architectures that subscribers/consumers also need to register their interests with; the event/message is fired off when available on the buffered message queue or topic. A message queue is a one-to-one or point-to-point architecture between message senders and message receivers; whereas a message topic is a one-to-many architecture between publishers and subscribers.

Regardless of the type of asynchronous architecture, the main purpose of this type of communication architecture is to provide a decoupling between the event/message, the publishers/producers, and the subscribers/customers. These are very popular architectures in distributed applications. Specific examples of implicit invocation architectures include, but are not limited to, JavaBean components, ActiveX components, .NET components, the Enterprise JavaBean (EJB) callback methods by the EJB container, the Common Object Request Broker Architecture (CORBA) callback mechanism, passing function pointers as parameters of function in method invocations in C++, Java XML SAX parser, and MS .NET Remote mechanisms.

8.2   Nonbuffered Event-Based Implicit Invocations

The nonbuffered event-based implicit invocation architecture breaks the software system into two partitions: event sources and event listeners. The event registration process connects these two partitions. There is no buffer available between these two parties.

The event-based implicit invocations (nonbuffered) is part of SmallTalk language where each object keeps its own dependency list. Any state changes of the object will impact its dependents. The diagram in Figure 8.1 shows the software architecture for the event-based implicit invocation in SmallTalk. The graphic View components register themselves with the interested event source Model via the event space. When the data is changed in the Model (event source) the target is notified via the event space and the target handles the event accordingly. These are the basics of the concept of event-based implicit invocation, which is the opposite of the direct explicit method invocation whereby the invoker must wait for the response from the called module; in this case, the invoker does not proceed until the called party responds. The MVC adopts this for the connection between model and view.

The diagram in Figure 8.2 depicts the explicit synchronous and implicit asynchronous connection architecture in a UML sequence diagram. The upper portion of the diagram demonstrates the synchronous invocation, while the lower portion shows the asynchronous one. In the latter, the service requester does not wait for the response; instead, it spawns a separate thread to receive the response from the service provider and resumes its

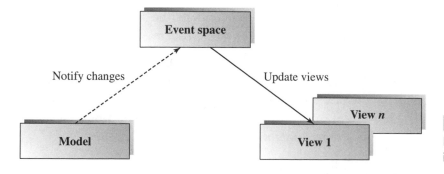

Figure 8.1

Event implicit invocations in SmallTalk

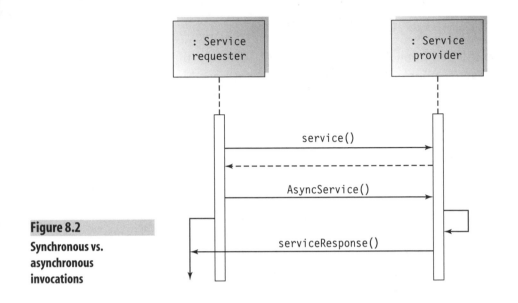

Figure 8.2

Synchronous vs. asynchronous invocations

own execution. The half arrow pointer in this portion of the figure indicates the asynchronous invocations. In many cases the service provider needs to spend a significant amount of computing time before it can reply to the requestors. That is also why asynchronous communication is necessary in many applications. In many other cases, such as a GUI interface application, there is no need to loop-check on the user actions due to the nondeterministic feature of applications. Event-driven asynchronous architecture better serves such applications, where events trigger and drive the computation.

A typical event-based implicit invocation class diagram is given in Figure 8.3. The event source class must provide mechanisms to register or deregister event targets and to notify event targets of the occurrence of the event. Event targets must specify the action in the `handleEvent()` method to respond to incoming events. Above the concrete classes are the interfaces for event source and event listener.

The event-based implicit invocation is a good solution for user interaction in a user interface application. Simple Java fragments that follow demonstrate how event sources and event targets (listeners) work together in an event-driven architecture for a user interface application.

```
package myEvent;
import java.applet.Applet;
```

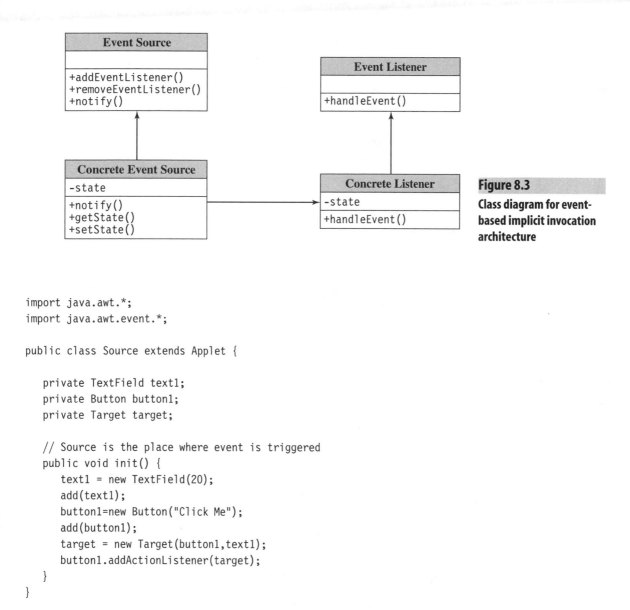

Figure 8.3

Class diagram for event-based implicit invocation architecture

```
import java.awt.*;
import java.awt.event.*;

public class Source extends Applet {

    private TextField text1;
    private Button button1;
    private Target target;

    // Source is the place where event is triggered
    public void init() {
        text1 = new TextField(20);
        add(text1);
        button1=new Button("Click Me");
        add(button1);
        target = new Target(button1,text1);
        button1.addActionListener(target);
    }
}
```

The Target registers with the event source by the following statement `button1.addActionListener(target)` where `target` is an object of class `Target`. The "Click Me" button is the event source. If it is pressed it will fire off an AWT event of `ActionEvent`, which will be intercepted by an `ActionListener` that has registered for it. In this case, the `Target` is the `ActionListener` where the `actionPerformed()` method specifies the event handling processing. The greeting message of "Hello <user>" will be displayed in the text field `text1` where the <user> is the user name typed in the text field before the button is pushed.

The screen shot below shows the word "Java" typed in the text field of the Applet and the button "Click Me."

The `Target.java` code is listed below. It specifies the actions which handle the `ActionEvent` event triggered by the button in the event source.

```
package myEvent;
import java.applet.Applet;
import java.awt.*;
import java.awt.event.*;

public class Target implements ActionListener {

    private Button button1;
    private TextField text1;

    public Target(Button b,TextField t) {
        button1 = b;
        text1 = t;
    }

    // Target is the event listener
    public void actionPerformed(ActionEvent event) {
        String msg = new String("Hello");
        if (event.getSource()==button1) {
            text1.setText(msg + " " + text1.getText());
        }
    }
}
```

After "Click Me" is pushed, a greeting message "Hello Java" is displayed in the text field.

An event can also be generic non-GUI related which users themselves can define. We call such events user-defined events.

The following Java fragments show a user-defined event-based architecture in Java. In the Java API, all events are subclasses of the EventObject class, regardless of whether they are built-in events or user-defined events. GUI event classes are subclasses of AWTEvent class or the Swing class, which is a subclass of EventObject. All the event listeners regardless of whether they are GUI built-in listeners or user-defined listeners are subclasses of EventListener.

Here is a user-defined event listener called MyListener.

```
public interface MyListener extends EventListener
{ void handleEvent(EventObject e); }
```

Next is a user-defined event object MyEventObject which is just like the GUI event object. This event object holds a long integer type of system time variable. It also provides a getTime() method to return the time when the object was created.

```
public class MyEventObject extends EventObject {
  long t1;
  public MyEventObject(Object o) {
    super(o);
    t1 = System.currentTime();
  }
  public long getTime(){ return t1;}
}
```

The target class Sink is a class of MyListener and handles the event by simply printing the time the event object holds.

```
public class Sink implements MyListener {
  ...........
  public void handleEvent(EventObject e) {
    System.out.println("Time is" + e.getTime());
  }
  ........
}
```

The event source class Source is a thread class so that the event source and event sink can run on different threads concurrently. This event source triggers a time event once every second. It also provides a registration vector for the event targets to register with this source. The addMyListener() method adds event targets to the vector. The triggerEvent() is the method used to create an event object with the current time and to scan the registration vector to notify all registered sink targets to handle the triggered event.

```java
public class Source implements Runnable {
  Vector v=new Vector();
  Thread thread;

  public Source(){
    Thread = new Thread(this);
    thread.start();
  }
  .....
  public void run() {
    while (true) {
      triggerEvent();
      try {
        thread.sleep(1000);
      } catch (Exception e) {. . .}
    }
  }

  public synchronized void addMyListener (MyListener l)
  {
    v.addElement (l);
  }

  void triggerEvent() {
    MyEventObject meo = new MyEventObject (this);
    for (int i = 0; i < v.length; i++) {
      MyListener wl=v.elementAt(i);
      wl.handleEvent(meo);
    }
  }
}
```

Here is the main bootstrap program that creates an event source object and an event target object, and then registers the target listener object with the event source object. If two threads are started, the conversation between the source and target will take place every second.

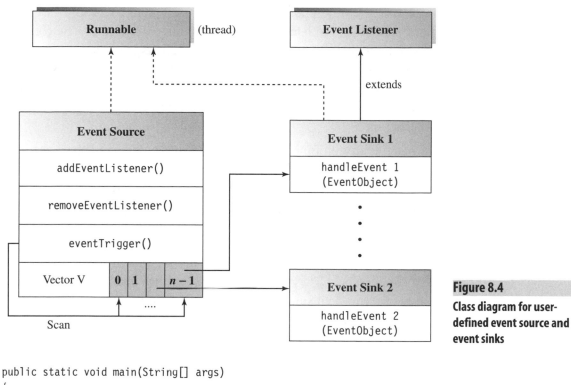

Figure 8.4

Class diagram for user-defined event source and event sinks

```
public static void main(String[] args)
{
   Source s1 = new Source();
   Sink t1 = new Sink();
   s1.addMyListener(t1);

   .
   .

}
```

The diagram in Figure 8.4 illustrates the concepts of user-defined event sources and event listeners (targets) that may be running in different threads concurrently.

An event can be declared either statically at compile time or dynamically at runtime. An event can be bonded with event listeners statically or dynamically, as well. We have only discussed static event declaration and static bonding. Dynamic event handler topics can be found in related professional books and articles.

Event-based implicit invocation architectures are found in many software application designs. The trigger function in the Oracle Developer database application is one example. Many IDE for CASE tools also apply the event-based connection, to handle editing functions, for example. The completion of the editing of a source file may trigger its compilation, or a new recompilation; this in turn triggers the relink processing, and so on. A related example is handling debugging: stopping at a breaking point may trigger the editor to take over so that a tester can check the current status of the program.

An example from business is a stock managing system whereby a user can set upper and lower threshold levels of a specific stock. When the stock value goes either too high or too low, the user will be notified automatically by the system and action will be taken automatically which can be configured by the user in advance. In an e-commerce system, when the inventory level of an item goes below the minimum stock level, the system is set to notify the contracted suppliers to order more items in order to keep the item in the stock. These are two typical applications where the event-handling approach is suitable.

Applicable domains of nonbuffered event-driven architecture:

- Interactive GUI component communication and integrated development environment (IDE) tools

- Applications that require loose coupling between components that need to notify or trigger other components to take actions upon asynchronous notifications

- The implementation of state machines

- When event handlings in the application are not predictable

Benefits:

- *Framework availability:* Many vendor APIs such as Java AWT and Swing components are available.

- *Reusability of components:* It is easy to plug in new event handlers without affecting the rest of the system.

- *System maintenance and evolution:* Both event sources and targets are easy to update.

- *Independency and flexible connectivity:* Dynamic registration and deregistration can be done dynamically at runtime.

- Parallel execution of event handlings is possible.

Limitations:

- It is difficult to test and debug the system since it is hard to predict and verify responses and the order of responses from the listeners. The event trigger cannot determine when a response has finished or the sequence of all responses.

- There is tighter coupling between event sources and their listeners than in message queue-based or message topic-based implicit invocation. Data sharing and data passing in the event object forwarded from event sources to event listeners also make the coupling tighter and somewhat hard to debug and test.

- Reliability and overhead of indirect invocations may be an issue.

Related architecture:

- PAC, message-based, MVC, multi-tier, and state machine architectures

8.3   Buffered Message-Based Software Architecture

The buffered message-based software architecture breaks the software system into three partitions: message producers, message consumers, and message service providers. They are connected asynchronously by either a message queue or a message topic. This architecture is also considered data-centric. In a message-based system, also referred to as a *fire and forget* system, a sender sends out a message that requires only a guaranteed message delivery reply. It is typically implemented as a message-oriented middleware (MOM) providing a reliable message service on a distributed system.

Message-based software architecture has long been in use. Messaging systems are used to build reliable, scalable, and flexible distributed applications supporting asynchronous communication. Messaging system architecture is essentially a peer-to-peer client-server architecture. The high degree of independency of components within the messaging system is one of its most important features. Its high scalability, interoperability in heterogeneous networks, and reliability also make the messaging system more popular.

Messaging-based architectures are widely used in the infrastructure for network management, telecommunication services, e-commerce, customer care, weather forecasting, supply chain management, banking systems, and many other systems. In addition, messaging systems are also used as bridges for system merging in the enterprise integration.

Many platforms provide message queue mechanisms, including Unix and Microsoft MQ, while others like IBM MQseries, Progress SonicMQ, JBossMQ, and FioranoMQ implement directly the Java Message Server (JMS). The BEA WebLogic JMS provides additional messaging flexibility over JMS. JMS is a typical API in J2EE platform that supports asynchronous messaging including Message-Driven Bean (MDB), a special type of enterprise JavaBean, that asynchronously consumes messages.

A message is a structured data with a message ID, message header, property, and a body. A typical example of a message is an XML document.

Messaging is a mechanism or technology that handles asynchronous or synchronous message delivery effectively and reliably. A messaging client can produce and send messages to other clients, and can also consume messages from other clients. Each client must register with a messaging destination in a connection session provided by a message service provider for creating, sending, receiving, reading, validating, and processing messages.

Messaging supports loosely coupled distributed communication between software components; this is similar to the implicit event-driven communication discussed earlier. However, a message receiver does not need to be available at the same time as the message sender in order for the communication to take place. In fact, the sender and receiver don't need to know each other's identity at all. The receiver, however, needs to know the message format and the message destination where the message is available.

Most messaging systems support asynchronous communication that delivers messages to a client as they arrive; thus, a consumer does not have to request messages in order to receive them.

Most messaging systems also support reliable message delivery that guarantees that the message is delivered exactly once.

This kind of messaging system is similar to email except that the producers and the receivers of an email message are human beings instead of software components.

Point-to-Point Messaging (P2P)   The message queue architecture is a point-to-point structure between producer and consumer. A P2P messaging archi-

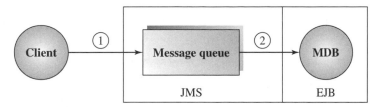

Figure 8.5
Message queue of JMS

tecture is composed of message queues, senders, and receivers. Each message is sent to a destination (a specific queue) which is maintained by the consumer; consumer clients extract messages from these queues. The queue retains all messages it receives either until the messages are consumed or until the messages expire. Each message has only one consumer, that is, the message is "gone" once it is delivered. This approach allows multiple message receivers but only one of them will receive the message as determined by the message service provider. A sender and a receiver of a message have no timing dependencies; the receiver can still receive the message even if it was not available when the sender sent the message. P2P messaging requires that every message sent to the message queue be processed successfully by a consumer. It is much more reliable than the simple event-listener based system discussed earlier.

The Message Driven Bean (MDB) of EJB is a consumer of the message queue supported by JMS. The diagram in Figure 8.5 shows the block diagram of Java Message Server (JMS) message queue. A message producer sends a message to the message queue destination which is taken by the MDB without timing restrictions.

Publish-Subscribe Messaging (P&S)   The publish-subscribe messaging architecture is a hub-like architecture where publisher clients send messages to a message topic that acts like a bulletin board. Message topic publishers and subscribers are not aware of each other. One difference between P&S and P2P is that each topic message can have multiple consumers. The system delivers the messages to all of its multiple subscribers instead of to a single receiver, as in the message queue system.

Publishers and subscribers have a timing coupling dependency. A message topic consumer must subscribe the topic before it is published unless the subscription is a *durable subscription* that is able to receive any topic messages sent while the subscribers are not active or not ready yet.

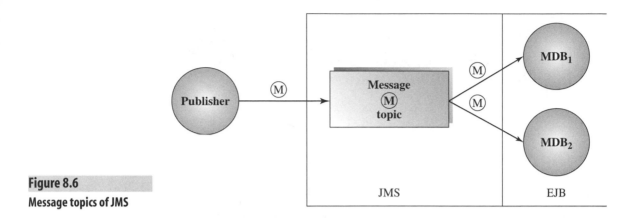

Figure 8.6

Message topics of JMS

Similar to event-based connection architectures, message-based connection architecture is mainly implemented by asynchronous communications (although it can also be synchronous). A software component can register a *message listener* with a consumer. A message listener is similar to an event listener. Whenever a message arrives at the destination, the provider delivers the message by calling the listener's onMessage() method, which performs the message handling operation just like the actionPerformed() method of the class ActionListener for AWT or Swing event in the Java API discussed previously.

Figure 8.6 describes the JMS message topics showing one published topic subscribed by multiple subscribers.

In most applications the JMS and the consumers (MDBs) can be remote distributed clients of the message queue or message topics. The MDB can also provide services to its own clients while it can access a database if necessary.

A message-based software application consists of the following parts.

1. *A messaging service provider or message server:* A messaging system that provides administrative and control features such as connection, session, and destination.

2. *Clients of message service:* Software components that produce and consume messages.

3. *Messages:* The objects that communicate information between message senders and message consumers.

Figure 8.7 and Figure 8.8 illustrate the JMS architecture, which supports both the point-to-point and the publish-subscribe messaging approaches.

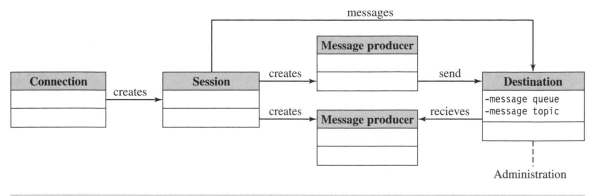

Figure 8.7

Class diagram for the message queue and message topic

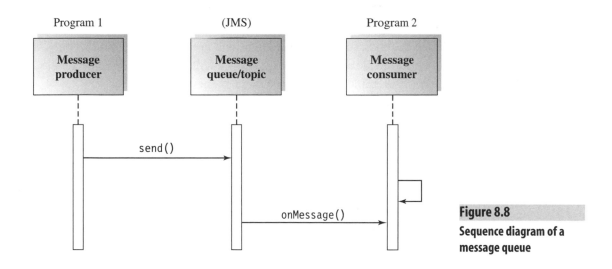

Figure 8.8

Sequence diagram of a message queue

Message clients (the message producer and message consumer) need to create connections to the message service provider and then create their session on the message server. The message destination (the queue or topic) is created by either administrator or by client programming.

The message producer generates a message and sends it to the destination queue or topic; the message consumer receives the message from the destination asynchronously by accepting the call OnMessage().

A *message listener* acts as an asynchronous event handler for messages just like the ActionListener for ActionEvent in the Java AWT API. The message

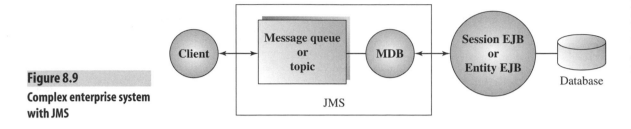

Figure 8.9

Complex enterprise system with JMS

listener has a method `onMessage()` which specifies message handling just like the `actionPerformed()` method of the `ActionListener`.

1. Create a connection to the messaging system provider.

2. Create sessions for sending and receiving messages.

3. Create `MessageProducers` to produce messages and `MessageConsumers` to receive messages.

Then the message-producing client will create messages and publish them to topics, while a message-consuming client will listen for messages associated with a topic and consume them as they arrive.

The MDB in Figure 8.9 plays the role of message listener. The `onMessage()` method will be called back whenever the message arrives at message queue or message topic destinations. Then the MDB can connect other session EJBs or entity EJBs on remote sites to let them take over the next distributed computation.

An enterprise web online business-to-business (B2B) application can use message-based architecture in situations like the following:

- The inventory component sends a message to the supplier component when the inventory level for an item drops below a certain level and needs to be replenished.

- The inventory component also sends a message to the business office component to prepare cash to purchase more inventory items and update the budgets.

- The supplier component sends a notification message to the catalog component to update the information after the supplier component gets more items in.

Academic retail, financial services, manufacturing, health services, and other settings can take advantages of messaging applications.

Applicable domains of message-based architecture:

- Suitable for a software system where the communication between a producer and a receiver requires buffered message-based asynchronous implicit invocation for performance and distribution purposes.

- The provider wants components that function independently of information about other component interfaces so that components can be easily replaced.

- The provider wants the application to run whether or not all other components are running simultaneously.

- The application business model allows a component to send information and to continue to operate on its own without waiting for an immediate response.

Benefits:

- *Anonymity:* provides high degree of anonymity between message producer and consumer. The message consumer does not know who produced the message (user independence), where the producer lives on the network (location independence), or when the message was produced (time independence).

- *Concurrency:* supports concurrency both among consumers and between producer and consumers.

- *Scalability and reliability of message delivery:* Reliability mechanisms include: control level setting of message acknowledgement; message persistence setting without loss; message priority level setting; and message expiration setting.

- Supports batch processing.

- Supports loose coupling between message producers and consumers, and between legacy systems and modern systems for integration development.

Limitations:

- *Capacity limit of message queue:* This is not an inherent limitation but an implementation issue that can be minimized if the queue is implemented as a dynamic data structure (e.g., linked lists). However, there is an absolute limit based on available memory. It is also difficult to determine the numbers of agents needed to satisfy the loose couplings between agents.

- Complete separation of presentation and abstraction by control in each agent generates development complexity since communication between agents only takes place between the control of agents.

- Increased complexity of the system design and implementation.

Related architecture:

- Event-based system, layered, multi-tier, and MVC

8.4   Summary

Implicit invocation architectures break the system into two parties: one party a publisher, sender, producer, source, or any other titles for event or message announcement, and the other a subscriber, receiver, consumer, target, or any other title with the same meaning for registering their interest and handling the events or messages. The communication between these two parties can be synchronous or asynchronous in a one-to-one (message queue), one-to-many (message topic, event-based), or many-to-one (event-based) mode. Thus, the implicit invocation architecture style bases its invariants on whether the event source or message sender know what components are interested in such events or messages; whether they care how the event target or message receiver will handle the event or message; and whether the two parties (source and target) are loosely connected.

This architecture style is commonly found in user interface design, e-commerce application design, and other distributed transactional business applications where the system involves many pairs of producer-consumer models that are loosely and asynchronously connected. The coupling between the sender and the receiver in message-based implicit invocation connected system is even looser than the event-based connected system because there are no time constraints dependency. A message receiver can still receive messages even if it is not running at the time the message was sent. In an event-based invocation system the event handler must be ready in order to be able to intercept an event and take an action upon that event.

This architecture style is commonly used in the connection between the Model subsystem and the view subsystem in an MVC or PAC architecture.

8.5 Self-Review Questions

1. Which of the following is one of the benefits of asynchronous architecture?

   a. Multiple independent agents

   b. Flexible GUI interfaces

   c. Multiple views

   d. Loose coupling of modules

2. Which of the followings is *not* typical design domain of the asynchronous architecture?

   a. Multiple agents in a distributed system

   b. Hierarchical structure

   c. Web server site application

   d. Java AWT and Swing

3. The testing of synchronous architecture is more straightforward than asynchronous architecture.

   a. True

   b. False

4. Implicit notification is often used in MVC architecture.

   a. True

   b. False

5. Multiple event targets can register with same event source.

   a. True

   b. False

6. An event can be either visible or invisible.

   a. True

   b. False

7. Coupling in message-driven architecture is even looser than in event-driven architecture.

   a. True

   b. False

8. A registered event target must be ready to handle the event when the event is fired off.

   a.   True

   b.   False

9. A message receiver is not required to be ready when the message arrives.

   a.   True

   b.   False

10. The notification of events or messages is different from local or remote method invocation.

    a.   True

    b.   False

11. Multiple consumers can consume a message on a message queue.

    a.   True

    b.   False

12. An event can be declared on the fly.

    a.   True

    b.   False

13. Message-based architecture is appropriate for a compiler in an IDE design.

    a.   True

    b.   False

Answers to the Self-Review Questions

1. d 2. b 3. a 4. a 5. a 6. a 7. a 8. a 9. a 10. a 11. a 12. a 13. b

8.6   Exercises

1. What is asynchronous application?

2. Typically, how many major partitions are there in an implicit invocation or asynchronous architecture? Explain why.

3. Describe the common features of asynchronous architecture.

4. Are web services or grid services asynchronous-oriented technology?

5. What are the problem domains for event-driven implicit architectures? Why?

6. What are the problem domains of message queue-oriented architectures? Why?

7. Are Java AWT GUI components examples of asynchronous architectures? Why?

8. Describe the limitations of asynchronous architecture.

9. Explain the advantages of event-driven invocation over message-driven invocation.

10. Explain the advantages of message-driven architecture over event-driven architecture.

8.7   Design Exercises

1. Design a software architecture for an online student registration waiting list system using the event-driven asynchronous architecture. When a course section is closed, the system must register students in a waiting list. When seats are available, students registered in the waiting list will be notified. Draw a block diagram, class diagram, and either a sequence diagram or collaboration diagram of your design, or both.

2. Design an event-driven software architecture for a GUI-oriented application. Draw a block diagram, class diagram, and either a sequence diagram or collaboration diagram, or both.

3. Design a software architecture for an inventory management system using the implicit invocation architecture. When the inventory has less than the minimum stock amount the system would notify the supplier to reorder more such items. Draw a block diagram, class diagram, and either a sequence diagram or collaboration diagram, or both.

8.8   Challenge Exercise

Design a stock market notification online system. A stock holder can set the upper and lower bounds on any stock he is interested in. Once the stock value goes above the up bound or below the low bound, the user should be notified. The user can register or unregister with a specified stock, and adjust the boundaries.

Suggested Reading

Jendrock, Eric, Jennifer Ball, Debbie Carson, Ian Evans, Scott Fordin, and Kim Haase. "The Java EE 5 Tutorial." October 2008. Sun Microsystems, http://java.sun.com/javaee/5/docs/tutorial/doc/.

CHAPTER 9

Interaction-Oriented Software Architectures

Objectives of this Chapter

- Introduce the concepts of interaction-oriented software architectures
- Describe the MVC and PAC architecture styles
- Discuss the application domains of interaction-oriented software architectures
- Assess the benefits and limitations of the interaction-oriented software architecture style
- Discuss other related architectures

9.1   Overview

More and more software applications involve user input/output interactions and specific user interfaces to software systems. In this chapter we focus on the software architecture that best supports user interaction in the application. We will also discuss software architectures for user interface design.

The interaction-oriented software architecture decomposes the system into three major partitions: data module, control module, and view presentation module. Each module has its own responsibilities. The data module provides the data abstraction and all core business logic on data processing. The view presentation module is responsible for visual or audio data output presentation and may also provide user input interface when necessary. The control module determines the flow of control involving view selections, communications between modules, job dispatching, and certain data initialization and system configuration actions. The key point of this architecture is its separation of user interactions from data abstraction and business data processing. Since there may be many view presentations in different formats, multiple views may be supported for the same data set. Even for a specific view presentation, the interfaces or views may need to change often, so loose coupling between data abstractions and its presentations is helpful and is supported by this style. The loose coupling connections can be implemented in a variety of ways such as explicit method invocation or implicit registration/notification method invocation. The control module plays a central role that mediates the data module and view presentation modules. All three modules may be fully connected.

This chapter presents two major style categories of interaction-oriented architectures: Presentation-Abstraction-Control (PAC) and Model-View-Controller (MVC).

These two models are similar in the sense that they propose three component decompositions. The Presentation module of PAC is like the View module of MVC; the Abstraction module of PAC looks like the data (or Model) module of MVC; the Control module of PAC is like the Controller module of MVC. Both MVC and PAC are used for interactive applications such as web online applications and distributed applications with multiple tasks and user interactions. They differ in their flow of control and organization. The PAC is an agent-based hierarchical architecture, whereas MVC does not have a clear hierarchical structure and all three modules are connected together.

The Apache Strut is a well-known pattern-based framework for MVC architecture that is widely used in web application design.

9.2   Model-View-Controller (MVC)

Most web developers are familiar with the MVC architecture because it is widely adopted for web server site interactive application design such as online shopping, surveys, student registration, and many other interactive service systems. MVC architecture is specifically used in applications where user interfaces are prone to data changes. MVC also typically supports "look and feel" features in GUI systems. The Java Swing components and Java Swing layout managers are designed using the MVC architecture.

This architecture was first introduced in Smalltalk-80. According to Glenn Krasner and Stephen Pope (1988):

> Model-View-Controller programming is the application of this three-way factoring whereby objects of different classes take over the operations related to the application domain (the model), the display of the application's state (the view), and the user interaction with the model and the view (the controller).
>
> Models: The model of an application is the domain-specific software simulation or implementation of the application's central structure.
>
> Views: In this metaphor, views deal with everything graphical: they request data from their model and display the data.
>
> Controllers: Controllers contain the interface between their associated models and views and the input devices (e.g., keyboard, pointing device, time).

In summary, the Controller manages the user input requests, controls the sequence of user interactions, selects desired views for output displays, and manages all initialization, instantiations, and registrations of other modules in the MVC system. The Model module provides all core functional services and encapsulates all data details. The Model module does not

Figure 9.1

MVC-I architecture

depend on other modules, and it does not know which views are registered with or attached to it. The View module is responsible for displaying the data provided by the Model module and updating the interfaces whenever the data changes are notified.

9.2.1   MVC-I

The MVC-I is a simple version of MVC architecture where the system is simply decomposed into two subsystems: The Controller-View and the Model. Basically, the Controller-View takes care of input and output processing and their interfaces; the Model module copes with all core functionality and the data. The Controller-View module registers with (attaches to) the data module. The Model module notifies the Controller-View module of any data changes so that any graphics data display will be changed accordingly; the controller also takes appropriate action upon the changes. The connection between the Controller-View and the Model can be designed in a pattern of subscribe-notify whereby the Controller-View subscribes to the Model and the Model notifies the Controller-View of any changes. In other words, the Controller-View is an observer of the data in the Model module. In Figure 9.1 the Controller and View are combined together to act as input/output user interface and the Model provides all data and domain services.

Let's look at a simple GUI example designed in MVC-I. The View has a GUI interface with two text fields; the user enters a new number in one of the text fields and the accumulated summation is displayed in the other. The summation is held in the Model module. The Model provides all business logics including all getter and setter methods. Whenever the data in the Model is updated, it will notify the registered GUI components of changes. Then the GUI components will update their displays. This is why we say that the data in the Model of MVC architecture is active rather than passive.

Actually, for this specific example there is no need to have a separated Model to notify the change because `actionPerformed()` can take care of all necessary changes. This example shows how MVC-I architecture works.

```java
// ViewController.java: ViewController makes a connection to the
// Model first. It sets up a GUI environment for input
// and output. It also attaches the display view of the
// textField to the Model by an attach() function,
// whenever user inputs a number in the textfield and
// hits a return key the actionEventListener requests
// service from the Model, performs business process,
// and reports the result.

package mvc1;
import java.awt.*;
import java.awt.event.*;
import javax.swing.*;

public class ViewController extends  JFrame  implements
    ActionListener {
    Model myModel;
    JTextField myInput;
    JTextField mySum;
    JPanel content;

  public ViewController(Model model) {
      myModel = model;
      myInput = new JTextField(5);
      mySum = new JTextField(15);
      content = new JPanel();
      content.add(myInput);
      content.add(mySum);
      setContentPane(content);
      myInput.addActionListener(this);
  }

 Public  void update() {
     mySum.setText(" " + myModel.getSum());
 }

  public void actionPerformed(ActionEvent e) {
     try  {
        myModel.add(myInput.getText());
```

```
        } catch (Exception ex)  { ... }
  }
}

// Model.java: The Model of MVC-I provides data and services, It
// provides mechanism for View/Controller to be
// registered and notified when any data is changed.

package mvc1;
import java.util.*;

public class Model {
  int sum;
  Vector listeners;

  public Model() {
     sum = 0;
     listeners = new Vector();
  }

  public void attach(ViewController vc) {
     listeners.addElement(vc);
  }

  public void notifyVC()     {
     for  (int i = 0; i < listeners.size(); i++) {
        ViewController vc = (ViewController)
                             listeners.elementAt(i);
        vc.update();
     }
  }

  public void add(String st) {
     sum += Integer.parseInteger(st);
     notifyVC();
  }

  public int getSum() {
     return sum;
     }
  }

// MVC1.java: application client instantiates the View/Controller
// and Model Attach View/Controller with the Model, and
// starts this event driven application.
```

```
import mvc1.*;
import javax.swing.*;

public class MVC1{
  public static void main(String[] args) {
    Model myModel = new Model();
    ViewController vc = new ViewController(myModel);
    myModel.attach(vc);
    vc.setTitle("my MVC-I");
    vc.setVisible(true);
  }
}
```

For a simple GUI application we can combine the View and the Controller. For a more complex GUI application, it is better to separate the View and the Controller. It is relatively easy to divide the View and the Controller in the previous example. Students can do it as an exercise.

9.2.2   MVC-II

The MVC-II architecture is a further development from the MVC-I architecture. The Model module provides all core functionality and data supported by a database. The View module displays the data while the Controller module takes input requests, validates input data, initiates the Model and the View and their connection, and dispatches tasks. The Controller and the View register with the Model module. Whenever the data in the Model module is changed, the View module and the Controller module are notified of the changes. In other words, the Model module plays an active role in MVC-II architecture as in the MVC-I. In MVC-II architecture, the View module and the Controller module are separate. This allows for the division of labor; for example, programming experts can work on the development of Controller while graphics interface design experts can work on the development of View. Also, because graphics interface technology is updated rapidly and business requirements are changed very often, it is much better to keep the View separated from the Controller. The MVC in Figure 9.2 is the same as the MVC-I in Figure 9.1 except that the Controller and the View are separated.

Figure 9.3 shows a class diagram for MVC-II. It is clear that C1 is paired with V1 and C2 is paired with V2 and all Controllers and Views are attached to the Model. The Model is supported by a database. You can see two classes in the Model: one is a collection type that aggregates (has) many other classes as part of it; the other represents a row in a database table.

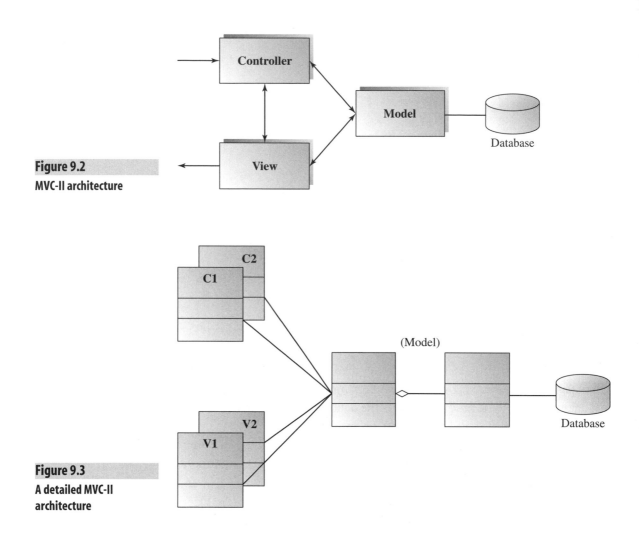

Figure 9.2
MVC-II architecture

Figure 9.3
A detailed MVC-II architecture

Figure 9.4 depicts a sequence diagram for a generic MVC architecture. After clients start up the MVC application, the Controller initializes the Model and View, and attaches itself and the View to the Model (this is called a registration with the Model). Later, the Controller intercepts a user request either directly from a command line or though the View interface, and forwards the request to the Model to update the data in the Model. The changes in the Model will trigger the Model to notify all attached or registered listeners of all changes, and the interfaces in the View will also be immediately updated.

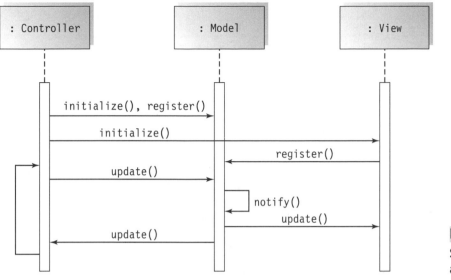

Figure 9.4

Sequence diagram for MVC architecture

The diagram in Figure 9.5 shows a typical MVC block architecture diagram in Java technology. The JavaServer Pages (JSP) is used in the View module development; the Java Servlet is used in the Controller module implementation; and the Java Bean, Java Enterprise Bean (EJB), and the Java Data Base Connectivity (JDBC) are used in the Model module development. Similar to Java technology, Microsoft ASP .NET technology is used for View development and ADO .NET for Model development. The Controller gets a request from the user via the GUI, or the command line interfaces and instantiates corresponding instances in the Model, selects the related Views for data display, calls business functions of the Model, and forwards the control to the View. The View gets the data from the Model and displays the data in the GUI interface.

The following example illustrates a simple implementation of an MVC-II architecture where there is only one Java class in each of the three modules of the MVC architecture. The MyBean JavaBean class plays the role of data Model; MyServlet Servlet class plays the role of Controller; and the fromServlet JSP plays a role of display *View*.

Figure 9.5 shows the architecture diagram of this web application. The myServlet Servlet sets an item value and stores this item in a JavaBean named myBean. It then transfers the control to a JSP page named fromServlet.jsp which retrieves the item from the myBean and displays it on a web page.

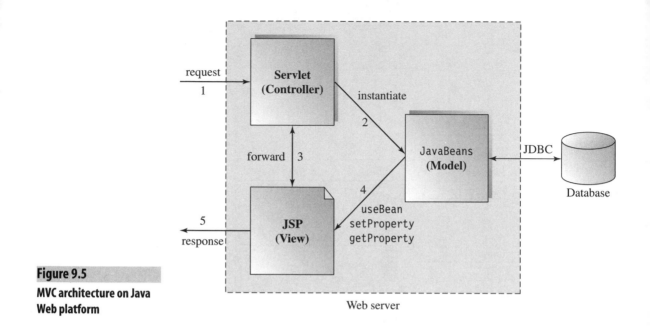

Figure 9.5

MVC architecture on Java Web platform

Whenever the data is changed the display is also changed. The following Java classes show a MVC-II template to provide more detailed explanations on the MVC-II architecture.

MyBean is a JavaBean class responsible for storing and providing data for business processing. This data JavaBean has one userName private property and two public methods to read from and write to this item property.

```java
// MyBean.java for Model in MVC-II
package myPackage;

public class MyBean {
    private String item;

    public MyBean(){ item = ""; }

    public void setItem(String item) {
        this.item = item;
    }

    public String getItem() {
        return this.item;
    }
}
```

The MyServlet Servlet class in the controller module sets the item property of myBean, stores this bean as an attribute (beanInfo) of the session
implicit object, and dispatches the control to fromServlet.jsp of the
View module.

```java
// MyServlet.java for Controller in MVC-II

import java.io.*;
import javax.servlet.*;
import javax.servlet.http.*;
import myPackage.MyBean;

public class MyServlet extends HttpServlet {
    public void service(HttpServletRequest request,
        HttpServletResponse response) throws
        ServletException, IOException {

        MyBean myBean = new MyBean();
        myBean.setItem("MVC");
        HttpSession session = request.getSession();
        session.setAttribute("beanInfo", myBean);
        RequestDispatcher rd;
        rd = getServletContext().getRequestDispatcher
                                ("/fromServlet.jsp");
        rd.forward(request, response);
    }
}
```

The fromServlet.jsp in the View module just retrieves the item property
stored in the myBean with the beanInfo id and displays it on the resulting page.

```jsp
// fromServelt.jsp for View in MVC-II
  <jsp:useBean id="beanInfo" class="myPackage.MyBean"
   scope="session"/>
  <html>
  <body>
 <b>Hello <jsp:getProperty name="beanInfo"
   property="item"/></b>
  </body>
  </html>
```

Applicable domains of MVC architecture:

  - Interactive applications where multiple views are needed for a single
    data model and the interfaces are prone to frequent data changes.

- Applications with clear divisions between controller, view, and data modules so that different professionals can be assigned to work on different aspects of such applications concurrently.

Benefits:

- Many MVC vendor framework toolkits are available.
- Multiple views synchronized with same data model.
- Easy to change or plug in new interface views, allowing updating of interface views with new technologies without overhauling the rest of the system.
- Very effective for developments if graphics, programming, and database development professionals are working in a team in a designed project.

Limitations:

- Not suitable for agent-oriented applications such as interactive mobile and robotics applications.
- Multiple pairs of controllers and views based on the same data model make any data model change expensive.
- The division between the View and the Controller is not clear in some cases.

Related architecture:

- PAC, and implicit invocation such as event-based, multi-tier architecture

9.3   Presentation-Abstraction-Control (PAC)

The PAC architecture is similar to MVC but with some important differences. PAC was developed from MVC to support the application requirement of multiple agents in addition to interactive requirements. In PAC, the system is decomposed into a hierarchy of cooperating agents. Each agent has three components (Presentation, Abstraction, and Control). The Control component in each agent is in charge of communications with other agents. The top-level agent provides core data and business logics. The bottom-level agents provide detailed data and presentations. A middle-level agent may coordinate low-level agents. Within each agent, there are no direct connections between the abstraction component and Presentation component.

The PACs three components concepts are applied to all concrete subsystem architectures. PAC is suitable for any distributed system where all the agents are distantly distributed and each agent has its own functionalities with data and interactive interface. In such a system, all agents need to communicate with other agents in a well-structured manner. PAC is also used in applications with rich GUI components where each of them keeps its own current data and interactive interface and needs to communicate with other components.

Of course, some concrete agents need all three components and others do not. For some middle-level agents, the interactive presentations are not required, so they do not have a presentation component. The control component is required for all agents because this is the only way for an agent to talk to another agent.

Figure 9.6 shows a diagram for a single agent in a PAC design. The Control component is a mediator between the Presentation component and the Abstraction component within the agent, and also a bridge between the agent itself and other agents, as well. The Presentation and Abstraction components are loosely coupled. The Presentation component is responsible for both data input and output in GUI interfaces where the data come from the Abstraction component. The Abstraction component is responsible for providing logical data concepts and services and encapsulating all detailed data manipulation.

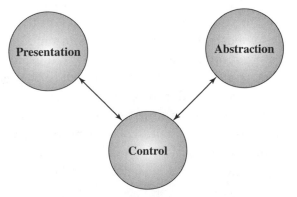

Figure 9.6
A single agent in PAC

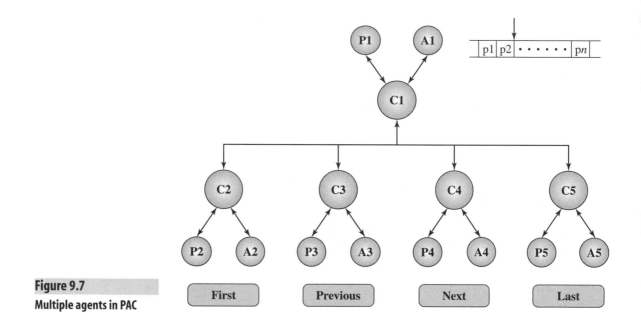

Figure 9.7

Multiple agents in PAC

Let's discuss how PAC works by using a simple example. We design a desktop presentation application that can browse and display presentation pages in a graphic document one at a time. The application provides four buttons to show the first page, last page, previous page, and the next page, respectively. The agent A1 (see Figure 9.7) has a connection to the data repository, which is the document file. This agent points to the current page in the document while agent P1 can display the current page in a specified format.

Assume that the current page is the second to last page in the document at this time. If the user clicks on the next button, the control agent C4 informs agent P4 to update its presentation; in this case, it also hides the next button since there is no next page after the last page. Agent C4 also informs agent A4 to update the data on the next button. After C4 handles all local processing, it contacts its parent agent, C1, to let it take over. After C1 gets the message from C4, it tells A1 to move the next page, which is the last page in the document, and then asks P1 to display that page. C1 also informs C5 to hide the last button since the current page is the last page (or let the last button stay based on the requirement specification). We can see that all the agents communicate via the controls. The data structure shown on the upper-right corner of Figure 9.7 indicates the pointer and data. Since

PAC2, PAC3, PAC4, and PAC5 are all buttons, they have very similar data and presentation functions such as hide, move-over, and gray-out features; their controls, however, are different.

The class diagram in Figure 9.8 represents the PAC architecture shown in the concept diagram of Figure 9.7.

The diagram in Figure 9.9 shows the interaction sequence in the example just discussed. When the next button is pressed to display the last page in the document, PAC4 and PAC1 react as follows:

> P4 informs C4 that the "next" button was pressed.
>
> C4 sends an update to A4.
>
> C4 informs P4 to update its presentation or shape.
>
> C4 contacts C1 (a top level agent).
>
> C1 sends an update to A1 to move the pointer to next (last page).
>
> C1 instructs P1 to display the last page.

Applicable domains of the PAC architecture:

- Suitable for an interactive system where the system can be divided into many cooperating agents in a hierarchical manner and each agent has its own specific assigned job.

- Suitable when the coupling among the agents is expected to be loose so that changes on an agent do not affect others.

Benefits:

- Support of multitasking and multiviewing

- Support agent reusability and extensibility

- Easy to plug in new agent or replace an existing one

- Support for concurrency where multiple agents run in parallel in different threads or on different devices or computers

Limitations:

- Extra time lost due to the control bridge between presentation and abstraction and the communication of controls among agents.

- Difficult to determine the correct number of the agents due to the loose coupling and high independence between agents.

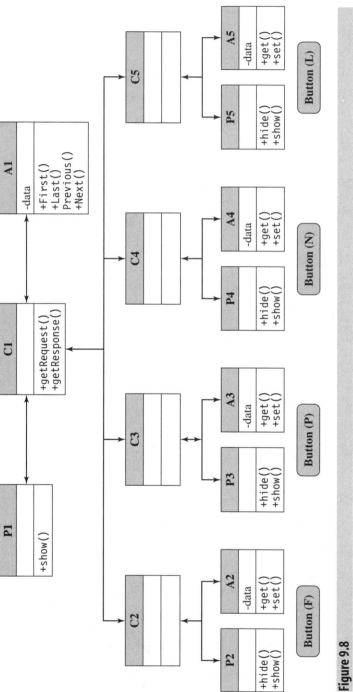

Figure 9.8

Class diagram for PAC

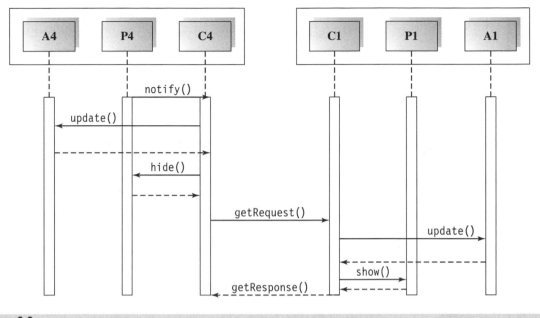

Figure 9.9
A sample sequence diagram for PAC

- Complete separation of presentation and abstraction by control in each agent generates development complexity since communications between agents only take place between the controls of agents.

Related architecture:

- Layered, multi-tier, and MVC

9.4 Summary

The MVC and PAC architectures are interaction-oriented. Both support the three-module decomposition of Presentation/View, Abstraction/Model, and Control/Controller. An important difference between the two styles is that the data in the MVC is active whereas the data in PAC is passive. Active data in MVC notifies the other two modules of any changes in the data; changes in passive data in PAC are under full control of the control component.

Although both of these two architectures are popular in interactive applications with GUIs, PAC is a better choice for such systems where subsystems require their own customized interactive interfaces. The MVC architecture is widely used in web application design, while the PAC architecture is widely used in agent-based distributed systems, where each agent has a specific task and interface. The PAC architecture is the right choice for distributed applications of wireless mobile communication systems since each device needs to have its own data and its own interactive interface, and also needs to communicate with other devices. A typical PAC software design is a networked traffic control management system that requires many mobile agents to monitor traffic and get data; display the analyzed data in graphics; coordinate the data from agents; and many other management tasks.

The PAC architecture is layered in a hierarchy where the top agent has access to the data repository, that is, it is global, while the bottom-level agents have their own local data and local interface. The middle-layered PAC agents coordinate the low-level agents. All communication is conducted by the control components of each individual agent. It is not realistic to have a single architecture style in a design problem.

9.5   Self-Review Questions

1. Which of the following is *not* a benefit of the MVC architecture?

   a. Supports multiple independent agents

   b. Provides flexible GUI interfaces

   c. Supports multiple views

   d. Supports loose data coupling

2. Which of the following is a typical design domain for the MVC architecture?

   a. Multiple agents in a distributed system

   b. Hierarchical structure

   c. Web server site application

   d. Web client site application

3. Traffic control agents in a city traffic management system may be designed using PAC.

   a. True

   b. False

4. Implicit notification is often used in the MVC architecture.

a.   True

b.   False

5. The data in the Model component of the MVC architecture is active.

a.   True

b.   False

6. The data in the Abstraction component of a PAC agent is passive.

a.   True

b.   False

7. PAC agents are loosely coupled.

a.   True

b.   False

8. The Abstraction and Presentation components in a PAC agent do not talk to each other directly.

a.   True

b.   False

9. The "Look and Feel" feature is well supported in the MVC architecture.

a.   True

b.   False

10. The PAC architecture is a hierarchically structured software architecture.

a.   True

b.   False

Answers to the Self-Review Questions

1. a 2. c 3. a 4. a 5. a 6. a 7. a 8. a 9. a 10. a

9.6   Exercises

1. What is an interactive application?

2. Typically, how many layers does PAC architecture contain?

3. Describe the features common to both the PAC and MVC architectures.

4. Describe the major differences between the PAC and MVC architectures.

5. What are the problem domains for MVC architecture?

6. What are the problem domains for PAC architecture?

7. Are Java AWT GUI components examples of PAC architecture?

8. Describe the limitations of PAC architecture.

9. Describe the advantages of MVC over PAC architecture.

10. Describe the advantages of PAC over MVC architecture.

9.7   Design Exercises

1. Design the software architecture for a student online registration system using the MVC architecture. Draw the corresponding block diagram, class diagram, and either a sequence or collaboration diagram.

2. Design the software architecture for a distributed traffic control system using the PAC architecture. Draw the corresponding block diagram, class diagram, and either a sequence or collaboration diagram.

3. Design the software architecture for a distributed game system using the PAC architecture. Draw the corresponding block diagram, class diagram, and either a sequence or collaboration diagram.

4. Design the software architecture for an online bookstore system using the PAC architecture. Draw the corresponding block diagram, class diagram, and either a sequence or collaboration diagram.

9.8   Challenge Exercises

1. Design the software architecture for a professional conference online registration system using the MVC architecture. The functional requirements include: announcement, call for papers, online paper submission, online paper reviews, paper notification, conference online registration, etc. Draw the corresponding block diagram, class diagram, and either a sequence or collaboration diagram. When designing a solution based on this architecture, be sure to consider how to increase performance, extensibility, and scalability.

2. Design the software architecture for an online distribution system for a business enterprise using the PAC architecture. Draw the corresponding block diagram, class diagram, and either a sequence or collaboration diagram. When designing a solution based on this architecture, be sure to consider how to increase performance, extensibility, and scalability.

References

Krasner, Glenn and Stephen Pope. "A Cookbook for Using the Model-View Controller User Interface Paradigm in Smalltalk-80." *Journal of Object-Oriented Programming*, Vol. 1, No. 3. SIGS Publications (1988): 26–49.

Suggested Reading

Buschmann, Frank, Regine Meunier, Hans Rohnert, Peter Sommerlad, and Michael Stal. *Pattern-Oriented Software Architecture: A System of Patterns.* Vol. 1. West Sussex, England: John Wiley & Sons Ltd., 1996.

Coutaz, Joëlle. "PAC, an Object-Oriented Model for Dialog Design." In: Bullinger, Hans-Jorg and Shackel, Brian (eds.) INTERACT 87 - 2nd IFIP International Conference on Human-Computer Interaction, Stuttgart, Germany, September 1-4, 1987, 431–436.

CHAPTER 10

Distributed Architecture

Objectives of this Chapter

- Introduce the client-server and multi-tier architectures
- Introduce the invocation and message broker architectures
- Introduce the service-oriented architecture

10.1   Overview

A distributed system is a collection of computational and storage devices connected through a communications network. In this type of system, data, software, and users are distributed. The subsystems or components within a distributed system communicate with each other using a number of methods including message passing, remote procedure calls, and remote method invocation. Two important elements of designing a distributed system are: *network topology*, the way in which entities are organized to form a connected network; and *communications mode*, the method by which components communicate with each other.

Many systems in the real world are naturally distributed. These systems are widely used in large enterprise environments such as a database system that enables data to be accessed remotely, a B2B system with its distributed suppliers and clients, or an SAP system to manage distributed resources. Distributed systems are everywhere.

A distributed system can be modeled by the client-server architecture, and this forms the basis for multi-tier architectures. Alternatives are the broker architecture such as CORBA, and the service-oriented architecture (SOA) such as web services and grid services. Key features of a distributed architecture are its service location transparency and its services reliability and availability. Additionally, there are several technology frameworks to support distributed architectures, including .NET, J2EE, CORBA, .NET web services, AXIS Java web services, and GloBus grid services.

Next, we discuss the technical details of various distributed architecture styles including client-server, multi-tier, broker, and service-oriented architecture.

10.2   Client-Server

The client-server model is the most commonly distributed system architecture. It is based on two communicating processes, usually running on different processors, and thus decomposes a system into two major subsystems: client and server. The first process, the client, issues a request to the second process, the server. The server process receives the request (serving data from a database, printing a document), carries it out, and sends a reply to the client.

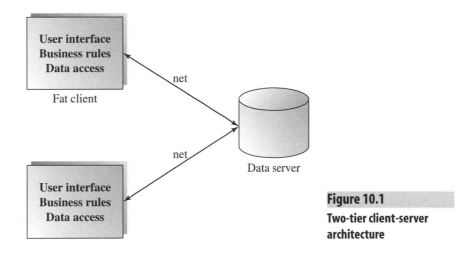

Figure 10.1
Two-tier client-server architecture

Figure 10.1 displays a sample two-tier client-server architecture. The front-end tier focuses on the user interaction, and the back-end tier focuses on business logic and database management.

The separation of client from data server releases clients from data query and management (such as SQL development) so that it supports the parallel developments for different tiers respectively.

Advantages:

- Separation of responsibilities such as user interface presentation and business logic processing
- Reusability of server components

Disadvantages:

- Lack of heterogeneous infrastructure to deal with the requirement changes
- Security complications
- Server availability and reliability
- Testability and scalability
- Fat clients with presentation and business logic together

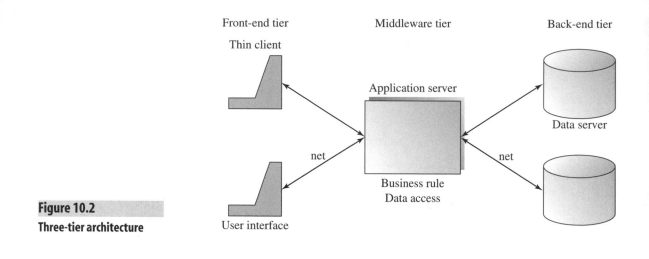

Figure 10.2
Three-tier architecture

10.3   Multi-tiers

The front-end tier in a multi-tier architecture, such as a three-tier architecture, is still the user interface presentation tier. The middle tier manages business logic and execution. The back-end tier usually handles database management. Multi-tier architecture is gaining popularity in today's enterprise applications. Figure 10.2 presents a sample three-tier architecture.

The advantage of multi-tier over the two-tier architecture is the enhancement of reusability and scalability by adding the middle tier. Any business-related changes are made only to the middle tier. For example, the middle tier in a three-tier architecture can have portable and nonproprietary design and implementation. The middle tier can also provide multi-threading supports for scalability. Multi-tier architecture also reduces traffic on the network. Its main disadvantage is testability due to the general lack of testing tools. Adding multiple servers in the system makes the server reliability and availability even more critical.

10.4   Broker Architecture Style

The broker architecture is a middleware architecture used in distributed computing to coordinate and facilitate communication between registered servers and clients.

Buschmann developed the broker architecture pattern to design a distributed system into components that interact by remote service invocations:

The Broker architectural pattern can be used to structure distributed software systems with decoupled components that interact by remote service invocations. A broker component is responsible for coordinating communication, such as forwarding requests, as well as for transmitting results and exceptions (Buschmann et al., 1996).

A broker can be either an invocation-oriented service, to which clients send invocation requests for brokering, or a document or message-oriented broker to which clients send a message (such as an XML document).

Better decoupling between clients and servers is one of the most important quality attributes for this architecture; client and server components are decoupled through the use of a broker. In other words, communication never takes place directly between the client and the server. A broker system is also called proxy-based system.

Servers make their services available to their clients by registering and publishing their interfaces with the broker. Clients can request the services of servers from the broker statically or dynamically by lookup. A broker component is responsible for coordinating communications—brokering the service requests, locating a proper server, forwarding and dispatching requests, and sending responses or exceptions back to clients. A broker acts as a policeman in a busy intersection who controls and interacts with the client components and server components. The connection between clients and servers is maintained by the broker. Common Object Request Broker Architecture (CORBA) is a good implementation example of broker architecture.

With the broker pattern, a distributed client can access distributed services simply by calling a remote method of a remote object just as if it were a local method call. This concept is similar to Remote Procedure Call (RPC) in Unix distributed structured programming and Remote Method Invocation (RMI) in Java distributed object-oriented programming. The distributed clients only need to obtain a reference to the appropriate object, instead of writing detailed code for protocol-oriented communication. In addition, the clients can dynamically invoke the remote methods even if the interfaces of the remote objects are not available at the compilation time.

The client has a direct connection to its client-proxy and the server has direct connection to its server-proxy. The proxy talks to the mediator-broker. The proxy is a well-known pattern for hiding low-level detailed communication processing such as data marshaling and unmarshaling, I/O port processing, and supporting location transparency. A client proxy resides in the client address space and implements the servant interface in this space. The client-proxy plays the role of mediator or interceptor, which intercepts the client's request, gets all arguments, packets it, marshals and formats the package in the format of communication protocol, and then sends it to the broker. For the same reason, there is another proxy on the server-side to free the server from knowing the location of its client and the details of the communication protocol.

Let's decompose the broker architecture into subcomponents:

- *Broker:* coordinates communications, passing on requests and returning replies. The broker stares all servers' registration information, including their functionality and services as well as location information. The broker provides APIs for clients to request, servers to respond, registering or unregistering server components, transferring messages, and locating servers.

- *Stub* (client-side proxy): mediates between the client and the broker and provides additional transparency between them. To the client, a remote object appears like a local one. The proxy hides the inter-process communication at protocol level, marshals parameter values, and unmarshals results from the server. The stub is generated at the static compilation time and deployed to the client-side to be used as a proxy for the client.

- *Skeleton* (server-side proxy): is also statically generated by the service interface compilation and then deployed to the server-side. It encapsulates low-level system-specific networking functions like the client-proxy and provides high-level APIs to mediate between the server and the broker. It receives and unpacks the requests, unmarshals the method arguments, and calls the appropriate service. When it receives the result back from the server it also marshals the result before sending it back to the client.

- *Bridges*: are optional components used to hide implementation details when two brokers interoperate. Bridges encapsulate underlying network detail implementation and mediate different brokers such as DCOM, .NET Remote, and Java CORBA brokers. They can translate requests and parameters from one format to another. A bridge can connect two different networks based on different communication protocols.

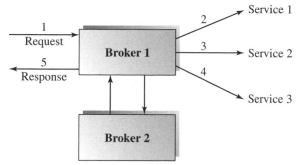

Figure 10.3
Broker model

- *Network:* connects components using designated protocol standards such as TCP/IP, OIIP, or SOAP. The request carries data in a message document or method invocation format.

The diagram in Figure 10.3 shows the objects involved in the broker system. A broker gets requests from clients and manages the requests by either forwarding them to service providers directly or dispatching the requests to another connected broker. Once it gets results back from the broker, it sends the results back to the clients. Many brokers can work together in a complex system as shown in Figure 10.4.

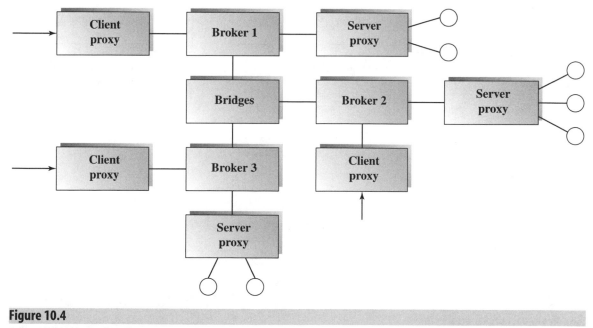

Figure 10.4

Connected brokers with client-server proxy

Figure 10.5 and Figure 10.6 show the class diagram and a sequence diagram of a broker architecture. We can see that the proxy pattern plays an important role in the broker architecture. A proxy is like a surrogate or placeholder for a server component providing a local interface to the real remote object.

Advantages:

- Server component implementation and location transparency
- Changeability and extensibility
- Simplicity for clients to access server and server portability

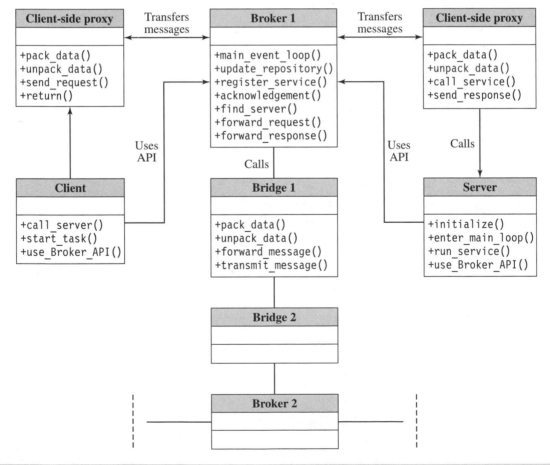

Figure 10.5

Class diagram for broker architecture

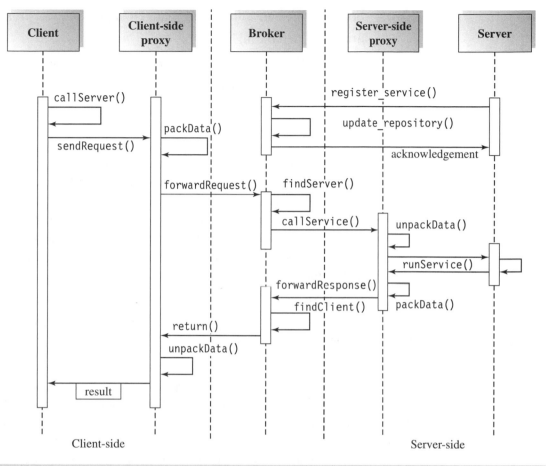

Figure 10.6

Sequence diagram for broker architecture

- Interoperability via broker bridges
- Reusability
- Feasibility of runtime changes of server components (add or remove server components on the fly)

Disadvantages:

- Inefficiency due to the overhead of proxies
- Low fault-tolerance
- Difficulty in testing due to the amount of proxies

10.4.1   Broker Implementation in the Common Object Request Broker Architecture (CORBA)

In this section we discuss the CORBA architecture, a typical broker architecture implementation. The diagram in Figure 10.7 shows an overview of the CORBA architecture.

Static Remote Invocation in CORBA

CORBA is an open standard for distributed, remote-method invocation computing schemes. It provides platform and language-independent middleware to integrate distributed applications, including legacy code. The services and operations that a CORBA object provides are specified in interfaces using the Interface Definition Language (IDL) so that clients can make requests without knowing the detailed implementation and location of the CORBA objects.

The Object Request Broker (ORB) protocol provides a software bus on the network for brokering the requests from clients and the responses from servers; the protocol also supports increased interoperability with other implementations.

CORBA object IDL specifications are compiled into a stub and a skeleton by the IDL compiler. The stub is deployed on the client-side while the skeleton is deployed on the server-side. The IDL stub has the responsibility to serialize and marshal client requests. The stub thus functions as a proxy for the distributed object, and it can receive a local call from the client to this distributed CORBA object. It talks to its partner skeleton deployed on the server-side,

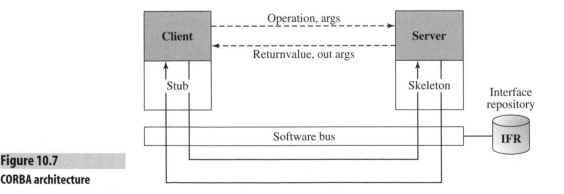

Figure 10.7

CORBA architecture

which in turn unmarshals the requests, dispatches the requests to the correct object, and sends the results back to the stub on the client-side via ORB.

Dynamic Remote Invocation in CORBA

CORBA also supports the Dynamic Invocation Interface (DII), which allows CORBA clients to use another CORBA object without knowing its interface information until runtime. Dynamic Skeleton Interface (DSI) is used by ORB to issue requests to objects that are implemented independently and for which the ORB has no compile-time knowledge of their implementation. Although the dynamic approach of DII and DSI is more flexible, they are always slower than their static IDL counterpart. The dynamic remote invocation mode was the only invocation mode available in the early version of CORBA. In some cases the IDL is not available at compilation time and the stub and skeleton cannot be generated at compilation time. For example, if a COM client wants to make a CORBA request or a DCOM object wants to provide its services on CORBA, a bridge interface is required to do the conversion. In the following we elaborate on some important notions of dynamic remote invocation in CORBA.

CORBA Interface Repository (IFR)

This repository keeps all registered IDL interface information such as method names, arguments, and types, and IDL identifiers for clients and servers to use in dynamic method invocation. The IFR can be updated by the IDL utility.

Dynamic Invocation Interface (DII)

This interface allows a client to dynamically discover the interface at runtime. DII provides all that is necessary for a client to generate a self-contained, self-described request that can directly access the ORB underlying the request mechanisms.

When a server has an IDL but clients have no knowledge of it, DII can work with the IDL static skeleton and the IFR. If the server implementation object by DII is registered with IFR, an IDL stub can be generated from the information on the IFR.

In summary, DII helps clients invoke remote object methods without the support of a stub proxy, but the client must create its own request by DII API, which incidentally is less efficient than static invocation.

Dynamic Skeleton Interface (DSI)

DSI is a dynamic skeleton that allows an ORB to send requests to an object implementation for which the ORB does not have static knowledge of the interface-type specification. DSI has the responsibility of dispatching incoming method invocations on the sever-side. A DSI CORBA implementation can be dynamically registered in IFR for clients to look up. Using either client IDL skeletons or dynamic skeletons makes no difference to a CORBA client.

Of course, a DII can also pair with a DSI for a true dynamic method invocation if the server and the client don't know anything about the IDL specification at compilation time. The IFR is the facility for servers to post their registrations and for clients to look up the registrations at runtime.

In short, DSI allows the ORB to forward requests to server objects without the support of skeletons.

10.4.2   Message Broker Architecture

A message is a packaged or formatted information such as an XML document sent and received between applications. A message broker is a Message-Oriented Middleware (MOM) server in a message-oriented distributed system. It performs message routing, message transformation, message invocation, security checking, and exception handling.

A message broker must be able to route messages from a sender to a receiver based on the content of the message. A broker can transform a

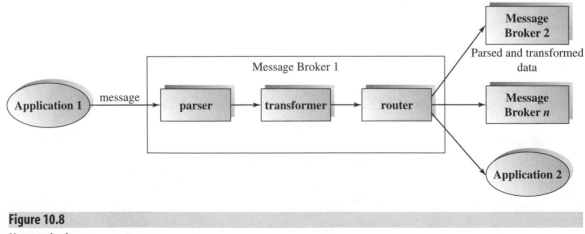

Figure 10.8

Message broker

message from one format to another to meet the different requirements of the sender and the recipient. A broker may also transform a message by modifying, inserting, merging, or removing some data elements in the message.

In addition to point-to-point messaging, a broker can also handle message distribution by publishing and subscribing. An application can publish on topics, and many applications can subscribe them on the broker.

A broker usually consists of three main parts: a front-listener subsystem that receives incoming messages based on the protocol used; the core broker subsystem that makes decisions on the message and dispatches the jobs; and the back-end subsystem that will finally perform business logic based on the incoming message.

There are commercial message broker systems such as WebSphere message broker, IBM MQSeries, Sun JMS, and others. Most message broker systems only provide asynchronous one-way communications, but some systems provide alternative communication semantics, including synchronous or asynchronous, one-way or two-way, and blocking or nonblocking communications.

A simple example of a message broker is email processing. When a business receives an email, the business application must analyze the heading of the email message, transform the message to some suitable format, and route the transformed message to a target destination for processing by a local application or via another remote broker.

A message usually falls into one of two categories: The Remote Procedure Call (RPC) category or the document category. In an RPC-oriented mode, the client knows the remote procedure or remote method; hence the message that the client passes contains the parameters to the remote procedure or method. In a document message mode, the client may not know the remote procedure or method that handles the message. The client just sends the message in an agreed-upon format such as XML or SOAP to a message broker and lets the message broker decide which procedure or method to invoke.

Advantages:

- *Reusability and maintainability:* Loose coupling between the client and server component leads to easy maintenance and extension on both sides.

- *Flexibility:* Invocation-oriented or document-oriented messaging; message heading and body can be altered for specific purposes.

Disadvantages:

- Overhead, indirection complexity, and difficulty in debugging and testing due to the new protocol stack added

10.5   Service-Oriented Architecture (SOA)

A Service-Oriented Architecture (SOA) starts with a businesses process. In this context, a service is a business functionality that is well-defined, self-contained, independent from other services, and published and available to be used via a standard programming interface. Software manages business processes through an SOA with well-defined, standard interfaces that can build, enhance, and expand their existing infrastructure more flexibly. SOA services can be extensively reused within a given domain or product line, even among legacy systems. Loose coupling of service orientation provides great flexibility for enterprises to make use of all available service resourses regardless of platform and technology restrictions.

The connections between services are conducted by common and universal message-oriented protocols, such as the SOAP web service protocol, which can deliver requests and responses between services loosely. A connection can be established statically or dynamically.

Figure 10.9 illustrates how SOA works. A client can find a service via a service directory and then accesses it in a service request-response mode.

A typical service-oriented application makes use of many available services using some flow control language (e.g., BPEL for web services). Such orchestration languages allow for specifying the sequence and logical order of the business executions based on the business logic. Figure 10.10 pres-

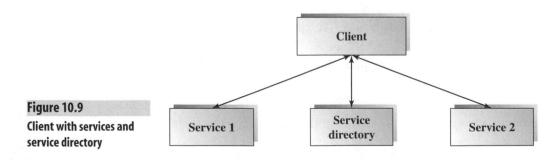

Figure 10.9

Client with services and service directory

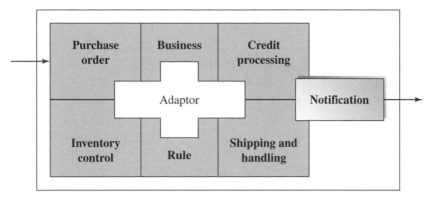

Figure 10.10
Service composition

ents a purchase business web service application that reuses some available web services such as purchase order, credit processing, inventory control, shipping and handling, and its own business logic processing. We can compose this application programmatically by embedding all these available web services to reduce the cost and time of software development significantly. The internal implementations of those atomic web services (e.g., credit processing and inventory control) can be changed over time as long as they stick to their public interfaces. Another positive feature is the reusability of all the atomic web services. Some services can be reused by other applications for which they were not originally designed. For example, the credit processing service can be sold to some other companies (e.g., a wedding planner) if they want to support online payment.

A complex service-oriented application can constitute many services in such a way that some are responsible for receiving requests, others for responding, and others that may not even be connected to external users at all (e.g., services #2 and #3 in the diagram in Figure 10.11).

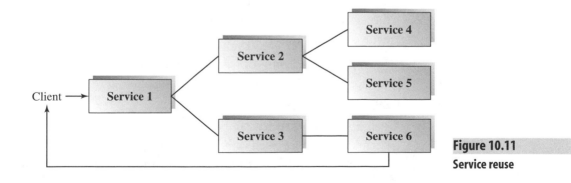

Figure 10.11
Service reuse

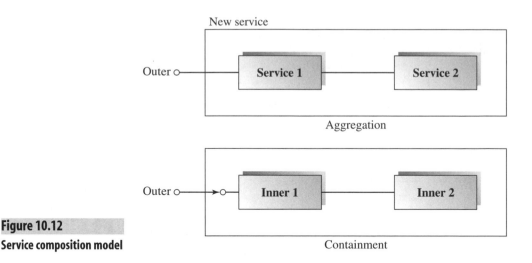

New service

Aggregation

Outer ○──── Service 1 ──── Service 2

Figure 10.12

Service composition model

Outer ○──────○─ Inner 1 ──── Inner 2

Containment

Coarse-grained services consist of multiple services working together coordinately. Via service aggregation and composition, services can be recursively constructed to satisfy more complex business needs. A new service can be built out of existing services using either the aggregation or containment structure afforded by OO concepts (as shown in Figure 10.12). An aggregation just extends one endpoint of a service to make a new interface of the new service. A containment has one interface that wraps all used services. In this way, an SOA is a way to organize and widely share business functions.

Advantages of SOA:

- *Loosely-coupled connections:* Loose-coupling is the key attribute of service-oriented architecture. Each service component is independent due to the stateless service feature. The implementation of a service will not affect its application as long as the exposed interface is not changed. This makes SOA software much easier to evolve and update.

- *Interoperability:* Technically, any client or service can access other services regardless of their platform, technology, vendors, or language implementations.

- *Reusability:* Any service can be reused by any other service. Because clients of a service need only to know its public interfaces, service composition and integration become much easier. This makes

SOA-based business application development much more efficient in terms of time and cost.

- *Scalability:* Loosely-coupled services are easy to scale. The coarse-grained, document-oriented, and asynchronous service features enhance the scalability attribute.

10.5.1   SOA Implementation in Web Services

A web service (as shown in Figure 10.13) is a service that communicates with other services or clients via standard protocols and technologies such as SOAP, XML, and HTTP. A web service is a message-oriented service that can deliver document-oriented messages as well as RPC messages. Because an XML-based message is semistructured, it makes a web service architecture universally accessible and flexible.

The two key specification standards for web service architecture are the Simple Object Access Protocol (SOAP) and the Web Services Description Language (WSDL). SOAP (as shown in Figure 10.14) provides a common message exchange format between clients and services, and also between services. The envelope specifies an XML namespace and an encoding style. The XML namespace specifies the names that can be used in the SOAP

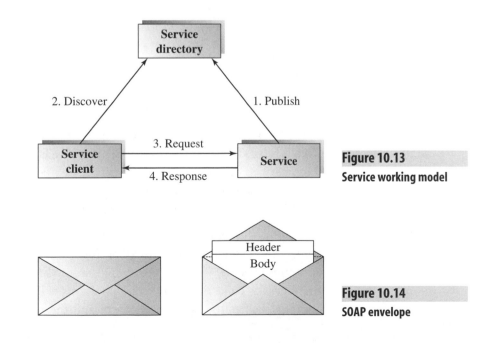

Figure 10.13
Service working model

Figure 10.14
SOAP envelope

message. XML namespaces serve similar purposes as .NET namespaces or Java packages—they allow the avoidance of name clashes.

The SOAP header may include security, source and destination location, and other elements that can be used by an intermediate service. The body contains the main part of the SOAP message; that is, the part intended for the final recipient of the SOAP message.

A SOAP message is an XML-based document that is independent of any platform and thus can be transported by many protocols, such as HTTP or SMTP.

The following is a SOAP message requesting the quote for a stock. The SOAP envelope <SOAP-ENV: Envelope> contains an optional <SOAP-ENV:Header> element and the required <SOAP-ENV: Body> elements. Clearly, the SOAP message specifies a quote that asks for the price of "My Life and Times."

```
<SOAP-ENV: Envelope  xmlns:SOAP-ENV=
    "http://schemas.xmlsoap.org/soap/envelope/"
    SOAP-ENV:encodingStyle=
    "http://schemas.xmlsoap.org/soap/encoding/">
    <SOAP-ENV:Header>
        <from>a_client</from>
            <to>a_target</to>
    </SOAP-ENV:Header>
    <SOAP-ENV:Body>
        <m:GetQuote xmlns:m="myURI">
            <name>My Life and Times</name>
        </m: GetQuote>
    </SOAP-ENV:Body>
</SOAP-Envelope>
```

Web Service Description Language (WSDL)

A WSDL document is an interface document that describes the interface of a web service. To access a web service, a client has to know the endpoint of a web service directly or indirectly via a web service registry repository where the Web service has registered. The interface information in the WSDL document helps build programmatic calls to the web service.

A WSDL document describes a web service as a set of "ports," or "endpoints," and the actions' signatures performed by the web service. Actions are represented by "operations," while argument data is represented by "messages." A collection of related operations is known as a "port type." A binding specifies the network protocol and the message format specifications for a particular port type. A binding binds a port with an IP address. A web service client first locates a WSDL document, finds the binding and network address for each port, and then calls the operations of this web service.

Here is a WSDL document for an online stock price search web service, where getStock is an operation of this web service declared in WSDL.

```
<operation name="getStock" ...
```

The input message is a symbol and the output message is the price for this operation.

```
<complexType>
    <all>
        <element name="symbol" type="string"/>
        <element name="price" type="string"/>
    </all>
```

The binding tag specifies the document style in the SOAP request.

```
<soap:binding transport=
  "transport=http://schemas.xmlsoap.org/soap/http"
. . .
```

The Business Process Execution Language (BPEL) is an XML-based description language for organizing existing web services to work together. BPEL describes the web services that participate in a process, the workflow of these web services, and interactions between them. For example, the following BPEL entry describes one of the services in the purchase order process: It receives a purchase order by an operation called purchaseOrder with a purchaseOrder port type which specifies its input and output messages from a participating web service partner link purchase. After the purchase order is received, the BPEL spawns the flow control into two concurrent flows: makeInvoice and scheduleShipping.

```
<sequence>
    <receive partnerLink="purchase"
        portType="lns:purchaseOrderPT"
        operation="PurchaseOrder"
        variable="PO">
    </receive>
    <flow>
        <invoke partnerLink="invoicelnk"
            portType="lns:invoicePT"
            operation="makeInvoice"
        />
```

```
        <invoke partnerLink="shippinglnk"
            portType="lns:shipping"
            operation="scheduleShipping"
        />
    </flow>
</sequence>
```

Figure 10.15 presents another simple purchase order as an example using BPEL composition. There are three vertical parallel flows in the middle box, indicating that all three flows are executed in parallel. The solid arrow line indicates the sequential execution of the connected web service from top to bottom. The arrow line between the flows indicates the constraints by other flows in the concurrent execution. For example, the total charge cannot be determined until the shipping and handling fee is determined. The diagram offers a clear picture of how BPEL uses web services to compose a business process application.

Figure 10.16 presents as another example an online travel agency system. It consists of four existing web services: airline reservation, car rental, hotel reservation, and attraction reservation. With built-in business rules and business strategy such as decision making and budget and schedule con-

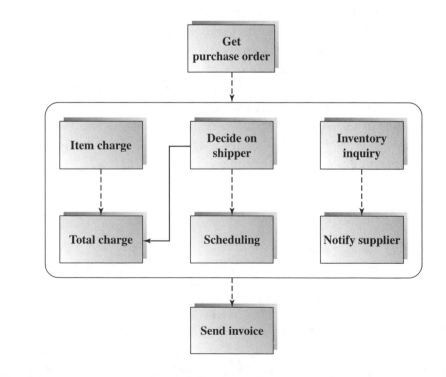

Figure 10.15

Web service compositions by BPEL

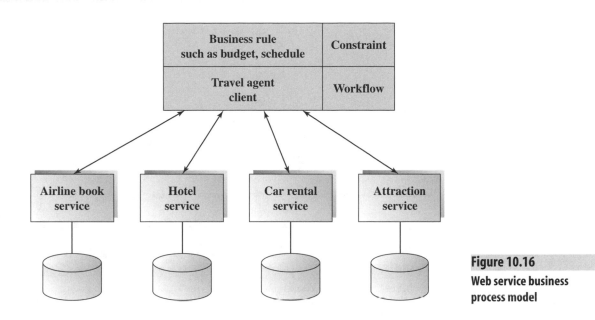

Figure 10.16
Web service business
process model

straints, the system should be able to make optimal decisions enabling clients to choose from a combination of airlines and hotels. BPEL can also be used to construct workflows among these web services. This system itself can provide a new web service for clients to use.

10.5.2 SOA Implementation for Grid Service Computing

Grid service computing is another implementation of SOA. Grid service computing makes use of all disparate resources spread over different locations via networks. It can provide both program services, such as web services and hardware services. Each grid can either be a computing grid supporting computational resources or a data grid supporting data integration, or both. Figure 10.17 shows a grid service architecture that manages all resources such as CPU, database, applications, storage, and network, by collective and visualizable management. A grid service scheduler coordinates the scheduling of all resource sharing.

When a client submits a job request, the service directory locates the service and lets the Grid service scheduler select the job that depends on the service availability. After the job is completed, the user will then be notified by the system.

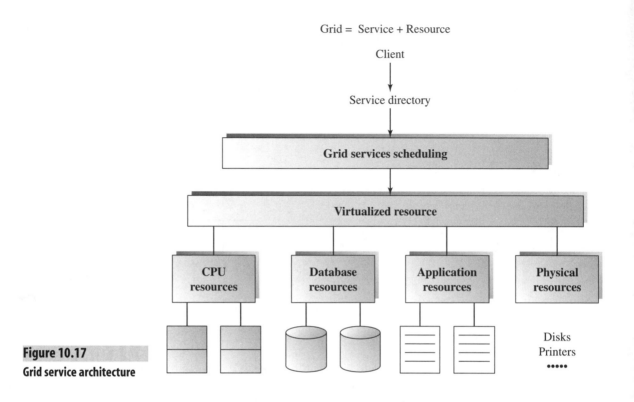

Figure 10.17
Grid service architecture

10.6 Summary

This chapter discussed the software architectures for distributed computing systems, those systems where data, users, and processing elements are all distributed over remote sites connected by networks.

Multi-tier architecture distributes and separates data and processing duties over different tiers so that each tier has its own responsibilities. It reduces message traffic on the network and increases system reliability.

The client-server architecture is widely used in current enterprise business and industry. Web server, data server, and application server are all examples of server tiers.

A broker, in the broker architecture, has the responsibility of brokering messages between remote components or other brokers so that a complex enterprise system may involve into multiple brokers, clients, and servers.

The CORBA, a primordial broker architecture implementation, is also a component-oriented architecture.

Service-oriented architectures are widely used in B2B enterprise business applications. Each service is a building-block component, such as web or grid service, which can be reused by other service components or other business process applications.

10.7   Self-Review Questions

1. Which of the following is *not* one of the benefits of distributed architecture?

   a.   Supports multiple independent agents

   b.   Scalability

   c.   Supports multiple views

   d.   Loose-coupling of modules

2. Which of the following is *not* a typical style of distributed architecture?

   a.   Client-server

   b.   Hierarchical structure

   c.   Broker

   d.   SOA

3. Client-server architecture in general is more scalable than the multi-tier model.

   a.   True

   b.   False

4. CORBA is an example of the broker architecture.

   a.   True

   b.   False

5. Web service is an example of SOA architecture.

   a.   True

   b.   False

Answers to the Self-Review Questions

1. c 2. b 3. b 4. a 5. a

10.8   Exercises

1. What is client-server architecture?

2. What is multi-tier architecture?

3. What are the benefits of broker architecture?

4. What are the benefits of SOA architecture?

5. Define the stack of standards for supporting web services.

10.9   Design Exercises

1. Design a three-tier, web-based, online bookstore application. The client front-end tier is a web browser that coordinates user account login and GUI interface. The middle tier is the application server that coordinates business logic such as shopping cart, transaction, checkout processing, and others. The back-end tier is a database server. The database stores all necessary information such as book catalog, customer, and order status information.

2. Design a travel agency application software using SOA. The application helps customers make travel plans including air, hotel, car rental, attraction visits, and time schedules. This application makes use of existing web services of airlines, car rentals, hotels, and attractions.

3. Design a stock exchange application using the broker architecture. Assume that the existing stockbroker legacy systems vary in platform, language, and technology. For example, some systems are implemented in Java and the others reimplemented in .NET.

10.10   Challenge Exercise

An enterprise company information system has heterogeneous infrastructure where many different software applications and databases are supported by many different operating systems. The headquarters include accounting, finance, and human resource offices and is located in New York. The Research and Development department is in Chicago. The sales departments are located all over the world. There are many distribution centers near the sales department. Find a solution to integrate the system software so that it will be easy to maintain and expand in the future. Which is better, broker architecture or service-oriented architecture? Explain the advantages and disadvantages of each solution.

References

Buschmann, Frank, Regine Meunier, Hans Rohnert, Peter Sommerlad, and Michael Stal. *Pattern-Oriented Software Architecture: A System of Patterns.* Vol. 1, West Sussex, England: John Wiley & Sons Ltd., 1996, 305–344.

Suggested Reading

Armstrong, Eric, Jennifer Ball, Stephanie Bodoff, et al. "The JMS API Programming Model." December 5, 2005. Sun Microsystems, http://java.sun.com/j2ee/1.4/docs/tutorial/doc/JMS4.html.

Orfali, Robert and Dan Harkey. *Client/Server Programming with JAVA and CORBA.* 2nd ed. New York: John Wiley & Sons, 1998.

Ort, Ed. "Service-Oriented Architecture and Web Services: Concepts, Technologies, and Tools." April 2005. Sun Microsystems, http://java.sun.com/developer/technicalArticles/WebServices/soa2/WSProtocols.html.

CHAPTER 11

Component-Based Software Architecture

Objectives of this Chapter

- Introduce concepts of the software components
- Discuss UML notations for component-based architectures
- Introduce principles of component-based design
- Introduce quality attributes of component-based design

11.1   Overview

Component-based software architecture divides a problem into subproblems each associated with component partitions. The interfaces of the components play important roles in the component-based design. The main motivation behind component-based design is component reusability: a component encapsulates the functionality and behaviors of a software element into a reusable and self-deployable binary unit. Designs can make use of existing reusable commercial off-the-shelf (COTS) components or ones developed in-house, and they may produce reusable components for future reuse. This increases overall system reliability since the reliability of each individual component enhances the reliability of the whole system via reuse.

There are many standard component frameworks such as COM/DCOM, JavaBean, EJB, CORBA, .NET, web services, and grid services. These target component technologies are widely adopted in local desktop GUI application designs such as graphic JavaBean components, MS ActiveX components, and COM components which can be reused by drag and drop. Many components are invisible, especially those distributed in enterprise business applications and Internet web applications such as Enterprise JavaBean (EJB), and .NET, and CORBA components. The combination of service-oriented and component technologies is getting more attention today; these include web and grid services.

A component is a deployable software package that can provide services to its clients; it may also itself require services from other components. A component remains self-contained and substitutable as long as its interface is unchanged.

A component-oriented design represents a higher level of abstraction than an equivalent object-oriented design; the former defines components and connections between them instead of classes and connections between classes. A component is a higher-level concept, usually incorporating more than one class. Thus, in component-oriented design we first identify all components and their interfaces instead of identifying classes and their relationships.

Component-oriented software architecture and design have many advantages over their traditional object-oriented counterparts. These include:

reduced time in market, lower development costs by reuse of existing components, and increased reliability with reuse of existing components.

The challenge is to design components in such a way as to make it possible to adapt existing components in order to reuse them. Product line architecture design helps with this as discussed in Chapter 14.

11.2   What Is a Component?

A component is a modular (cohesive), deployable (portable), replaceable (plug-and-play), and reusable set of well-defined functionalities that encapsulates its implementation and exports it as a higher-level interface. Szyperski defines a software component as a unit of composition with a contractually specified interface and explicit context dependencies only (Szyperski, 2002). That is, a software component can be deployed independently and is subject to composition by third parties. In the generic model in Figure 11.1 a component is represented by a box the inside of which is its implementation. The dark boxes on the boundary represent the exported interface elements, and the "plugs" sticking out represent required explicit context (usually plugged into another component's interface). The diagram on the right shows how a (larger) component is implemented by interconnecting other components. This larger component can in turn be connected to another component. In this way, a "system" built out of a "network of components" is itself a component.

A component represented in UML 2.0 notation is shown in Figure 11.2.

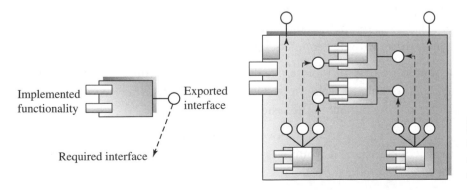

Figure 11.1

General concept of a component and nested composition

Figure 11.2

UML component notation

The circle interface symbol, called provided port, represents the services the component provides; the cup-like interface symbol, called required port, represents the services the component requires from other components. The ports may be connected synchronously or asynchronously, or connected via I/O streams.

A UML component can be mapped to any target technology component. An EJB component is packaged in a .JAR archive file. A Java web component is packaged in a WAR archive file. A remote distributed component is accessed by the "lookup" command for the component's deployment name. A .NET component is deployed as a .DLL dynamic linked library file that is accessed by the "Using" directive in .NET client code. A JavaBean component is deployed as a JAR file and is accessed by "`import <package>.*`" directive in Java client code.

Why use components? Reusability, productivity, composability, adaptability, scalability, reliability, and many other features make component-oriented design and development very useful especially in enterprise frameworks.

Because a component is developed for reusability it must have a clear functionality and be self-contained. Components must be designed and developed for easy reuse. Components should, therefore, be very reliable.

Since detailed coding is significantly reduced by the adoption of a component architecture, the approach increases productivity in the software development process. Instead of development by programming, it will be possible to construct a new component or new software by component composition with development kits.

It should be easy to replace or adapt any existing components. It should also be possible to scale the service capacity by replacing components to increase functionality in the system.

The diagram in Figure 11.3 shows a simple component composition where the client component requires (gets) services from a server component via the server's provided port.

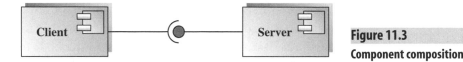

Figure 11.3
Component composition

A component may contain a set of collaborating classes grouped together in packages. A component-oriented architecture emphasizes building systems out of existing components chosen from a reusable library. First, let's look at a simple Java component example. It is specified in a package named counter. Packages can be deployed as single units.

Here is a Java Counter interface with its abstract methods.

```
package counter;

interface Counter {
    public void setCount(int c);
        public int getCount();
        public void inc();
}
```

Class CounterImpl1 is a possible implementation of interface Counter:

```
import counter.*;

class CouterImpl1 implements Counter {
    private int count;

    public void setCount(int c){ count = c;}

    public int getCount(){ return count;}

    public void inc() { count ++; }
    }
```

The interface exposes all the operations of the component while the class implements this interface. A client can use this component as follows:

```
CounterImpl1 myCounter  = new CounterImpl1();
myCounter.inc();
```

The first line can be replaced by using another implementation component ConterImpl2 without any change to the rest of code if both CounterImpl1 and ConterImpl2 implement the same interface Counter.

```
CounterImpl2 myCounter  = new CounterImpl2();
```

The interface separates the implementation of a component from its clients. We can easily convert a Counter implementation class to a JavaBean by following the JavaBean convention, compile the source code for JavaBean, and generate file CounterImpl.class. We know a Java Bean is a deployed component of a java class just like the MS DLL components. It is necessary to create a manifest file to specify this Java class as a bean. The manifest file becomes part of the Java component JAR file. At this time we can use any bean development tools such as Bean Builder or NetBean Visual Studio to load this bean into the tool library and reuse it. The deployed component also can be placed in any directory as long as it is on the classpath. The following screenshot shows the composition of a button component and a counter component, whereby counter is able to display the counts that the button has been pressed. This is a simple form of composition of two components. This composition can be implemented by many Java IDE tools listed above.

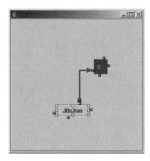

We can also build the Counter component using CORBA technology, deploy it on any CORBA compatible server, and access it by remote clients. A CORBA component can work together with other components. Here is a CORBA interface definition of the Counter component:

```
module Counter {
    interface Count {
        attribute long  count;
        long inc();
    }
}
```

This IDL interface definition can be mapped into a Java package and interface, and implemented by Java classes or mapped to other language implementations so that clients can use this component.

```
package counter;

public interface CountOperations  {
    int count();
    void count(int newCount);
    int inc();
}
```

In addition to the above file, idlj produces more files such as Count.java, a subclass of this interface, implementing all the operations in the interface.

In this section we introduced component concepts illustrating their implementation using several target technologies. During component-oriented design we focus on abstract component specification, which can then be mapped into any target component for implementation.

11.3 Principles of Component-Based Design

11.3.1 Connections of Components

The software system is decomposed into reusable, cohesive, and encapsulated component units. Each component has its own interface that specifies the required ports and provided ports; each component hides its detailed implementation. In other words, each component can be seen as a black box building block grouping functionalities and data cohesively as a module (package).

Connectors connect components, specifying and ruling their interaction. Component interaction can take the form of method invocations, asynchronous invocations such as event listener and registrations, broadcasting, message-driven interactions, data stream communications, and other protocol specific interactions. The interaction type is specified by the interfaces of the components.

Figure 11.4 shows a component-based software architecture. The manager component gets service support from a single component (requests) and a combined service component subsystem (Service 1 and Service n), and the latter gets data access service from a database. The whole software system is a set of components connected by their interfaces. Each component may be replaced or updated without any changes of the other part of the system.

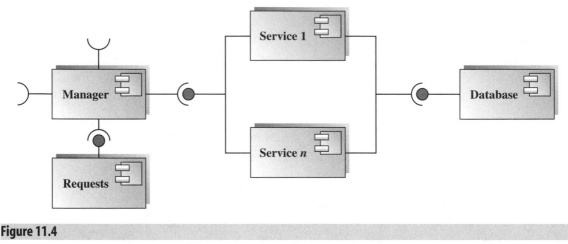

Figure 11.4

UML component-based architecture

There are three categories of connections:

- *Ball and cup (b2c or c2b) connection:* connects two internal or two external components

- *Ball to ball (b2b) or cup to cup (c2c) delegation:* connects an external ball (cup) port to an internal ball (cup) port

- *I/O stream connection*

All above connections can be direct method invocation, implicit (indirect) event-based invocation, or message-based notification. The stream connection is often used for network connection, file read, and file write operations.

The component-oriented software architecture is an architecture style that can be applied to both system and partial system design. Component-based software design is design by contract. The contract specifies the interface between the component and its clients.

To support reusability, one of the most important features of components, we can substitute any component in the system if the new component provides no less than what the old component provides and requires no more than what the old component required.

During the design we consider not only reuse or adaptation of existing components but also the construction of new reusable components.

Components are building blocks just like classes are in the object-oriented paradigm. Class diagrams are the blueprints in object-oriented design; other diagrams refer to, and exist within, the context of this overall class structure.

In a component-based design approach, it is necessary to first identify all components (instead of locating classes first). In most cases, several iterations are required to identify all components. We need to refine the component-based design step-by-step to meet all the requirements, make maximum use of available components, and make all new components necessary for future reuse. Once all components are identified and their interfaces designed, we can move ahead to design the classes that conform each component.

We can see that component-based software design starts from a more abstract level than does OO design.

11.3.2   Component-Level Design Guidelines

Use case modeling and business concept modeling of the project are available before the design phase. Use case diagrams describe user interactions with the system which indicate all necessary operations (interfaces) of the component. We can map use case diagrams to the provided service interfaces of the first-cut component specification.

The business concept diagram depicts the relationships of the business process entities in the domain. We can extract the business process entities that can exist independently without any associated dependency on other entities. We can recognize and discover these independent entities as new components. The current component needs the provided services from these new discovered components. In this way, we can also map the business concept diagrams to the required service interfaces of the first-cut component specification.

A collaboration is any identifiable *slice of functionality* that describes a meaningful service involving, in general, several concepts. A collaboration can be seen as *the implementation of a use case*. Thus, for each use case U, there will be a collaboration diagram "encapsulated" in a component C (one or more sequence diagrams will be drawn to exercise the use case through scenarios). Figure 11.5 illustrates the component implementation of use case U (that happens to lay in between two other use cases).

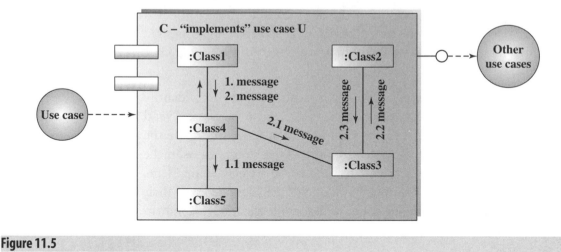

Figure 11.5

Use case component implementation

At the first design step, we derive a first-cut component design that defines the number of components. We know what services each component can provide at this stage. In the next step we need to find out what services each component requires in order to provide its own services. Some required services may be available but some others may not. We need to refine the design, which may result in new component specifications and additional interface ports for existing components.

Following these two steps we get a new component specification with its provided service interface (from step 1) and its required service interfaces (from step 2). We also get other new components, which will need to be refined. We need to repeat these steps until no more new components are left.

UML is a good design tool for component-based software design. To present the event-driven behavior time sequences, not only component and class diagrams, but also dynamic diagrams such as sequence collaboration diagrams are needed. One class may be used in many components, and one component may need many collaborating classes. One component may be reused many times in the software system, and one software system needs many components to work together.

We don't need to address any specific target component technology in the design phase since the component software architecture can be mapped to a target technology later during the implementation phase.

Let us now look at a problem domain to see how to apply component-based software architecture in its design. The software is used to manage clinic appointments. The requirement is described as follows.

A clinic has a dozen family doctors. Each doctor has a daily schedule with 15-minute time slots. A patient can make an appointment with any doctor. Patients may change or cancel their appointments. New patients are welcome. All appointments include patient name, doctor name, data, time slot, reason, and insurance policy. Patients must pay any copayment for the office visit at the sign-in time and the accounting office will bill the rest of the charges.

Assume that we know the system requirements from the analysis process. The system requirements come with text documents, UML diagrams such as a use case diagram, and a business concept diagram. The analysis class diagram may also be available. The use case diagram shown in Figure 11.6 provides a partial description of the scenario. The reader can refine it further.

The business process concept diagram shown in Figure 11.7 describes the possible situations. Each doctor has many daily schedules; any doctor can mark off any unavailable slots on the daily schedule so that patients can select available slots from the schedule when making an appointment. A doctor's daily schedule consists of many appointments with different individuals. Each appointment must connect with the billing system. One

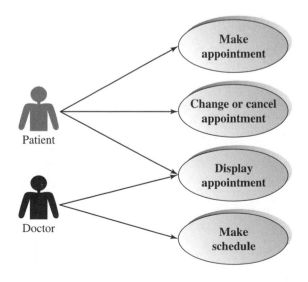

Figure 11.6
Use case for clinic appointment system

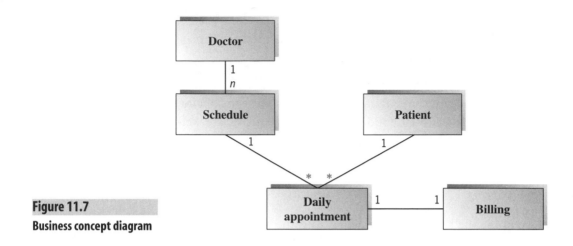

Figure 11.7

Business concept diagram

patient may have at most one daily appointment. This diagram shows the domain entities and business concepts.

The component-based design produces a draft solution for software development based on the requirement analysis. It involves top-down refinement iterations. For example, the first-cut component architecture shows all top-level components; then each subsequent refinement iteration will break down a large and complex component into a number of subcomponents until all component elements match some reusable components or are suitable to be created anew.

Assume there is no class diagram available. We refine the business concept diagram with the following process.

First, identify the independent entities, those that can exist alone without any dependency on other entities (Cheesman and Daniels, 2001). Doctor

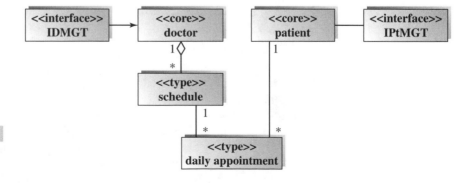

Figure 11.8

Identification of components

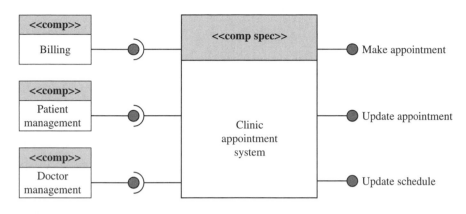

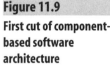

Figure 11.9

First cut of component-based software architecture

and patient are such entities. A schedule belongs to a doctor and is derived from appointments; daily appointments are generated from patient-doctor schedules. The UML notation for interface type or core type is "<< >>". The <<core>> type can exist independently, and each core type has a management interface to the core type. The other types are derived types that cannot exist independently. We focus on the core types and complete the interface management types first.

Figure 11.9 depicts the first-cut of a component-based software architecture for this business process problem domain. There are two levels of components: clinic appointments at the top, and billing, patient, and doctor management components on the next level.

Each core type entity is transformed to a component element that provides services to the root controlling component. Each use case is transformed into an interface provider for users to interact with. Billing may be another system, which can then be designed in the same manner: break it down into many subcomponents and establish corresponding interfaces. The patient component and the doctor component are used to manage persistent data. The clinic appointment system component itself has a lot of business logic to manage. If it is too complicated, we can refine it following the same guidelines as a separate subsystem.

We can conduct the top-down component-based design as shown in Figure 11.10. We can also do the architecture design from the bottom up if the class diagram is available. We can group related classes into a component and work out the interface of this component. Sometimes a component-based software design needs a glue component to integrate multiple ones into a single component so that they can work together.

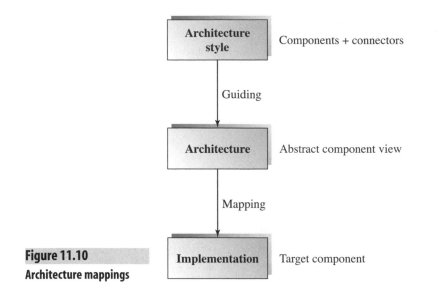

Figure 11.10
Architecture mappings

Applicable domains of component-based architecture:

- Applications where the interface contracts between subsystems are clear

- Applications that require loose coupling between the components and where many reusable components are available

- Suitable for the class library system organization (.NET class library and Java API are built in component architecture)

Benefits:

- Reusability of components.

- System maintenance and evolution; easy to change and update the implementation without affecting the rest of the system.

- Independency and flexible connectivity of components.

- Independent development of components by different groups in parallel.

- Productivity for the current and future software development.

- Many OO design tools can also be used for component-based software development.

Limitations:

- It can be difficult to find suitable available components to reuse.
- Adaptation of components is an issue.
- Few component-oriented dedicated design tools are available.

Related architecture:

- OO architecture, distributed architecture, SOA

11.4   Summary

Component-based software architecture is an extension of object-oriented architecture. Its basic unit is a component in component-orientation instead of classes in object-orientation.

Component is a higher level of abstract concept than class. A component may consist of many related classes stored and deployed in the same binary assembly. The interface of a component plays the role of contract between its implementation and its clients; hence the approach is also called a contract-oriented software architecture. The first step in component-based software design is to identify first-cut components and specify all necessary connections among these components. The connections are conducted via the interfaces of components.

UML component diagrams are useful to specify the topology configuration of connected components. Dynamic UML diagrams are also needed to describe the dynamic behaviors of the assembly of connected components.

An abstract component-based software architecture is ultimately mapped to a target technology component architecture that will be implemented by that technology.

Component-based software design has many advantages over object-oriented design in the quality attributes of reusability, productivity, reliability, scalability, portability, and others. The challenges for adopting a component-based architecture include the adaptation between components, the determination of component unit, and finding suitable existing components.

11.5   Self-Review Questions

1. Which of the following is *not* a benefit of component architecture?

    a. Concurrency

    b. Interactivity

    c. Incrementalism

    d. Productivity

2. Which of the following is *not* a benefit of component architecture?

    a. Performance

    b. Interactivity

    c. Evolution-Adaptability

    d. Reusability

3. CCM is a target technology for component technology.

    a. True

    b. False

4. Each component may have its provided ports and required ports from other components.

    a. True

    b. False

5. Each component must have its provided ports and required ports.

    a. True

    b. False

6. The provided interface ports may be in synchronous or asynchronous modes.

    a. True

    b. False

7. A component architecture can be derived from use case analysis and business concept diagrams.

    a. True

    b. False

8. Core type classes can be recognized as a new component.

    a. True

    b. False

9. A core type component does not depend on any other classes.

    a. True

    b. False

10. The interaction operations in the use case diagrams should be included as part of provided interfaces of components.

    a. True

    b. False

Answers to Self-Review Questions

1. a, b   2. a, b   3. a   4. a   5. b   6. a   7. a   8. a   9. a   10. a

11.6　Exercises

1. What is a software component?

2. Why are components needed?

3. What is component-oriented architecture and design?

4. What is component reusability?

5. What is component deployment?

6. List at least three target component technologies that you know.

7. Is Java API component-oriented?

8. Is .NET class library component-oriented?

9. Is a .jar or .DLL file a component?

11.7　Design Exercises

1. Design a component software architecture for an ordering system involving customer, order, order line, item (product), and billing.

2. Design a student registration system with component-oriented methods where a student can register courses with session number in certain terms with a certain instructor. A student can modify or cancel a registration.

3. Design a hotel reservation system with component-oriented methods where a customer can reserve hotel rooms in a specific

hotel within the hotel chain headquarters. Customers may change or confirm their reservation.

11.8   Challenge Exercises

1. Continue the design of the online payment system and the motel reservation system at the end of Chapter 3. After identifying the subsystems in the problem domain, identify the components for the subsystems and specify the connection between the components. Recall that components and layered architecture are often used together to design a large-scale software.

2. Use the same design strategy and software architecture to design an online textbook exchange store.

References

Cheesman, John and John Daniels. *UML Components: A Simple Process for Specifying Component-Based Software.* Addison-Wesley Professional, 2001, 83–119.

Szyperski, Clemens. *Component Software: Beyond Object-Oriented Programming.* 2nd ed. Component Software Series. Addison-Wesley, 2002, 49–56.

Suggested Reading

Wang, Andy Ju An and Kai Qian. *Component-Oriented Programming.* Hoboken, NJ: John Wiley & Sons, 2005.

CHAPTER 12

Heterogeneous Architecture

Objectives of this Chapter

- Introduce a general methodology of making architecture decisions
- Summarize the benefits and limitations of each architecture style
- Demonstrate how to apply the general principles in case study cxamples

12.1   Overview

In practice, multiple architecture styles often have to be used in the same project. Imagine yourself as the architect of a medieval castle. It is unlikely that the same architecture style can be used for all parts of a castle (e.g., moat, tower, drawbridge, curtain wall, castle hall, residential buildings for civilians). Similarly, for a large-scale software project, heterogeneous architecture styles are used to combine benefits of multiple styles and to ensure quality and appropriateness.

This chapter provides a case study on the heterogeneous architecture. It examines the analysis and design of a relatively large-scale project (an online computer vendor and manufacturer) using the time-tested "divide and conquer" approach. The case study will help you to review knowledge obtained in previous chapters and to practice the general principles in a more realistic design.

12.2   Methodology of Architecture Decision

A successful army commander has to take all factors into account before sending soldiers out. Similarly, the responsibility of a good software architect is not to work out one feasible solution, but to determine which architecture best suits the business needs. A number of architecture styles have been covered, including the data flow architectures (batch sequential, pipe filter, process control), data centric architectures (repository, blackboard), hierarchical, implicit asynchronous communication, interaction-oriented, distributed, and component-based architectures.

Given the large number of alternative architecture styles available, how do you choose the right one that will achieve the project goals optimally (e.g., with the minimal cost)? This section guides you through a brief introduction of the general methodology of determining software architecture under given system constraints.

The process of selecting the architecture of a software system is closely related to requirements analysis. The requirements of a system, the priority of each requirement, and the system constraints (project budget, release date, etc.) all determine the architecture to be used, even if it might not be the most elegant, the fastest, or the most economical. The chosen architecture must be "optimal" and not necessarily focus on one particular aspect of the system constraints. Take the design of an operating system as an example. The layered architecture and its variants are widely adopted by designers of many operating systems, such as Mac OS, OS2, Unix and its variations, and the various versions of the Windows operating system. One strength of the layered architecture is robustness, and this is critical for an OS; since errors do not propagate from one layer to another, if an upper layer crashes it will not affect bottom-layer services.

Figure 12.1 presents a simplified architecture selection process combined with requirement analysis. When a project starts, the system analysts and

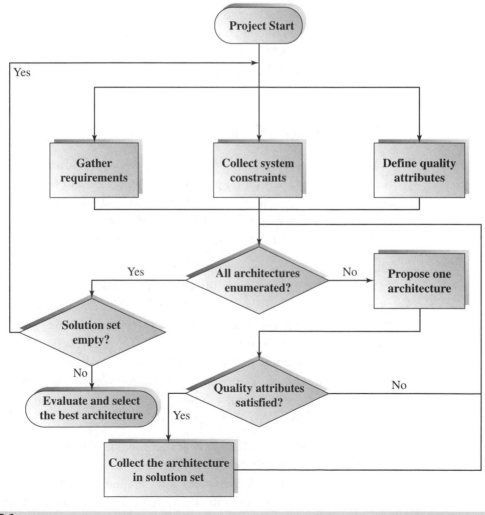

Figure 12.1

Flowchart of the architecture selection process

software architects interact with the project stakeholders, collecting project requirements, identifying system constraints, and defining system quality attributes. Then software architects decompose functionalities and propose feasible architecture styles. For each proposed architecture design, required functions are mapped to the components of the architecture. When all required functions are satisfied, quality attributes are evaluated against the architecture design. The results, together with the architecture design, are documented and collected in a set of candidate solutions. The process is repeated for all possible architecture styles and the results evaluated. If none of the proposed architecture designs work, system analysts must talk with stakeholders about project requirements changes such as extended deadline, increased budget, or fewer functional requirements. When the set of requirements and system constraints is refined, the whole process starts all over again, until the most appropriate architecture is identified (or the project is terminated).

12.3   Quality Attributes

While the overall pattern of the architecture selection process is clear, how it is implemented can vary a great deal depending upon the practitioners. An especially challenging step in the process is identifying and evaluating project quality attributes. The success of this step depends on the expertise and experiences of software architects and system analysts.

Quality attributes are an essential part of the nonfunctional requirements of a system. It is the responsibility of system analysts to put together a complete list of quality attributes before the detailed design process can begin. For most computer systems, quality attributes often include *efficiency* (time efficiency, resource economy), *functionality* (completeness, security, interoperability), *maintainability* (expandability, modifiability, testability), *portability* (hardware independence, software independence, installability, reusability), *reliability* (error tolerance, availability), and *usability* (understandability of code, user interface, learnability).

Each system, with its specific application domain, may have special requirements for quality attributes. System analysts need to interact with stakeholders to identify the relative importance of quality attributes. Notice that, even for the same type of software systems, different stakeholders might prefer different quality attributes. For example, operating systems on IBM mainframes, which are widely deployed in banks, have very high standards on maintainability, reliability, and security. However, efficiency and usability may be of less concern. On the other hand, some stakeholders may prefer efficiency over security.

In many cases, quality attributes can be quantified. For instance, to define the performance attribute of an online media broadcast server, many factors can be defined and evaluated quantitatively, such as bandwidth, throughput, latency, loss rate, and jitter rate. For other quality attributes, such as understandability and reliability, qualitative evaluation may be also converted to quantitative values. Comments such as "excellent" and "bad" can be mapped to numerical points in a scale of 100.

When all quality attributes are represented quantitatively, software architects can enumerate feasible architecture designs and evaluate each quality attribute for each design. As each quality attribute is assigned a weighting factor, defined during the earlier requirement analysis, a total score can be calculated for each design. When the evaluation process is complete, the design with the highest score can be selected.

Figure 12.2 is a simple example of quantitative evaluation of architecture designs. Suppose that the system analysts on a project identify five quality attributes during the requirement analysis: performance, reliability, usability, reusability, and cost-effectiveness. Each of the quality attributes is assigned a percentage weighting factor; for example, performance accounts for 50% of stakeholder concern among all quality attributes. For each quality attribute the evaluation is represented using a value between 0 and 100.

	Performance (50%)	Reliability 10%	Usability (10%)	Reusability (10%)	Cost-Effect. (20%)	Sum
Design 1	10	90	90	80	100	51
Design 2	80	80	20	90	70	73
Design 3	30	80	30	90	60	47
Design 4	20	20	20	20	100	36
Design 5	90	10	10	30	60	62

Figure 12.2
Sample quantitative evaluation of quality attributes

A weighted score can be calculated for each design. For example, the total score of Design 1 is calculated as follows:

$10*50\% + 90*10\% + 90*10\% + 80*10\% + 100*20\% = 51$

By comparing the total scores of all designs, we find that the choice is Design 2.

Once a quantitative evaluation framework is defined, software architects can proceed with the architecture design with the following two steps:

1. Choose a proper architecture style.

2. Furnish the details of the architecture design; for example, when the pipe-filter style is chosen, software architects still have to determine what the filters will be and how to connect them.

12.4   Selection of Architecture Styles

The selection of architecture styles usually depends on the expertise of software architects. However, one helpful tool is Grady Booch's initiative to create the *Handbook of Software Architecture* (Booch, 2004). It inventories software systems and discusses applications of various architecture styles. For developers working on routine projects (e.g., web applications, relational database applications, online games, traffic control, etc.), the handbook is a fast and convenient way to find related projects in the same application domain and learn about architecture styles that are already in use. [Also, progress in product line architectures is promising (see Chapter 14).]

However, general direction on how to select architecture style based on project requirements and constraints does exist. Figure 12.3 presents a concise comparison of the architecture styles introduced in this book and enumerates quality attributes. Each cell denotes whether an architecture style meets the corresponding quality attribute as follows: "+" signifies good, "++" signifies very good, "-" signifies bad, and "—" signifies very bad. An empty cell denotes no explicit judgment for the style/attribute pair in the general case. By examining the architecture style against each required quality attribute in Figure 12.3, and the application domain of each architecture style, a software architect can gain a rough idea of the applicability of an architecture style in a project.

12.5   Evaluation of Architecture Designs

Next we address the second step in architecture selection: how to evaluate an architecture *design*. There are many systematic evaluation approaches, such as ATAM (Architecture Trade-off Analysis Method), SAAM (Software

	OO	Batch sequential	Pipe and Fitter	Process Control	Repository	Blackboard	Main/Subroutine	Master/Slaves	Layered	Virtual Machine	Event-Based (non-buffered)	MsgPassing (buffered)	MVC	PVC	Client-Server	Multi-tier	Broker	Service Ori, Arch. (SOA)	Component-Based
Learnability	-	+	+	-	-	-	-	-	-	-	+	+	+	+	+	+	-	++	++
User Interface	+																+		
Understandability				-				-	+		+	+					+		
Availability									+	+							+	+	
Error-Tolerance									+	+									
Reusability	+	-	+		+	+	-	-	+	+								++	++
Installability										+							+		
Software Independence	+									++								++	+
Hardware Independence				+					+	++							++	++	
Interoperability		-	-				-				+	+	+	+		+		++	++
Security							-		+	+						+			
Completeness	+																		
Space Economy	+	-			+	+	+			-		-				-	-		
Time Economy	+			+	+	-	+	+	-	-						-	-	-	

Figure 12.3

A fact sheet of architecture styles

Architecture Analysis Method), and ARID (Active Reviews for Intermediate Designs). This section briefly discusses the application of the SAAM approach (Kazman, Abowd, Bass, and Clements, 1996).

The general idea of SAAM is to evaluate candidate architecture designs using a collection of scenarios. A design scenario represents an important usage of a system and reflects the viewpoints of stakeholders. Notice that a scenario is similar to, but not the same as, a use case. A use case captures the required usage of the system; however, a scenario may contain situations that are not included in the current scope of the project. For example, to evaluate the modifiability of an online registration system of a university, one scenario could be: What should developers do when the internal data representation of a graduation application package is changed? This is a scenario used in SAAM, but not a use case of the system.

The SAAM analysis process generally consists of three stages:

1. Define a collection of design scenarios that cover the functional and nonfunctional requirements. Quality attributes should be reflected.

2. Perform an evaluation on all candidate architecture designs, using the collection of scenarios.

3. Perform an analysis on the interaction relationship among scenarios.

The following case study demonstrates the first two stages in SAAM. The case study is based on the taxpayer example in Chapter 4. Assume that you are going to design an online tax processing system for the Internal Revenue Service (IRS). Operators input the information of each taxpayer into the system, which is recorded in an instance of a class like *AmericanLawyer* and *AmericanProfessor*, based on the occupation of the taxpayer. One instance of the *IRS* class is used to process tax information for each taxpayer. Two candidate architecture designs (both of OO style) are presented in Figure 12.4. The stakeholders are interested in the following quality attributes:

- *Expandability:* Over time, more occupation types could be added into the system, such as *AmericanFarmer*, *AmericanBusinessOwner*, etc.

- *Performance:* Since millions of cases could be processed each day during peak times, time efficiency is very important. However, space efficiency is of less concern because the stakeholders have

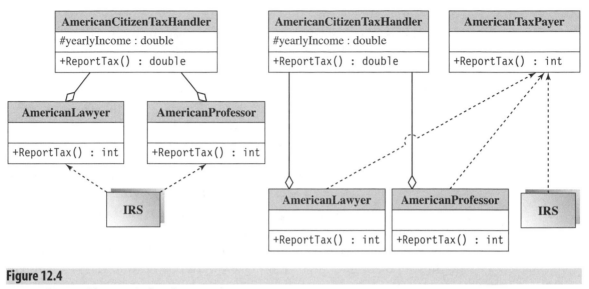

Figure 12.4

Two candidate architecture designs for IRS

enough funding to purchase computer storage (which is cheaper each day).

- *Modifiability:* The format of tax forms and the method of calculating tax rates change every year. The system should be adaptable to such changes.

To evaluate the two candidate designs in Figure 12.4, the following three scenarios are designed:

- *Scenario 1:* Add one more occupation, called *AmericanFarmer*, into the system. This scenario tests the expandability of the system.

- *Scenario 2:* Perform a virtual exhaustive testing on the system. How will the system behave if it has to process one million taxpayers per day? The *IRS* object includes a list of one million taxpayers, and it has to process each one by calling the ReportTax() operation. This scenario tests the performance of the system.

- *Scenario 3:* Alter the tax rate calculation algorithm in ReportTax(), for example, to change the rules of itemized deduction. This scenario tests the modifiability of the system.

Now consider how to evaluate the two designs in Figure 12.4.

Scenario 1: In Design 1 (on the left of Figure 12.4), if a new class *American-Farmer* is added, the code of the *IRS* class has to be modified. When iterating through the list of taxpayers, the *IRS* object has a big switch case to test the type of each taxpayer instance and calls the corresponding operation. A case has to be added into that switch case statement. In Design 2 (on the right of Figure 12.4), programmers can simply insert the new class file of *AmericanFarmer*, and all other classes remain intact. Obviously, Design 2 beats Design 1 in Scenario 1.

Scenario 2: It is easy to see that the two architecture designs are similar in performance. Design 1 will have a slightly higher overhead in deciding which ReportTax() operation to call based on the type of taxpayer instance. The greater the number of occupation types in the system, the longer the switch case statement and the larger the overhead. Design 2 does not have this problem due to polymorphism, whose extra overhead is a constant value. However, their difference in overhead is negligible compared with the complexity of tax rate calculation. Hence both designs perform equally on Scenario 2.

Another question to consider is whether or not the two designs will both pass the test of Scenario 2. One million cases have to be processed per day, which amounts to 11.57 cases per second. This goal could roughly be met if no heavy I/O is involved. However, if additional functions are required (e.g., to generate an automatically filled out tax report for each case), this could easily surpass the capability of both architecture designs. Hence, both designs may have performance issues when additional functional requirements are added.

To improve the time efficiency, duplication of the current designs can be considered (as shown in Figure 12.5). A task dispatcher accesses the sequential user data and distributes the data to a number of IRS offices. Each IRS office is essentially a deployment of Design 2 in Figure 12.4. Notice that the architecture can be easily expanded to introduce more IRS offices to achieve further performance gains. The task dispatcher can also be replicated because there is no interdependency relationship among taxpayer cases. Figure 12.5 is essentially a batch sequential architecture style.

Scenario 3: Both designs in Figure 12.4 will perform equally in Scenario 3. If the tax calculation algorithm changes, the *AmericanCitizenTaxHandler* class has to be modified in both designs.

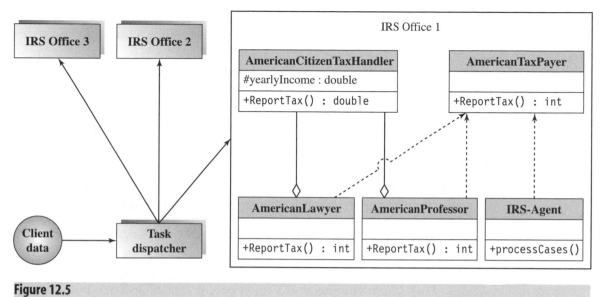

Figure 12.5
Task dispatcher for parallelism

	Scenario 1 (Expandability)	Scenario 2 (Time Efficiency)	Scenario 3 (Modifiability
Design 1	−	−	+
Design 2	+	−	+
Design 3	+	+	+

Figure 12.6
SAAM analysis results

Figure 12.6 summarizes the results of the SAAM analysis on the two architecture designs in Figure 12.4 and the one in Figure 12.5.

12.6   Case Study: Online Computer Vendor

This section presents a case study on how to construct the design blueprint for an *online computer vendor* (OCV). The resulting system is called OCVS, in which the last "S" stands for "System."

The business goal of an OCV is to minimize the price of products and increase the satisfaction rate of customers via the latest technology. An OCV sells computers directly to customers via the Internet. Customers directly specify what they need online. When an order is received, parts are assembled to meet the customer's requirements. Direct selling allows the removal of middlemen and dealers, and hence reduces the cost of product. Just-in-time (JIT) manufacture is used to minimize inventory cost and maximize manufacturing efficiency. Parts are ordered only when required. The whole order processing and product manufacturing process is monitored by a computer system (OCVS), and accurate orders of parts are sent to suppliers every day so that the requirements on parts can be precisely met. The success of OCV relies on the computer system, which bridges the information among all departments and maximizes the efficiency of the whole organization in its entirety. The general requirements of the OCVS are outlined as follows:

1. **Requirement 1** A web portal is provided to customers to place orders. An order can be highly customized where a customer can set the configuration of products step-by-step. Customers can check out directly via the shopping cart or save the shopping cart for later use. Credit card is the only acceptable payment method. The web portal can serve 10,000 customers simultaneously.

2. **Requirement 2** A subsystem is provided to product designers. When a product is released, the designer can input the basic configuration of the product into OCVS. A design can also specify the configuration process of the product. When the specification of a new product is done, the corresponding web pages should be automatically generated in OCVS. Inventory and the subsystem for assembly lines can also incorporate the information immediately.

3. **Requirement 3** A subsystem is to assist assembly lines. Each worker on an assembly line is equipped with a computer system that describes in detail the job that the worker has to perform.

4. **Requirement 4** An automatic inventory management subsystem is developed to track the inventory. An automatic scheduler reports the estimated number of parts required every day. The reports, if approved by business managers, are converted to parts orders to suppliers.

5. **Requirement 5** The OCVS should bridge information among all departments to maximize organizational efficiency. The departments involved include order processing, manufacturing and shipping, product design, and business strategy.

6. **Requirement 6** The required quality attributes of OCVS include:

   - *expandability*, so that new products (and their configuration process) can be easily added into the system;

   - *modifiability*, to allow for modifications of internal representation of products and configuration processes over the time, since the business rules (e.g., parts usage prediction), product web pages, and configuration process will go through frequent changes;

   - *availability and reliability*, especially for the modules that interact with customers and the manufacture assembly lines; and

   - *time efficiency*, for all modules to cope with the requirement of producing one million PCs per year. Peak time requirement of its customer web portal is to support 10,000 customers simultaneously at any given time.

The next task is to construct a feasible architecture design blueprint of OCVS. Follow a top-down strategy: provide the overall architecture design first and then decompose system into components, where the design of each component is furnished.

12.6.1 Overall Architecture Design of OCVS

Recall that the process of architecture design contains two steps: (1) selection of architecture styles, and (2) architecture design. We now have to make decisions on architecture style(s) of the overall structure of OCVS. There are many architecture styles from which to choose, and some of them can be screened out easily. Figure 12.7 illustrates the screening process. OCVS does not fall into the application domain of many architecture styles listed, such as process control (which favors embedded systems), pipe and filter (which requires data streams between components), main/subroutine (which does not support distributed architecture), MVC (which suits the web portal component of OCVS only), and so on.

Since pure batch sequential and repository styles do not work for OCVS in isolation, they are combined as one candidate (heterogeneous) architecture style. Hence, after the initial screening in Figure 12.7, the candidate architecture styles are: (1) batch sequential + repository, (2) layered, (3) multitier, (4) service-oriented architecture (SOA), and (5) component-based architecture (CBA).

	Architecture	Reasoning
OO	OO	**Ruled out:** OO is not proper as an architectural style at the overview level for a complex system.
Data	Batch Sequential	**Candidate:** suitable for order processing process. **Limitations:** low efficiency.
Data	Pipe and Filter	**Ruled out:** data transferred among departments is not stream-oriented.
Data	Process Control	**Ruled out:** OCVS is not in this application domain.
Data Centric	Repository	**Candidate:** suits the needs for storing customer data and product configuration. **Limitations:** the pure repository model forbids communication among system components.
Data Centric	Blackboard	**Ruled out:** OCVS is not in the application domain. Debugging and testing are difficult.
Hierarchy	Main/Subroutine	**Ruled out:** OCVS has to support multiple tasks (e.g., order process-ing, inventory management and prediction, etc.). There is no need for a central coordinator.
Hierarchy	Master/Slaves	**Ruled out:** similar to Main/Subroutine.
Hierarchy	Layered	**Candidate:** the services of OCV can be classified into layers.
Hierarchy	Virtual Machine	**Ruled out:** OCVS is not in this application domain (e.g., machine simulation and porting of existing systems).
Implicit Interact.	Event-Based (non-buffered)	**Ruled out:** OCVS does not fall in this application domain (e.g., GUI applications).
Implicit Interact.	MsgPassing (buffered)	**Ruled out:** OCVS does not fall in the application domain.
Interaction	MVC	**Ruled out:** Although the Web portal subsystem, which interacts with customers, may be a good candidate using MVC, the OCVS system has many other noninteractive subsystems. Hence MVC is not the most appropriate architectural style for OCVS.
Interaction	PVC	**Ruled out:** similar reason as MVC.
Distribution	Client-Server	**Ruled out:** the model does not suit the multiple components and multiple tasks of OCVS.
Distribution	Multi-tier	**Candidate:** similar to layered system.
Distribution	Broker	**Ruled out:** low efficiency and difficulty in testing.
Distribution	SOA	**Candidate:** suits loosely coupled services and departments.
Component	Component-Based	**Candidate:** suits loosely coupled services provided by OCVS. Its architecture is very similar to SOA, except that SOA provides service directory (such as UDDI) to locate services, which is not needed here. **Limitations:** data representation may not be as flexible as XML (semi-structured) representation in SOA.

Figure 12.7

Screening of architectural styles for OCVS

Two pairs of architecture styles are very similar: layered vs. multi-tier and SOA vs. CBA. Multi-tier architecture can be simply regarded as the layered architecture style in a distributed system. First you have to break the tie between SOA and CBA.

12.6.1.1 SOA vs. CBA

In both SOA and CBA, components ("services" in SOA) have well-defined interfaces. CBA is an older technique than SOA, which is mainly supported by middleware techniques such as CORBA. In addition, CBA has weaker directory services than those provided in SOA (such as UDDI, the Universal Description, Discovery, and Integration services).

However, in the case of OCVS, CBA does have its own advantages. First, as all components are well-known and not typically published to the outside world, the extra service broker and location services such as the UDDI in SOA are not needed by OCVS. Second, efficiency can be a concern in SOA implementation. Although greater flexibility is provided by the use of XML in parameter passing, SOA is essentially stateless and lacks the capability of passing remote object references. All remote object references have to be serialized, which creates much larger network overhead for SOA implementations (Brown, Johnston, and Kelly, 2002). In addition, the network overhead of passing the same message by SOA is significantly greater than CBA. Therefore, considering the requirements of OCVS, the CBA architecture style is preferred.

12.6.1.2 Final Decision on Architecture Selection

The decision is made to select component-based architecture (CBA) over the other alternatives. The batch sequential to data repository is ruled out due to the following argument: Batch sequential is suitable for order processing; however, it supports the workflow of one particular task only. OCVS has to perform several major tasks concurrently.

With multi-tier view you can use the following three tiers to model the system: (1) front-end, (2) business model, and (3) database. Notice that many functional units, such as Web portal and manufacturing system, have to be broken down into three tiers and their components mixed in the same tier. Hence, logically the system does not look like a clear-cut choice for this style. The preceding comparison leads to the choice of CBA.

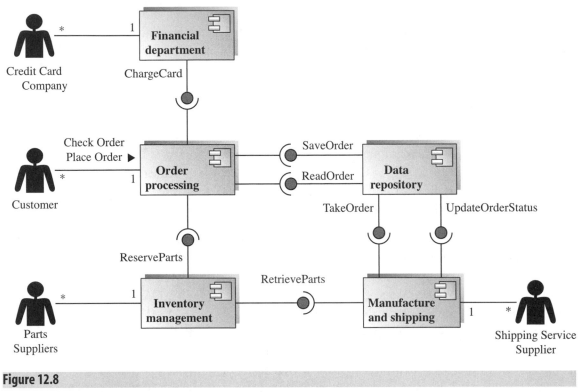

Figure 12.8

Overall architecture of OCVS

Figure 12.8 presents the architecture design of the overall structure of OCVS. The system generally consists of five components: *Order Processing, Data Repository, Inventory Management, Manufacture and Shipping,* and *Financial Department.* Note that each component may be deployed on one or more computers, and the overall OCVS system is a distributed system. There are four actors that interact with OCVS: *Customer, Parts Suppliers, Credit Card Company,* and *Shipping Service Supplier.* Components interact with each other via remote procedure call. For example, when the *Order Processing* department finishes the order transaction of one customer, the *SaveOrder* interface of the *Data Repository* is used to save the order. In the meantime, the *ReserveParts* interface of *Inventory Management* is used to reserve parts for that order. Later the *Manufacture and Shipping* component will *TakeOrder* from *Data Repository,* and *RetrieveParts* from *Inventory Management.* The *Manufacture and Shipping* will periodically *UpdateOrderStatus* to *Data Repository* so customers can trace order status. When an order is finished, *Shipping Service Supplier* will be contacted to deliver products to customers.

The next task is to evaluate how the architecture design in Figure 12.8 satisfies the requirements of OCVS. **Requirement 1** (customer Web portal) is mapped to the *Order Processing* component. **Requirement 2** (insertion of product configuration) is not satisfied by the architecture design yet. System analysts and software architects may suggest removing this requirement. The argument is that to achieve Requirement 2, a specific product description language has to be defined and the corresponding language interpreter has to be implemented. Since OCVS does not release more than 20 products per year, there is no need to build a product description language and interpretation system. A more convenient way is to insert product configuration modules into the order processing system manually by the system engineer. **Requirement 3** (computer assisted manufacture system) is mapped to the *Manufacture and Shipping* component. **Requirement 4** (smart inventory management) is mapped to the *Inventory Management* component. **Requirement 5** is reflected in the design of the overall structure where the *Data Repository* component takes charge of maintaining live data.

Requirement 6 is about quality attributes. The expandability requirement can be solved by manual addition of product configuration modules into the *Order Processing* component (not as good as the product description language solution, but much less costly). Time efficiency and availability can be achieved through replication of components, for example, *Order Processing* and *Data Repository* components. The only quality attribute that is not handled well is modifiability. When internal data representations of customer profiles or order details are changed, *Data Repository* and other correlated components have to be modified. The SOA architecture might do a little better due to the semistructured XML. However, the modifiability is traded for the time efficiency and convenience of implementation.

Next we will address the architecture design of *Order Processing, Inventory Management*, and *Manufacture and Shipping* components. The discussion of *Financial Department* and *Data Repository* is omitted here because the design is straightforward: *Financial Department* contacts credit card companies for charging cards, and *Data Repository* is a simple wrapper class of relational databases.

12.6.2   Architecture Design of Order Processing Component

The *Order Processing* component is similar to the *Order Processing System* (OPS) discussed in Chapter 4 and the JSP/Servlet MVC II example discussed in Chapter 9. In summary, the *Order Processing* component naturally falls into the application domain of web-based interactive architecture style. There are two choices of interactive architecture: MVC and PAC. MVC model is chosen due to its simplicity.

As requested by the stakeholders of OCV, it should be relatively easy to add new product information and product configuration process into the *Order Processing* component. To achieve this, the overall structure of the component is organized using component-based architecture, where each component represents the set of correlated JSP pages, Java Servlet classes, and the corresponding Java Beans for a certain "stage" during a shopping session. These components do not invoke any functions of each other, and the only type of association among them is that one component might forward (i.e., redirect) to another.

Figure 12.9 presents the overall structure of the *Order Processing* component. Notice that there are multiple components for product configuration

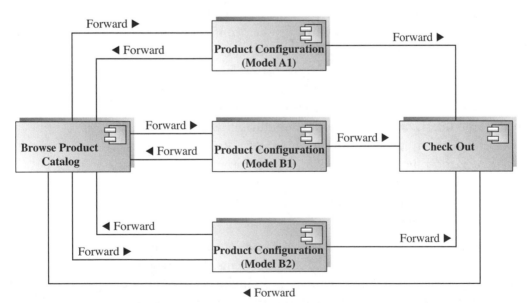

Figure 12.9

Major components of the *Order Processing* component

(e.g., A1, B1, and B2). If a new product is released, the corresponding configuration component can be inserted into the *Order Processing* component with all other product configuration components and the *Check Out* component remains intact. Only the *Browse Product Catalog* component will need to be recompiled if a new product is added.

The architecture design of the *Browse Product Catalog, Check Out,* and *Product Configuration* components will be similar. All of them use the Model-View-Controller (MVC) architecture, which allows separation of presentation and business logic, and hence the flexibility in extension and modification. The basic idea of MVC is to use a model to maintain the data of the system, a view for presenting the data, and a controller to serve as a middleman between view and model. MVC can be implemented on many platforms including both .Net and Java. For example, on Java platforms, JSP pages are usually used as View, Java Servlet classes are used as Controller, and Java Bean objects and back-end databases are used as Model. The architecture design of the *Product Configuration* component is presented in Figure 12.10.

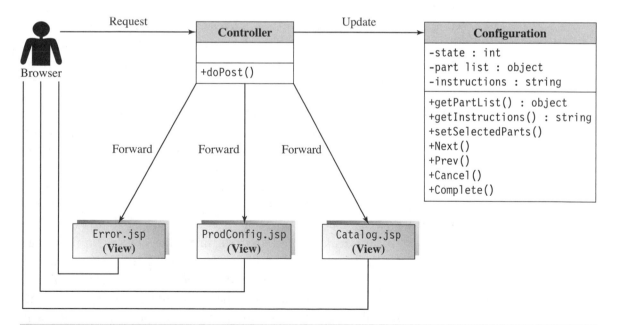

Figure 12.10

Architecture design of *Product Configuration*

In Figure 12.10, the "View" of a *Product Configuration* component consists of three JSP pages, one for displaying error message, one for displaying product catalog (actually a part of the *Browse Product Catalog* component), and the last one (`ProdConfig.jsp`) for interacting with a customer in each step of the configuration process. Each JSP page has static HTML contents, designed by graphic designers, which may change frequently. The dynamic contents are set by the *Controller* Servlet. For example, the step number of configuration process, instructions for the configuration step, as well as a list of parts by different vendors for the customer to choose from, parameterizes `ProdConfig.jsp`. All these contents are eventually retrieved from the model, a Java Bean called *Configuration.*

The model shown in Figure 12.10 works as follows. After the customer selects one product model in the *Browse Product Catalog* component, the controller of the *Browse Product Catalog* redirects the browser to `ProdConfig.jsp`. The *Controller* Servlet is created and it, in turn, creates the model *Configuration* bean. Then the `ProdConfig.jsp` page helps the customer to configure the computer step-by-step—selecting CPU model, memory type and size, graphic card, etc. A customer can choose to advance to the next step, or go back to the previous step. When a step is finished, the list of parts that are selected during that step is forwarded to *Controller* and then to *Configuration.* When the whole configuration is completed and confirmed by the user, the *AddToCart* request is sent to *Controller* and central database will be updated.

The choice to implement the modules of the *Product Configuration* is obvious, that is, object-oriented paradigm. A state machine diagram can capture the design of configuration beautifully, and one example is shown in Figure 12.11. Each state of the state machine diagram represents one step in the configuration. When the state machine enters one state, the part list variable is set correspondingly for that step. Users can step backward and forward between states. From each state, a call of the *Cancel* operation causes the state machine to end up in the final state. Notice that the design in Figure 12.11 does not furnish all the details. For example, to allow customers to step backward, a stack should be established to record the history of selected parts. When the state machine advances to the next state, the latest parts list submitted by the customer should be pushed into the stack; when the state machine steps backward, a pop operation should be conducted. Another problem with the current design is that from each state the

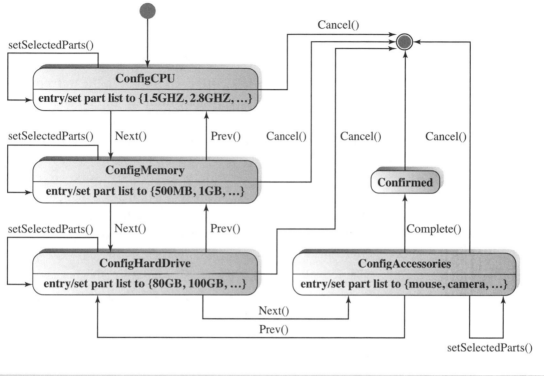

Figure 12.11

State machine diagram of the *Configuration* class

Next transition should be disabled if the user has not submitted the selected parts for that step. You can refine the design in Figure 12.11.

12.6.3   Architecture Design of Inventory Management

As shown in Figure 12.8, the *Inventory Management* component has the following responsibilities:

- It maintains the records of all parts (e.g., CPU, memory chip, hard drive, monitor, etc.). The warehouse of OCVS is managed digitally. Each item has a full record in the database system of *Inventory Management* and each item (not its *type*) has a unique barcode.

- It allows customers to reserve parts for an order. When a reservation succeeds, the barcodes of the reserved items are associated with the order. Customers receive an immediate response when parts they ordered are not available. When a customer steps backward in product configuration, the reservation locks on the corresponding parts are released by invoking the *UndoReserve* operation.

- It allows the *Manufacture and Shipping* component to check out parts by calling *RetrieveParts*. Each worker in the warehouse has a working desk equipped with a computer and a barcode scanner. When the remote invocation of *RetrieveParts* occurs, the *Inventory Management* generates a job order, which specifies the items to check out and their destination, and assigns a barcode and an internal mail package box for the job order. A worker receives a job order via computer, selects the required items, assembles the product, and then sends it out. Whenever an item is put into a package, its barcode first has to be scanned. When the package box arrives at *Manufacture & Shipping*, the barcode of the package is scanned again to confirm the completion of the job order.

- It routinely examines the inventory of all parts. Based on the history of inventory, it issues a daily order for each type of parts to suppliers. Each supplier has established a transaction server that conforms to the supply-chain interface of OCVS.

From the above requirements, it is easy to infer that the inventory management should include:

- a database which maintains information on all parts stored in the warehouse;

- a controller system which is able to accept remote invocation from the *Order Processing* and *Manufacture and Shipping* components; and

- satellite computers (with barcode scanners) that are used by the workers.

The next step is to decide how to organize these modules. The application domain of the *Inventory Management* soon leads to a heterogeneous architecture style: the combination of data repository and client server styles. The block diagram in Figure 12.12 displays the general structure of *Inventory Management*. Both the *Inventory Management Controller* and *Satellite Computers* interact with a relational database for insertion, removal, and update of computer parts records. The relationship between the *Satellite Computer* and *Inventory Management Controller* is client/server. The *Inven-*

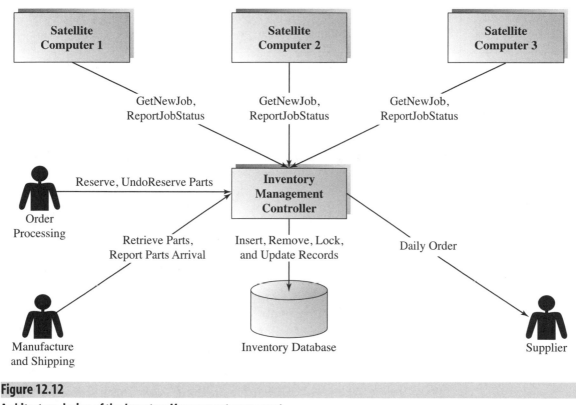

Figure 12.12

Architecture design of the *Inventory Management* component

tory Management Controller keeps a list of job orders. When a *Satellite Computer* has completed one job, it retrieves the details of another job order and displays the job to worker.

Clearly, the *Inventory Management Controller* can be developed using the OO paradigm, and the *Satellite Computer* can be developed using MVC architecture (as it interacts with workers). We will examine the design details of these two modules as exercises.

12.6.4   Architecture Design of Manufacture and Shipping Component

The last task of this chapter is the architecture design for the *Manufacture and Shipping* component. This subsystem has to manage the information flow of the manufacture department, which is responsible for producing over one million PCs per year.

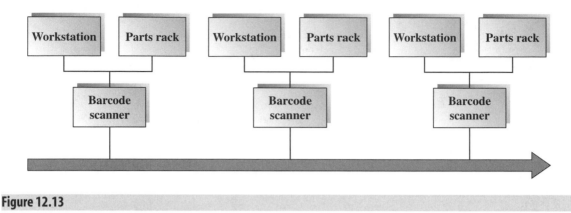

Figure 12.13

An intuitive diagram of OCVS assembly line

Background   The major equipment of the manufacture department is its assembly line.

The major idea of an assembly line is to take advantage of the economic principle of "division of labor." If managers break down the use of labor into well-defined, specialized, and repetitive tasks, they can greatly increase the efficiency of the output. The structure of an OCV assembly line is presented in Figure 12.13. Its major component is the conveyor belt, which moves materials forward. Multiple stages are attached to the conveyor belt (the number of stages can vary and can be adjusted dynamically). The hardware of each stage consists of the following:

- A workstation that provides the space for workers to assemble parts. The workstation is equipped with a computer (called "stage computer") that displays job details to operators and allows operators to send messages to central controller (e.g., reporting testing failures, malfunction of parts, etc.).

- A parts rack to hold the parts required for the stage. The inventory department fills the parts rack. With the assistance of OCVS, it guarantees that when a computer chassis arrives at one stage, the required parts at this stage are already in the parts rack.

- A barcode scanner which is used: (1) to check in parts when they are delivered by the inventory department; (2) to check in computer chassis when it arrives; and (3) to check out computer chassis when the job is completed at this stage.

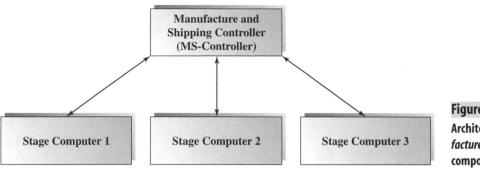

Figure 12.14

Architecture of *Manufacture and Shipping* component

Overall Structure of Manufacture and Shipping Component The project goal is to coordinate the information flow to expedite the production process. The scope of the *Manufacture and Shipping* component includes the central controller that interacts with other components of OCVS, and the stage computers (with barcode scanner); control of the conveyor belt pulley is out of the scope.

Given the requirements and the nature of the assembly line, one natural choice for the overall structure of the *Manufacture and Shipping* component is the client-server architecture, shown in Figure 12.14. The server part in the design is called *MS-Controller*.

Design of MS-Controller Recall that the responsibilities of the *MS-Controller* are: (1) to interact with *Order Processing* and *Inventory Management* components for smooth supply-chain; and (2) to manage all stage computers to coordinate the manufacture process, such as displaying job details to operators when a computer chassis arrives to the stage or accepting exception reports from operators.

Since *MS-Controller* bears many responsibilities, a layered architecture can be used to simplify its design. The basic idea is to split *MS-Controller* into three layers: (1) a communication layer that accepts messages sent by stage computers and communicates with other remote components such as *Order Processing* and *Inventory Management*; (2) a core engine layer that handles requests from stage computers and controls the whole manufacturing process; and (3) a business logic layer that defines and interprets business rules.

Figure 12.15 shows the architecture design of *MS-Controller*. The communication layer has to communicate with remote computers/components.

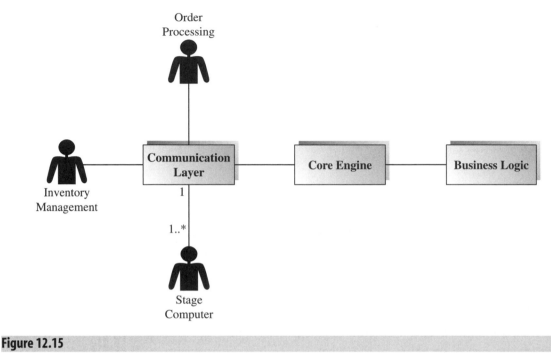

Figure 12.15

Architecture design of *MS-Controller*

Requests from the outside world are forwarded to the core engine to be processed. The business module sitting behind parameterizes the processing by the core engine.

The next step is to drill down to the design of the three modules of *MS-Controller*. The design details of *Communication Layer* and *Business Logic* are left to you as assignments. In the following, the focus is on the design of the *Core Engine*.

The *Core Engine* has to perform many different tasks. For example, when the assembly lines are started, it is responsible for retrieving the daily job orders from the *Data Repository*. If anything goes wrong (e.g., sound card malfunctioning), the *Core Engine* has to send instructions to the stage for taking remedial actions (e.g., to pull the product off the line and to temporarily stop all products of the same model number). There are several

Event	Action
Assembly Line Started	Retrieve the list of orders of the day. Send requests to inventory for parts.
Parts delivered at one stage	Based on the part barcode, find the order that uses it and update the information. When all parts are ready, trigger the "all parts ready" event.
All parts ready for an order	Schedule the job to one of the assembly lines in the department. Consult the business logic about the split of manufacture process and then map the "logical stages" of the process to physical stages attached to the assembly line.
Chassis arrived at one stage	Send instructions and job details to the stage workstation computer (e.g., which parts to be used, the barcode of the parts, and how to install them).
Parts malfunction	Send instruction: "Pull the chassis off the line. Continue to work on the next job. Replacement part will arrive in 10 minutes." Send emergency parts retrieval requests to inventory. Count the number of failures of the same parts. If the number exceeds a certain threshold, trigger the "Parts Quality Problem" event.
Parts Quality Problem	Pull all products with problematic parts off the assembly line. Raise issues to management.

Figure 12.16

Sample events and handlers of *Core Engine*

feasible alternatives for the design of *Core Engine*. These include the blackboard and event-based architecture styles. However, the best solution is to use the buffered message architecture. The message registration service can be easily set up using messaging services such as Java Message Service. Then events can be added into the message registration service, and the handlers are registered. Figure 12.16 presents some sample events and the corresponding actions to be taken.

An outstanding feature of the buffered message system is its flexibility. New events and handlers can be defined conveniently without interrupting the existing modules. Although the architecture decision of the *Core Engine* is to use the buffered message style, its detailed design can be conveniently implemented using the OO approach.

12.7   Summary

Choosing the best architecture design for a software system is indeed an art. This chapter introduced several methodologies for making architecture decisions and evaluating alternative architecture designs. The general principles were practiced in a case study of building an online computer vendor system. Various architecture styles such as the component-based, service-oriented, batch sequential, model-view-controller, client-server, data repository, and buffered message systems were considered in its design. You are encouraged to complete the unfinished modules of the online computer vendor system. Remember: expertise comes from experience!

12.8   Self-Review Questions

1. Which of the following is used to evaluate architecture designs?

   a.   ATAM

   b.   SAAM

   c.   ARID

   d.   ALL

2. Which of the following is true about heterogeneous architecture?

   a.   There is no mixed architecture style at one abstraction level.

   b.   Heterogeneous architecture implies increased time efficiency.

   c.   If the general structure of a system is connected using one architecture style, and each component can use a different one, this is one example of heterogeneous architecture.

   d.   None

3. Modifiability and expandability are essentially the same quality attribute.

   a.   True

   b.   False

4. SAAM relies on use cases to test an architecture design.

   a.   True

   b.   False

5. There is always an architecture design that can meet all requirements.

    a. True

    b. False

6. Service-oriented architecture is stateless, while component-based architecture is not.

    a. True

    b. False

7. Batch sequential architecture is generally more time efficient than pipe and filter.

    a. True

    b. False

8. It is beneficial to integrate architecture design with the process of requirements analysis.

    a. True

    b. False

9. Event-based architecture is a good candidate for interactive systems with graphic user interface.

    a. True

    b. False

10. Blackboard architecture is difficult to debug.

    a. True

    b. False

Answers to the Self-Review Questions

1. d 2. c 3. b 4. b 5. b 6. a 7. b 8. a 9. a 10. a

12.9 Exercises

1. List the application domain of every architecture style that is introduced in this book.

2. Is there any difference between modifiability and expandability? Explain.

3. Give one scenario for which batch sequential architecture is a better choice than pipe and filter.

4. Give one scenario for which service-oriented architecture (SOA) is a better choice than component-based architecture (CBA).

5. Give one scenario for which event-based architecture (non-buffered) is a better choice than the message passing architecture (buffered).

12.10   Design Exercises

1. Use the SAAM approach to evaluate the modifiability of the design in Figure 12.9.

2. Finish the detailed design and implementation of the *Production Configuration* component (in Figure 12.10) using JSF/Servlet/JavaBean.

3. Finish the detailed design of the *Configuration* class in Figure 12.11.

4. Complete the detailed design of the *Inventory Management System* in Figure 12.12 using the OO paradigm.

5. Select a proper architecture style for the *Business Logic* module in Figure 12.15.

6. Enumerate three more events and the corresponding actions that can be listed in Figure 12.16.

12.11   Challenge Exercises

1. Assume that the stakeholders ask for an additional module in the *Manufacture and Shipping* component. The module should provide a graphical user interface that allows business managers to adjust the mapping of a manufacturing process (of a product) to the stages of assembly lines. Choose the architecture style for this module and furnish the detailed design.

2. Assume that OCV has expanded its business and sells 50 million PCs per year. Every year, OCV brings over 50 new products to the market. Now the support of **Requirement 2** (which was discarded in the original design of OCVS) has been an urgent task. How would you expand the existing OCVS system to make the following a reality?

"**Requirement 2**: A subsystem shall be provided to product designers. When a product is released, the designer can input the basic configuration of the product into OCVS. A design can also specify the configuration process of the product. When the specification of a new product is done, the corresponding web pages should be automatically generated in OCVS. Inventory and the subsystem for assembly lines shall also incorporate the information immediately."

Think of the architecture style for the new module. Furnish the detailed design of the module and implement your design using JSP/Servlet.

References

Booch, Grady. *Handbook of Software Architecture*, 2004, http://www.handbookofsoftwarearchitecture.com/ (accessed November 2008).

Brown, Alan, Simon Johnston, and Kevin Kelly. "Using Service-Oriented Architecture and Component-Based Development to Build Web Service Applications." A Rational Software White Paper. Rational Software Corporation, 2002, 8–9. http://www-128.ibm.com/developerworks/rational/library/content/03July/2000/2169/2169.pdf.

Kazman, Rick, Gregory Abowd, Len Bass, and Paul Clements. "Scenario-Based Analysis of Software Architecture." *IEEE Software*, Vol. 13, No. 6. Los Alamitos, CA: IEEE Computer Society Press, 1996, 47–55.

Suggested Reading

Shaw, Mary. "Heterogeneous Design Idioms for Software Architecture." IWSSD '91: Proceedings of the sixth international workshop on software specification and design. Los Alamitos, CA: IEEE Computer Society Press, 1991, 158–165.

Garland, Jeff and Richard Anthony. *Large-Scale Software Architecture: A Practical Guide Using UML*. Wiley, 2002.

CHAPTER 13

Architecture of User Interfaces

Objectives of this Chapter

- Introduce the look and feel and the usability of user interfaces
- Discuss the design considerations
- Demonstrate the enabling technology

13.1   Overview

Any software system is a service. A good service must satisfy the user's expectations. From the user's viewpoint, the first impression of a software system is its user interface (UI). Due to the fact that any software system should accept inputs, conduct computations, and display outputs, the user interface mainly performs two functions. One is accepting the user's inputs (input data or control commands), and the other is displaying the outputs (or the current states of the software system). Even a batch software system, such as a software system for a numeric computation, has at least one command, "run," and a display of the computational results.

As we discussed in Chapter 3, we have introduced a "user interface view" into the 4+1 view model, which we compiled with the "scenario view." In other words, the user interface of a software system is a very important portion of the system, just like a wrapper is a very important part of a candy. Why is it so important?

In some sense, the user interface could be the most important part of a software system. No matter what the internal architecture of the software system is, users will first see the architecture of its external user interface. The users' choices for a software package are very often based on what is offered by the user interface of the software. A good user interface will attract the user while a bad one may cause a market failure against the competition of the software system. In this sense, the user interface is the external, and possibly the only, visible aspect of the underlying software system.

As a "language" for describing the software to users, the user interface has its syntax and semantics. The syntax includes the component types (textual, icon, button, etc.) and their composition (organization and layout). There are no rules, like grammar rules, that can be used to check the correctness of the syntax of the user interface; instead we use the look and feel to summarize it. The semantics of the user interface includes the linkages between the components of the user interface and the functionalities associated with the software system. A good user interface should help the user to understand the software system easily, without misleading information, and attract the user to use the software system joyfully without mistakes. Usability summarizes the semantics of the user interface.

Software in different domains may require different styles of its user interface. A calculator requires only a small area for displaying numeric numbers but a big area for commands. A text editor needs a big area for displaying information but a small area for commands. An Integrated Development Environment (IDE) for software development requires a complicated menu system, a property listing, a palette for holding all UI components, and a panel for accepting UI components with a drag-and-drop method. A web page, a web application, or a web service needs forms, links, tabs, etc. A computer game needs a totally different user interface. However, no matter which kind of user interface it is, every user interface supports accepting commands and displaying information.

Based on the appearance, we group user interfaces into three styles: static, dynamic, and customizable. Additionally, based on the way commands are issued, we divide user interfaces into three categories: textual, graphical, and other kinds, such as voice. In general, the textual user interfaces are being faded out.

This chapter primarily discusses the graphical user interfaces. In the discussion, we will mainly focus on the common architecture and design principles. The topics include: (1) evolution of user interfaces; (2) look and feel of user interfaces; (3) usability of user interfaces; (4) design considerations; and (5) enabling technology. Through these topics, we will evaluate and analyze the existing user interfaces, and then synthesize the observations to draw common principles. Finally we will discuss the design considerations and enabling technologies as solutions for realizing the requirements of user interfaces.

13.2   Evolution of User Interfaces

The architecture of user interfaces supports its look and feel and usability aspects. The evolution from textual user interfaces to graphical user interfaces can give us an idea about why the look and feel and the usability came to be. Let us take a calculator in a software version as an example. In the early days, before calculators became commercial hardware products in the market, many students had developed software calculators with a command line. (Using the DOS prompt panel, we can experience what the command line is today.) When the software calculator is running, the user types in the command "add 5 10 <Enter>", and the screen displays the computation result. This was the first type of interface for interactive systems. It was known as command-line interface. A large number of systems have been developed with command-line interfaces, particularly operating systems. Users of some operating systems still prefer using this kind of textual command line user interface today.

The command-line interface uses a command language. Creating a command language processor is usually easier than implementing a graphical user interface. However, users have to learn and memorize the command language. It is not suitable for casual and inexperienced users. In addition, users inevitably make errors in expressing commands so that the language processor must include error handling and message generation facilities.

To overcome these drawbacks, a listing of commands was used. When the calculator starts running, a set of commands was listed as a group of "choices" like this:

1. addition

2. subtraction

3. multiplication

4. division

5. …

When the user clicks one of the number keys on the keyboard and types in two operands, the calculator will display the corresponding computation result on the screen. The entire screen is for listing the commands, displaying the input data, and showing the output results. The display moves up line-by-line along the screen when the user issues more commands.

Today's calculator, for example the Windows calculator shown in Figure 13.1, looks totally different. A dedicated small window is used for showing the numeric numbers. Buttons and check boxes represent all commands (functions). The user points and selects buttons and check boxes to operate these commands.

These two versions of user interfaces, namely the textual command-line and the graphical point-and-click user interfaces, have a different syntax (look and feel) while their semantics are the same; both of them access the same internal functionalities behind the textual listing or the buttons.

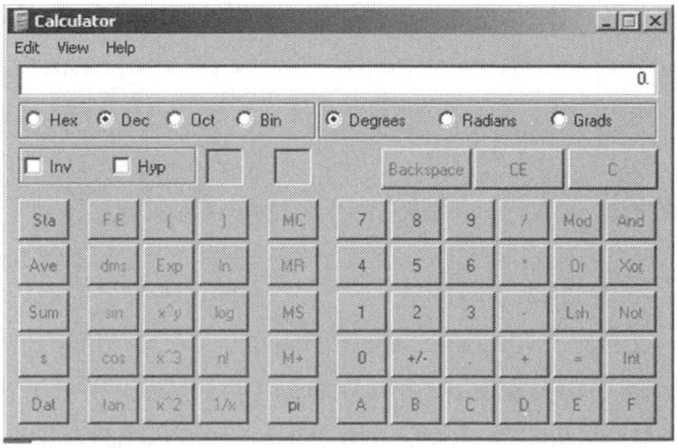

Figure 13.1
The Windows calculator

Imagine that we map all functions supported by the Windows calculator shown in Figure 13.1 to a command listing, the listing will contain about 40 lines or so. Users have to browse the entire list each time to find the function they need. Not only is the list display a mess but selecting a command from the long listing is a tedious and error-prone task. Thus, the graphical user interface is more meaningful and easier to use than the text-based user interface.

From this example we also can see that a user interface itself, especially the graphical user interface, is sophisticated software. It needs codes not only for displaying, arranging, and laying out all buttons, labels, and components but also for linking these elements in the user interface with the internal functions of the software. This example also reveals a separating principle: to separate the view (user interface) from the logic (computations). The internal architecture of a software system follows the logic of the application specifications. Its user interface is the view of the logic of the software. We may have the same logic for the computations but different views for different users. If we would like to design a calculator for a blind person, we need another kind of user interface.

Fortunately, many programming languages, such as Visual Basic, Java, etc., provide built-in components and layout managers for implementing user interfaces. In addition, many IDEs support drag-and-drop metaphors for making the implementation of graphical user interfaces easier. However, organizing these components to form a user interface can be an art. We need to understand this art and the way to map it into an engineering practice. The points of this understanding mainly include what kind of components should be used, how to arrange them in a proper fashion in terms of its syntax (look and feel), and what the architecture of the user interface should be in terms of its semantics (usability, consistency, and integration).

13.3   Look and Feel (Syntax) of User Interfaces

The syntax of user interfaces refers to its appearance, or its look and feel. As we have previously mentioned, the arrangement of a user interface is an art. There are no engineering "rules" that can be used to check its "correctness," like grammar rules used to check the syntax of a programming, or even a spoken, language. The design and implementation of the look and feel are based on the belief that most humans know how to appreciate artwork. In general, graphical user interfaces have three styles: static, dynamic, and customizable.

13.3.1   Static Style of User Interfaces

The static style of user interfaces refers to those user interfaces that have statically "prefixed" components and compositions. The Windows calculator shown in Figure 13.1 is a typical example. The components used on the user interface include button, radio button, and check box. All these components are arranged into three rows and two columns. The frequently used digits and commands are in the right-hand column. The infrequently used commands, including scientific, statistic, and memory access commands, are in the left-hand column. The digits [0–9] are grouped into a panel that is almost the same as the digit panels on other popular devices like phones. The digits [A–F] will be activated only when the user selects the "hex" (hexadecimal) operation. Different colors identify different clusters of commands or data. The key "Sta" will pop-up a hidden window that extends the functionality of the user interface. All these arrangements together form the architecture of the user interface. The architecture provides context for the content and tells us what we can do. The architecture also illustrates the syntax of the user interface. In addition, the "Help" menu is one of precious tools for helping users find tutorials and hints on using the system.

Many user interfaces fall into this style, such as text editors and IDEs for software development. In general, these user interfaces are well-defined, in the sense that they are usually developed by professionals, and many are commercial products. Secondly, the IDEs have a clearly defined application domain and serving targets, that of supporting program development with a selected programming language; an IDE deals with a certain set of menus, such as File, Edit, Search, Build, Run, and so on. The organization and layout of these user interfaces of IDEs and Editors can be summarized in the following.

- **1D layout:** This simply has only one menu bar that supports fundamental functions for editing—such as MS Notepad, MS Word, and so on—and leaves central space for information editing. The menus usually have pull-down menus and walking menus, as shown in Figure 13.2. They could be considered as 2D layout, but the menu system appears along the x-direction only as a 1D layout.

- **2D layout:** besides a menu system along the x-direction, there are certain left or right panels along the y-direction for arranging more tool bars or for displaying properties. Some of them also use the bottom portion for displaying status. TextPad, Visual Basic editor, and Paint are some examples of this kind, as shown in Figure 13.3.

- **3D layout:** a menu along the x-direction, toolbars along the y-direction, and tabs or more multiple choices along the z-direction, such as Eclipse, Java Studio IDEs, and .NET studio, and the like, as shown in Figure 13.4.

- **4D layout:** The user interface of Maya (Figure 13.5) is one example. It has a menu along the x-direction, toolbars along the y-direction,

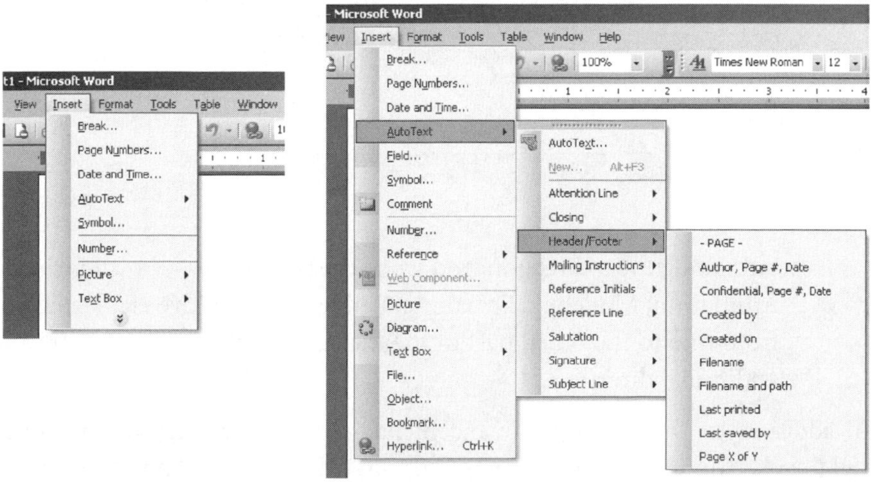

Figure 13.2

Pull-down menu (left) and walking menu (right) in MS Word

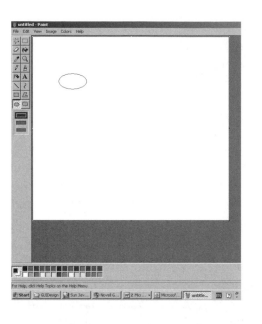

Figure 13.3

2D layout in a user interface (Paint)

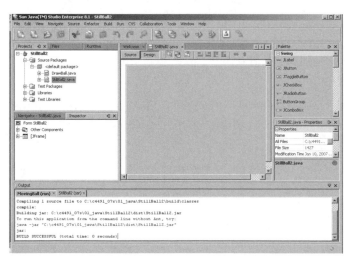

Figure 13.4

3D layout in a user interface (Java Studio Enterprise 8)

tabs along the *z*-direction, and when the menu-sets—which include Animation, Modeling, Dynamics, Rendering, and Live etc.—change from one to the other, part of the menu is changed. This creates an additional direction.

In addition to these "static" arrangements, many user interfaces include right-click, context pop-up menus, pop-up windows, or "hot keys" that extend the "static" layouts. Some of them summarize important actions,

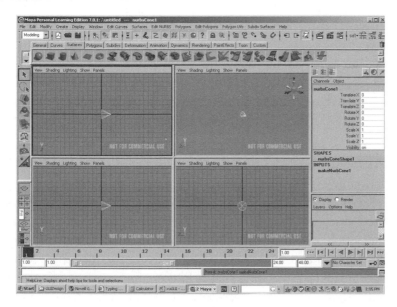

Figure 13.5

4D layout (Maya)

which were originally spread throughout different menus and now are pulled together in one place, while some of them introduce new commands.

With the rapid increase of mobile or handheld devices, such as cell phones and personal digital assistants (PDAs), a new kind of user interface is becoming popular. Due to the fact that handheld devices impose limitations, such as small screen size, limited screen resolution, and cumbersome input mechanisms, their user interfaces should be categorized as page-based or layer-based. The user has to search page-by-page or layer-by-layer for the required button and information. These user interfaces are still pre-arranged but embed more intelligent designs.

13.3.2   Dynamic Style of User Interfaces

Websites allow users to ask, browse, and search for information that the user would like to obtain. This kind of user interface also provides menus, tabs, and some static links. Specifically, these user interfaces leave space for displaying information, and the information may embed many "dynamic" links, known as hyperlinks. These dynamic hyperlinks are not part of prefixed UI components but are dynamic occurrences of components that guide users from one web page to another or from one website to the world. Consequently, a website needs to accept a user's query, conduct searching, and display the results with further searching links that dynamically depend on the displayed contents. A browser (e.g., MS Internet Explorer) can be used to access any available web object uniquely linked by the Unified Resource Locator (URL). Today, almost all organizations have their own websites and so do many individuals. These websites provide different content and embedded hyperlinks to guide users to search more URLs.

Web pages, with their hyperlinks and displayed content, need to have a structure, an organization, and a labeling system. The structure determines the appropriate levels of granularity for the information units. The organization involves grouping those components into meaningful and distinctive categories. The labeling system can be used for figuring out what to call those categories for the series of navigation links that lead to them. Since many web pages belong to organizations and individuals, a web page could be designed and implemented by professionals or laymen. Some websites provide logical structures that help users find answers and complete tasks with relative ease. Others lack any intelligible organization and are difficult to navigate. In other words, the assessment of the quality of this kind of user interface often mixes the concept of the "traditional" user interface with the information structure of the contents.

With the rapid growth of the Internet and wireless networks, e-business and m-business are based on web applications and web services and are increasing rapidly. Their user interfaces are the environment in which online users conduct communication, information searches, and transactions. They are not only web pages with hyperlinks but they also dynamically support users' interactive input and output. These user interfaces deal with more complicated software systems, supported by the so-called three-tier architecture, and depend on the dynamically changed market and business logic. Their look and feel should satisfy both customers' and entrepreneurs' expectations.

13.3.3   Customizable Style of User Interfaces

A developing trend of user interfaces is the customizable style. This style of user interface is tightly integrated with the entire software system. A simple example is the Windows calculator shown in Figure 13.1. The user interface of the calculator has a menu labeled "View." Click this menu item and a pull-down menu pops up with an option: "Standard" or "Scientific." If the user selects "Standard," the calculator will provide a much simplified user interface without the sophisticated scientific functions, as shown in Figure 13.6. That is, such a customizable user interface can make the calcu-

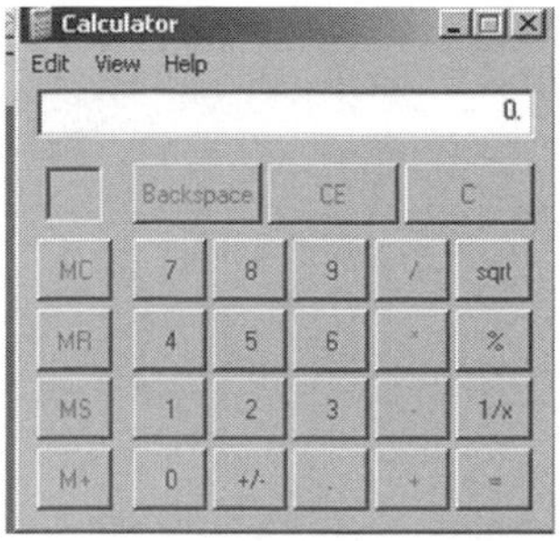

Figure 13.6

The "Standard" version of Windows calculator

lator easy to be used either by pupils in elementary schools or by scientists for their research.

This means that the entire software system supports all needed functions with a specific customizable user interface. Many user interfaces that belong to the static style also have some setting functions for customizing the user interface appearance, such as text colors, contents of tool bars, etc. However, they do not change the functionality provided via the user interface.

More customizable user interfaces are being developed. Eclipse and NetBeans are typical examples. These software systems have a main part and a set of plug-in modules. The modules can be attached for increasing functionality of the entire system. For example, NetBeans is used for developing Java applications. It has attachable modules for developing specific software including Mobility Pack, Visual Web Pack, Enterprise Pack, C/C++ Pack, Profiler, and UML modeling. When these modules are added, the user interface is tailored accordingly.

Figure 13.7 shows the user interface of the NetBeans IDE after adding some plug-in modules. This type of design provides a lot of benefits for users. We can imagine that in the future, users will only pay a small amount for buying (or free-downloading) the main body of a software system. Whenever they need additional functions, they can buy, rent, or freely download some extra modules. This style of user interface can satisfy users' expectations. The numerous widgets available for the Mac OS Dashboard interface are another good example.

13.3.4   No User Interfaces

Ultimately, user interfaces as we known them today, may be replaced by new technology such as multitouch sensors, brain electrode connections, as well as audio input that can be used to interactively access the underlying computers without static user interfaces (Han, 2006).

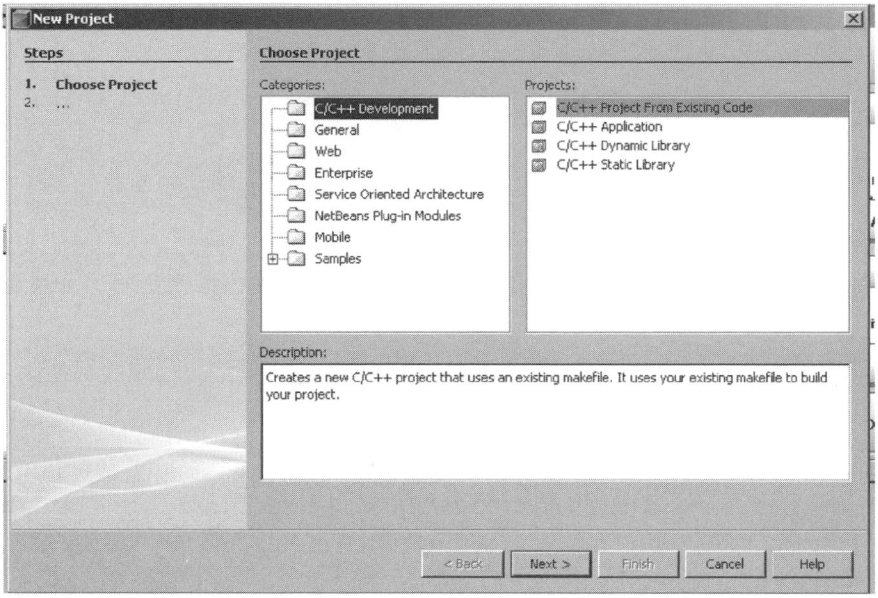

Figure 13.7

After adding plug-in modules (NetBeans)

Multitouch sensing enables a user to interact with a system with more than one finger at a time, as in chording and bimanual operations. Such sensing devices are also inherently able to accommodate multiple users simultaneously, which is especially useful for larger interaction scenarios such as interactive walls and tabletops. The technique is force sensitive, and provides unprecedented resolution and scalability that can be used to create sophisticated multipoint widgets for displaying panels large enough to accommodate both hands and multiple users. This technique offers the ability to make computing more accessible to children, seniors, and populations unfamiliar with traditional computer interfaces.

13.4 Usability (Semantics) of User Interfaces

The semantics of user interfaces mainly refers to usability, consistency, and integration (Torres, 2001). Usability is the key attribute that determines the quality of a user interface. Whatever the software system, be it a simple calculator, an IDE, or a website, a beautiful user interface does not mean that the software system has a high degree of usability. An engineering student may only derive 30% usability from the standard version of the Windows calculator shown in Figure 13.6 because the standard version does not support required functionalities for scientific calculations. At the same time, an elementary school student may derive only 50% usability from the scientific version of the Windows calculator shown in Figure 13.1 because the student never uses the advanced scientific functions. The customizable interface of the calculator, which can switch from the "standard" version to the "scientific" version, illustrates an idea that significantly increases the usability of the interface. That is, the usability of a user interface depends not only on the architecture of the user interface and the entire software system, but also refers to the needs, experiences, and capabilities of the system users.

Usability also includes information presentation since the purpose of most systems is to input commands and watch for new information returned by the system. Presentation may simply be a direct representation of the input information, such as text in a word processor, or it may present the information in some other more meaningful way, such as information returned by web pages as images or even videos. This is an important point in the dynamic style of user interfaces.

The usability of a user interface reflects the usability of the entire software system. Web pages where partial user interface is embedded in the contents of the information require structure, organization, and a labeling system. Their combinations support "findability." Thus, if users cannot find what they need through a combination of browsing and searching, the website fails. A properly designed information architecture is required to effectively support findability (Rosenfeld and Morville, 2002). As we can imagine, information architecture is a mixture of science and art; designers have to deal with the complexity and ambiguity of natural languages, and they must rely on their experience, intuition, and creativity. An important factor that increases complexity is related to the exponential growth of information. A study at the University of California at Berkeley found that the world produces one to two billion gigabytes of unique information per year (Rosenfeld and Morville, 2002). The classification of the information is built on the foundation of natural languages. Unfortunately, natural languages are inherently ambiguous. For example, if a paper has an "Information Technology" phrase in its title, should the paper belong to the discipline of IT (information technology), IS (information systems), or CS (computer science)? Similarly, how should a paper with "Information Security" in its title be categorized? The labeling system can also be misleading if labels are buzzwords of categories. There are no classification systems that can create unique categories.

Additionally, users often lack a clear idea of what they may be looking for and they also have an uncertain category labeling system in mind. Furthermore, embedded hyperlinks are often idiosyncratic and personal in nature. They provide browsing paths for you to find what you like, but after tracking a certain number of links you may find that you either entered an unexpected website or you could not find a way back to your starting point.

13.5   Design Considerations of User Interfaces

Based on the preceding discussion, a user interface can be viewed as a mixture of engineering and art. Human beings know how to appreciate artwork. However, individuals have their own angles from which they view it. All of this makes the design and implementation of user interfaces difficult. Nevertheless, from the evaluation of existing user interfaces and the analysis of the syntax and semantics of user interfaces, we can at least find a direction for designing a "best" user interface. That is, a user interface that is both user and service-providers oriented. In order to approach this direction, the user interface should be customizable, component-based, and apply the separating rule: to separate the user interface from the underlying software logic. Consequently, the following major design considerations and implementation processes are key.

- **User-centered:** As pointed out previously, user interface design must take into account the needs, experiences, and capabilities of the system users. A user interface must be a user-centered product. The key is to apply the user-centered methodology that involves users early and often throughout a product's development. It means involving users in all processes including planning, identifying requirements, design, construction, product evaluation, and deployment. In order to understand users' needs, prototyping is an essential step. The prototype of a user interface should be available to users, and feedback from users should be incorporated into the final product.

- **Intuitive:** No matter how many variants there are, the central attributes remain the same: simplicity, intuitiveness, and usability. The "best" user interface is one that people can figure out how to use quickly and effectively even without instructions. Graphical user interfaces are better than textual user interfaces in the sense that a graphical user interface usually consists of windows, menus, buttons, and icons, and is operated by using a mouse. The layout of these components is usually consistent, and over time users learn hidden and advanced features. Once a user establishes a comfortable interaction approach, the experiences can be transferred across other graphical user interfaces.

- **Consistency:** Designers must consider the physical and mental limitations of users of the software system. They need to recognize the limitations on the size of short-term memory and to avoid overloading users with information. User interface consistency reduces the probability of errors. Consistency supports usability. User interface consistency refers to either or both syntax and semantics. Consistency means that the software system is expected to be consistent with itself and with other software on the same platform or in related domains. An interface's commands and menus should have the same format, parameters should be passed to all commands in the same way, and command punctuation should be similar. For example, a user interface cannot be designed to have a panel for [0–9] digits with a digit order that is different than some common devices like a phone's digits panel. Even in two user interfaces, it is not advisable to use "Alt + a" to mean "Accept the input" in one user interface and to mean "Abort the transmission" in another. The interface should use terms and concepts drawn from the experience of the anticipated class of users; should be consistent in that comparable operations can be activated in the same way; should not have behaviors that can surprise users; should include mechanisms to allow users to recover from their mistakes; and should incorporate some form of context-sensitive user guidance and assistance.

- **Integration:** Integration is another important factor that supports the usability of user interfaces. The software system should integrate smoothly with other applications. For example, different editors in the Windows operating system, such as MS Notepad and MS Office applications, can use "Clipboard" commands (Cut, Copy, and Paste) to directly perform data interchange. MS Word can launch the PDF (Adobe Portable Document Format) package to convert documents from Word to PDF format. The printing manager can send the data to a printer and also to a file. Maya's import and export commands can accept an image file created by other applications or export a scene file to other software systems. The Paint software can convert an input GIF (Graphics Interchange Format) image to different formats like JPEG (Joint Photographic Experts Group). The Java Studio Enterprise IDE can draw a UML (Unified Modeling Language) diagram based on the code of a project. These integrations extend the usability of one application, enhance the usability of the other, and greatly impact the design and organization of the user interface.

The integration of a user interface is also reflected in the usage of its components. In what situation is a radio button or a check box a proper choice? Under what conditions is a slider a better choice than a radio button? The answer depends on the nature of the functions of the software.

- **Component-oriented:** In addition to consistency and integration, component-oriented architecture should be applied in the design of the user interface. A user interface is a sophisticated software system. Some software systems contribute 50% of their code to the user interface. Therefore, the design of the user interface will have the same requirements as the design of the main body of the software system. It is important that a user interface be modular, incorporating the component-oriented philosophy. Modules can be easily modified and replaced without ramifications to other parts of the system. For example, an IDE system is able to plug-and-play components, such as a word spelling checker, a coloring subsystem, a compiler, or a library of a different programming language. Gradually, these well-defined software components can be manufactured as reusable and adaptable components for common sharing.

- **Customizable:** Customizable user interfaces require that the architecture of the entire software system be based on component-oriented philosophy in order to incorporate plug-in modules. Let us take the Eclipse IDE as an example. The architecture of the Eclipse software package is based on Eclipse Modeling Framework (EMF), which unifies Java, XML (Extensible Markup Language), and UML technologies so that they can be used together to build better customizable and integrated software tools. Extensibility and integration are its paramount goals. It allows many different people to independently extend the software in ways we could not even previously imagine. For supporting its customization, its integration includes user interface integration (the ability of independent extensions to contribute to a single user interface) and asset integration (the ability of the persistent files produced and used by various extensions to be managed by common resource management mechanisms). The development work in Eclipse is divided into three main projects: the Eclipse Project, the Tools Project, and the Technology Project. The Eclipse Project is divided into three subprojects: the Platform, the Java Development Tools (JDT), and the Plug-in Development Environment (PDE). The Tools Project defines and coordinates the integration of different sets of categories of tools based on the Eclipse platform. The Technology Project provides an opportunity for researchers, academics, and educators to become involved in the ongoing evolution of Eclipse. The Eclipse Platform is a framework for building IDEs. It is described as "an IDE for anything, and nothing in particular." The addition of specific tools (plug-ins) extends the framework and collectively defines a particular IDE.

A plug-in in the Eclipse IDE is a component or basic unit of function. A plug-in includes everything needed to run the functionality provided in a manifest file, named plugin.xml, which declares the interconnections to other plug-ins, among other things. The Eclipse core includes a class, named `Plugin`, which represents a plug-in component. The attribute plugin on the top-level of the class `Plugin` can be identified in the manifest file. When a plug-in component is used for the first time, an object of the `Plugin` class is instantiated. Through the object, the plug-in's resource bundle, its location, and the platform's logging facilities can be accessed (Budinsky et al., 2004.)

- **Separation:** User interfaces are tightly integrated with the underlying software system through their architecture for supporting the system. However, they are intended to be separated from the logic of the system through its implementation for increasing reusability and maintainability.

According to the MVC (Model-View-Controller) model, if we separate the View (the user interface) from the Model (the logic of the software system), then based on the same functionalities of the software system, we can design different user interfaces depending on the system users' needs, experiences, and capabilities. The same set of data could be displayed using different information representation, such as data shown as either a bar diagram or a pie diagram. This separation allows designers to change the information representation on the user's screen without having to change the underlying computing functions and the logic of the system. In addition, requirements of the user interface team will not be tightly coupled with the requirements of the logic design team. This criterion is especially important for those service providers who deal with a dynamically changing environment, such as the market and the business logic. Therefore, this criterion has been widely used in the design of web applications and also is important for general user interfaces such that the same internal functionality of software may support textual, graphical, or other kinds of user interfaces for satisfying users' needs.

- **Information representation:** The same data or information can be represented in using different shapes, colors, digital or analog signs, and so on. For making design decisions, a number of factors must be taken into account: (1) Is the user interested in precise information or in the relationships between different data values? If precise numeric information is required, information should be represented as text or tables. If the relationship is more important than the numeric data, then graphical diagrams are preferred. (2) How quickly do the information values change? Should the change in a value be indicated immediately to the user? If the information values are changed quickly and the user should observe the changes immediately, text display or slider type of graphical display with scales should be used. (3) Must the user take some action in response to a change in information? Depending on whether the user is interested in relative or absolute changes, graphical or textual display is preferred and an action mechanism should be provided, such as a button or a menu. Dynamically varying numeric information is usually best presented graphically using an analog representation like gauge displays in car dashboards.

Very large amounts of information are better visualized graphically. The presentation may be used to navigate through the information or as a way of exposing relationships that are not obvious from the raw data. Examples include weather information, a model of a molecule, etc. Systems for information visualization rely on high-performance computers, color graphics, and some specialized equipment, such as a virtual reality helmet display, data glove, and the like.

- **Friendliness:** Friendliness is embedded in any aspects listed previously, from the look and feel to the usability. Besides supporting a complete set of functions including redo functions, customizable settings, hot keys, and so on, it should also include features such as tutorials, search engines, help facilities, or updating links.

- **Summary:** In summary, the user interface should satisfy five major principles, with the acronym SAPCO: simple, aesthetic, productive, customizable, and other (Torres, 2001).

  - *Simple* means that a user interface does not require use of a book or online help in order to get started with simple tasks. It is sufficiently intuitive that a user need only be told once how to operate using the user interface.

  - *Aesthetic* refers to appearance and appeal. For example, all components in the user interface are arranged symmetrically, following a popular style, and clearly cut into groups based on their roles from very frequently used to very rarely used, or from very simple functions to very complicated functions.

  - *Productive* indicates that a minimal number of work steps can accomplish a task. A user interface should be able to tolerate small mistakes, such as supporting redo functions, and following conventions, such as mouse left-click, right-click, single-click, double-click, and drag-and-drop.

  - *Customizable* allows individual users to select from various available forms in order to suit personal preferences and needs, including customizable user interfaces, settings, and status lines.

- *Other* implies that beyond these principles there are countless other principles available. The majority are variants of the SAPC.

13.6 Enabling Technology

As discussed in Chapter 1, software architecture is regarded as "the description of elements that comprise a system, the interactions and patterns of these elements, the principles that guide their composition, and the constraints on these elements." This description also applies to the software architecture of a user interface, with regards to its elements and compositions. This is mainly a design aspect; traditionally, enabling technology belongs to the implementation aspects. However, due to the fact that the drag-and-drop metaphor is widely used and can automatically generate required codes for all UI components and their compositions in user interfaces, designers can directly use the metaphor to build up a blueprint for a user interface. Thus, selecting and using an enabling technology is no longer a "pure" implementation aspect. More importantly, as we have discussed, organizing components to create a user interface can be an art. We need to understand this art and determine how to map it into an engineering practice. The points of this understanding include what type of components should be used, how to arrange them in terms of syntax (look and feel), and what the architecture of the user interface should be in terms of semantics (usability, consistency, and integration). Therefore, both user interface designers and implementers need to have the required knowledge of enabling technologies and how to apply them in creating a user interface. Here, we will focus on the relationships between the principles we have discussed and what can be used to realize these principles, which is the goal of this section.

Some customizable and component-oriented graphical user interfaces, such as Eclipse or NetBeans IDEs, are built from the ground up with a module- or component-oriented architecture. This kind of architecture not only deals with software module integration but also with user interface integration, or the ability of independent extensions to contribute to a single user interface. To realize this integration, the graphical user interface itself must be made of components.

Currently, many programming languages directly support the design and implementation of user interfaces by integrating components. The Java programming language is one of these kinds of programming language. Java is a "pure" object-oriented programming language. It has three editions: the Java 2 Enterprise Edition (J2EE) supports enterprise applications, the Java 2 Standard Edition (J2SE) is suitable for general purpose applications, and the Java 2 Micro Edition (J2ME) can be used for developing applications for handheld devices, such as PDAs and cell phones. All three editions have rich sets of UI components for making graphical user interfaces, layout managers for organizing the components according to the designer's requirements, and listeners that listen to the events when users access the components in the graphical user interfaces. Listeners trigger event handlers to perform the functions of the corresponding components. That is, the components and layout managers fulfill the look and feel needs of a graphical user interface, while the events link the users' actions with the internal logic of the software system. This loosely coupled mechanism makes the customizable user interfaces and the separating principle possible. With its popularity, many powerful IDEs that support Java programming language come in handy for using the drag-and-drop metaphor to build up user interfaces. Designers can directly describe the look and feel of a user interface easily.

In J2SE edition, Java provides two packages for all GUI components. One package is `java.awt` (Abstract Windows Toolkit), which contains all components that are automatically mapped to platform-specific elements through their respective agents, known as peers. These components are prone to platform-specific bugs because the peer-based approach relies heavily on the underlying operating system. AWT is fine for developing simple graphical user interfaces, but not for developing comprehensive GUI projects. Since Java 2, the `java.awt` GUI components were replaced by a more robust, versatile, and flexible package known as `javax.swing`. Swing components are painted directly by Java code, except the components `java.awt.Window` and `java.awt.Panel`. Swing components rely less on the underlying platform and are referred to as lightweight components. These components are categorized and described in the following subsections.

13.6.1 Containers

The package `javax.swing` provides the three top-level container classes, `JFrame`, `JApplet`, and `JDialog`. Each Java GUI has at least one top-level container. This top-level container is the root of a containment hierarchy.

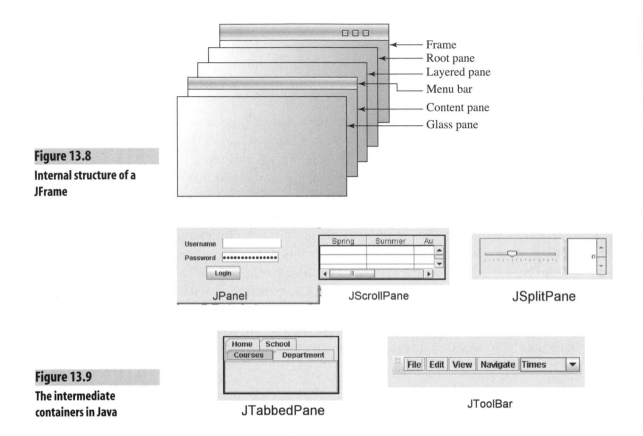

Figure 13.8

Internal structure of a JFrame

Figure 13.9

The intermediate containers in Java

JFrame is used for standalone Java applications, while JApplet is widely used in Web applications. The internal structure of a JFrame has four layered panes as shown in Figure 13.8. The root pane, layered pane, and glass pane are required to organize the menu bar and the content pane. The content pane is the main container in all frames, applets, and dialogs which adds all visible components in that top-level container.

Swing provides several general-purpose intermediate containers as shown in Figure 13.9. These intermediate containers can group related components together as a unit by using any layout manager. The one most often used is JPanel. Others include JScrollPane that provides scroll bars around a large of extendable component; JSplitPane that displays two components in a place, letting the user adjust the amount of space for each of them; JTabbedPane that contains multiple components but shows only one at a time; and JToolBar that holds a group of components in a row or column, allowing the user to drag it.

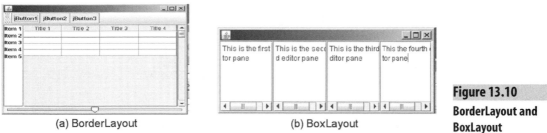

(a) BorderLayout   (b) BoxLayout

Figure 13.10
BorderLayout and
BoxLayout

13.6.2   Layout Managers

All container classes have layout managers for general use. The layout managers include BorderLayout, BoxLayout, CardLayout, FlowLayout, GridBagLayout, GridLayout, AbsoluteLayout, and NullLayout. Every content pane is initialized to use a BorderLayout. In Figure 13.10, a BorderLayout (a) places components in up to five areas: top, bottom, left, right, and center. All extra space is placed in the center area. A BoxLayout (b) puts components in a single row or column. It respects the components' requested maximum sizes and also lets designers align components.

A CardLayout lets designers implement an area that contains different components at different times. A CardLayout is often controlled by a combo box. The state of the combo box determines which panel (card) the CardLayout displays. In Figure 13.11, (a) shows card 1 that contains a JTextArea component in a CardLayout, while (b) shows card 2 that contains a JTable in the same CardLayout. A FlowLayout is the default layout

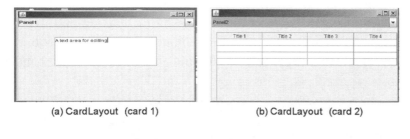

(a) CardLayout (card 1)   (b) CardLayout (card 2)

(c) FlowLayout

Figure 13.11
CardLayout and
FlowLayout

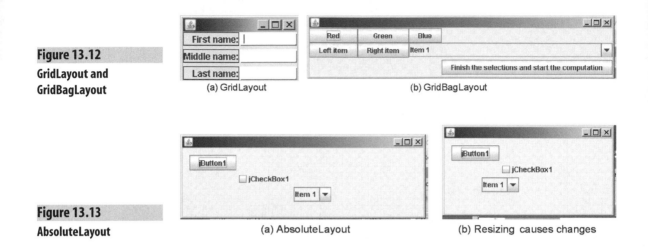

Figure 13.12

**GridLayout and
GridBagLayout**

(a) GridLayout   (b) GridBagLayout

Figure 13.13

AbsoluteLayout

(a) AbsoluteLayout   (b) Resizing causes changes

manager for every JPanel. It simply lays out components in a single row, starting a new row if its container is not sufficiently wide, as shown in (c).

In Figure 13.12 a GridLayout (a) simply makes a group of components equal in size and displays them in the requested number of rows and columns. A GridBagLayout (b) is a sophisticated and flexible layout manager. It aligns components by placing them within a grid of cells, allowing some components to span more than one cell. The rows in the grid can have different heights, and grid columns can have different widths.

An AbsoluteLayout, shown in Figure 13.13, lets designers specify an absolute location for components. The components can be moved around and resized using their selection border. An AbsoluteLayout is particularly useful for making prototypes since there are no formal limitations and designers do not have to enter any property settings. The NullLayout shown in Figure 13.14 is similarly useful for making prototypes since it means no layout management for components. However, both Absolute-Layout and NullLayout are not recommended for production applications

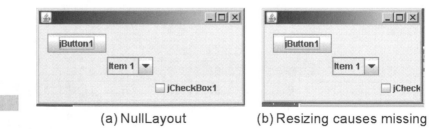

Figure 13.14

NullLayout

(a) NullLayout   (b) Resizing causes missing due to the fact that the fixed locations and sizes of components do not change when the environment changes. For example, if the size of the container changes, the location of some components may be changed arbitrarily under the AbsoluteLayout manager as shown in Figure 13.13(b), while some components may be partially missing under the NullLayout manager as shown in Figure 13.14(b).

13.6.3   Major UI Components

All subclasses of the JComponent class are the components needed for building graphical user interfaces. These UI components can be added into containers, such as JFrame, JApplet, and JPanel as previously described.

To illustrate, some selected components are depicted as follows. A Button is a component that triggers an action event when clicked. Swing provides JButtons, JRadioButtons, JCheckBoxes, (shown in Figure 13.15), and JToggleButtons. JRadioButtons support a mutually exclusive choice while JCheckBoxes support a multiple choice.

For making a choice from a list of items, Swing provides JComboBoxes and JLists (shown in Figure 13.16). A JComboBox will pop-up a list of items when users click on the expanding arrow so that it saves the space of user interfaces. A JList explicitly displays a set of items. Both components allow single or multiple selections.

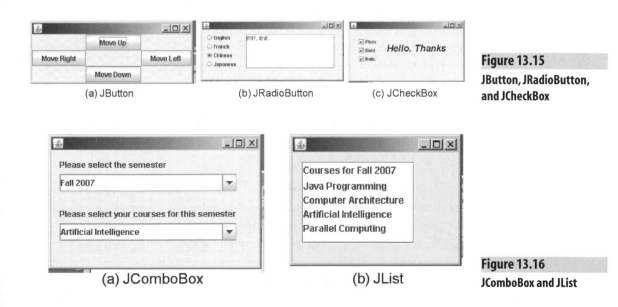

(a) JButton   (b) JRadioButton   (c) JCheckBox

Figure 13.15
JButton, JRadioButton, and JCheckBox

(a) JComboBox   (b) JList

Figure 13.16
JComboBox and JList

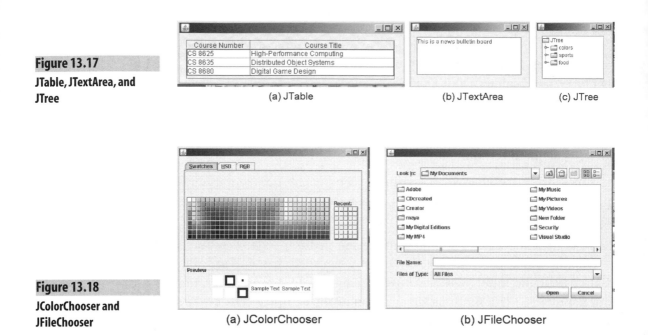

Figure 13.17
JTable, JTextArea, and JTree

(a) JTable   (b) JTextArea   (c) JTree

Figure 13.18
JColorChooser and JFileChooser

(a) JColorChooser   (b) JFileChooser

For organizing texts, Swing provides JTables, JTextAreas, JTrees (shown in Figure 13.17) and JTextFields.

Swing supports two major choosers as shown in Figure 13.18. The JColorChooser organizes all colors for selections. It is composed of two separate areas. One area is a set of color chooser panels with three panels that allow a color chooser to be selected among Swatches, HSB, and RGB. The other area is a preview panel that visually communicates the selected color. JColorChooser is typically displayed in a dialog box, but since it is a component, it can be contained in any container. The JFileChooser supports three display modes: file only, directories only, and files and directories. It comes with both single and multiple selections. Specific files or types of files can be filtered from a file chooser.

Understanding these components and their layout managers helps designers decide when and how to use these components and their compositions for designing a graphical user interface. Moreover, in J2EE edition, JavaServer Faces supports UI components for developing web applications and services; in J2ME edition, it supports specially designed UI components available for developing GUIs for a variety of mobile devices.

13.6.4 Event Listeners

Event listeners are the linkages between the UI components and the internal logic of the software system. Functions of a UI component are triggered by users' actions, such as entering the mouse into the area of the component, clicking on the component, or exiting from the area of the component. The process for making the component accept users' actions, called events, and performing its functions takes three phases. The first phase, the register phase, occurs at compile time. In this phase, the component is registered with an event listener. The event listener has an event handler. The functions of the event handler are the codes in the event handler. Designers and implementers design the functions and provide the codes during compile time. The second phase, known as the capture phase, happens at runtime. When users access a component, such as clicking on it, the event is captured by the event listener. The event listener stimulates the event handler. This brings in the third phase, the action phase, to perform the functions of the component, such as invoking the internal logic of the software system for the users. That is, graphical user interface design and implementation is based on the event-driven philosophy.

From this description we can see that the Java event model consists of three types of elements: the event object (the signal), the source object (the component that fired the event), and the event listener object (the event handler for performing the functions). Different types of components associate with different types of events. Different types of events are generated by different users' actions. Each of the events has a corresponding event listener.

13.6.5 A Case Study

Let us take the standard version of Windows Calculator as an example. By using the IDE of NetBeans, we can design and implement the graphical user interface of the Calculator easily as shown in Figure 13.19. The IDE has a palette on the rightmost column of its GUI containing all JComponents defined in Swing. The middle column of its GUI is the design form of a JFrame or a JPanel. Simply drag-and-drop the components from the palette and put them on the form; a graphical user interface of the Calculator will be built up quickly. In Figure 13.19, we have placed a JMenubar with a JMenu, a JTextfield, and seven JButtons. The properties of each component, such as the label text, the color, the size, etc., can be edited in the properties window located on the rightmost column of the IDE's user interface.

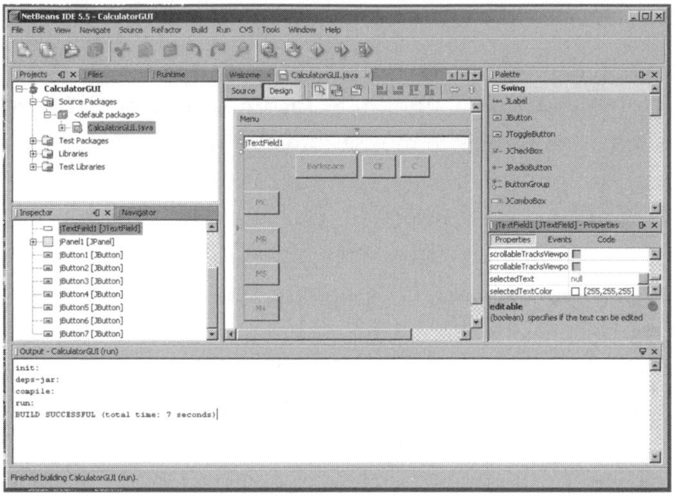

Figure 13.19

Implementing the GUI of a Calculator using NetBeans

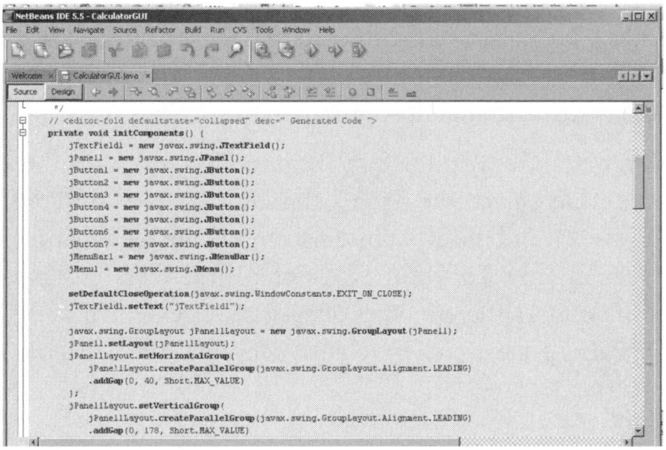

Figure 13.20

The codes of the Calculator are generated automatically.

At the same time when the component is placed on the JFrame, the corresponding codes are generated automatically by the IDE as shown in Figure 13.20. This step sets up the look and feel of the graphical user interface in implementation.

After the layout of the components, the next step is to build up the linkage between the components in the user interface with the functionalities of the internal logic of the software system. As discussed in the previous section, this takes three phases. For example, if users click the button with the label "C" (Clear) in the GUI of the standard calculator, then all information

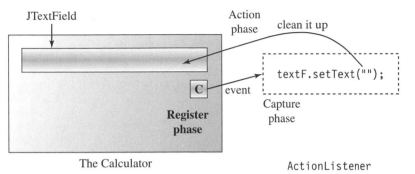

Figure 13.21
Three phases of an event listener

displayed in the JTextField will be erased. This is done by an ActionListener that has been associated with the button "C". The ActionListener has an actionPerfomed() event handler, which will erase all information displayed on the JTextField as shown in Figure 13.21. Further discussion of the implementation of event listeners is beyond the scope of this chapter.

13.7   Direct Manipulation

All user interfaces that we have discussed to this point belong to a type of user interface known as direct manipulation interface. It allows users to interact with objects via the use of a pointer. Almost all user interfaces of word processors or screen editors fall into this category. The information space of word processors is composed of a sequence of paragraphs that are presented to the user as a document. To insert text, the cursor is positioned at the appropriate place in the display and text is typed. Users get immediate feedback on their actions. Mistakes can often be detected and corrected quickly. Many actions performed using choices on menus are available via direct manipulation. For example, dragging a document icon to a desktop printer icon directly prints the document. Other actions, such as move, copy, delete, and link, are also performed via direct manipulation.

Another example of direct manipulation interfaces is a form-based interface. This kind of user interface is gaining popularity with the increasing popularity of web applications and web services. Figure 13.22 shows a web application for conducting a survey. It asks users to fill out a form by typing in the information requested. Validations can be applied with each field to ensure that the data input is in the correct form, such as an email address field. This kind of user interfaces can also be easily implemented by using an IDE with drag-and-drop metaphor, such as Java Studio Creator and Eclipse.

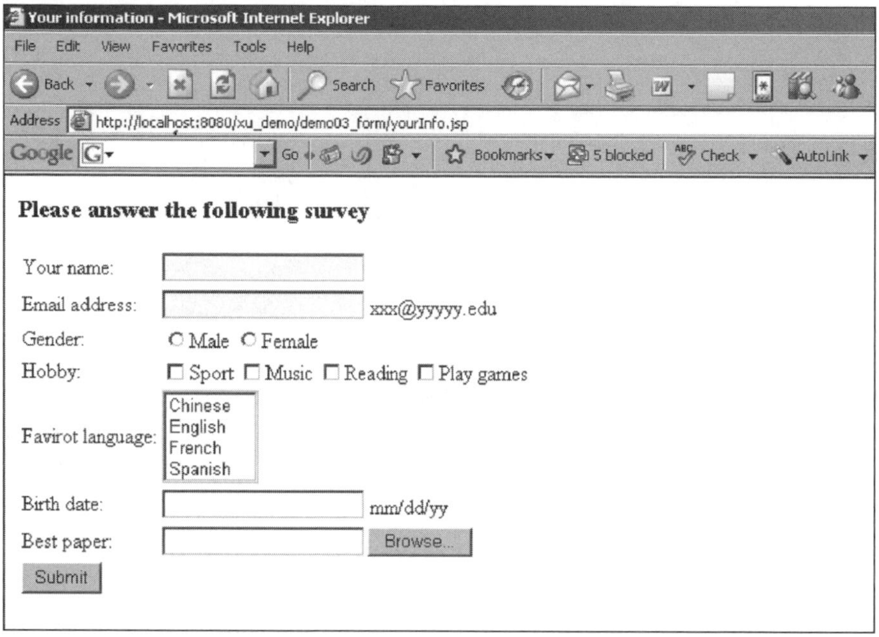

Figure 13.22
A form-based user interface

Direct manipulation supports users to interact with the software through direct actions. Modifications to the presented information immediately change the state of the system and the displayed information. Its advantages include:

- Learning time is relatively short due to its simplicity.
- It is intuitive and users are not intimidated by it.
- Mistakes can often be detected and corrected quickly.

Other kinds of manipulations include clipboard, shortcut keys, access keys in menus and dialogs, and mouse-keyboard augmentations. Although useful, these mechanisms are not considered essential features of graphical user interfaces.

13.8   Evaluation of User Interfaces

Part of the software system quality assurance process is concerned with an evaluation of the user interface design. This evaluation focuses on the defects in user interface features, the usability of the interface, and the degree to which it meets users' requirements.

Possible usability attributes of a user interface include:

- How long does it take a new user to become productive with the user interface? For example, a new user can master the usage of the user interface in a three-day training seminar.

- What percentage of the user interface components and the system functions are usable for users? For example, some components of the user interface and functions of the system are "redundant."

- What is the user's observation of the look and feel of the user interface? For example, the user may operate the user interface without looking at it, the system is well implemented with consistency and integration, and the system uses colors to distinguish important information.

- How effective is the user interface at recovering from user errors? For example, the system can check spelling and automatically correct spelling errors. The system can format source codes and automatically import packages. The system can redo 50 step actions.

- Can the user interface be customized and adapted to a new environment? For example, the user interface can be switched from one version to the other for different users. The user interface can incorporate additional components with plug-and-play.

- How well does the system response match the user's work practice? For example, a right-click context sensitive menu saves user's actions.

- How tolerant is the system of user error? For example, what happens if the user accidentally clicked two components or hit three keys at the same time? Will the system be aborted?

- Is the user interface complete? For example, the system also includes a user guidance, tutorials, and help tools.

Systematic evaluation of a user interface design can be an expensive proposition. Surveying users via questionnaires or some other simple methods can be relatively cheap. Simpler approaches can use a group of volunteers to discover and correct many problems of the user interface design and implementation.

13.9 Summary

User interfaces are an integral part of a software system. Sometimes, it determines the market value of the software. There are two major kinds of user interfaces: textual and graphical. In general, users better recognize graphical user interfaces. The quality of a user interface is characterized by its look and feel and its usability. Quality results from a mixture of engineering practice and art. All user interfaces are serving users, including information providers, in certain circumstances. Therefore, a user interface is a user-centered design product. Consequently, design and implementation of user interfaces must satisfy users' requirements. In addition, user interfaces themselves usually are sophisticated software. Their design and implementation should follow the general software principles, including object-oriented and component-oriented architecture.

13.10 Self-Review Questions

1. A user interface is mainly for accepting inputs, conducting computations, and displaying outputs.

    a. True   **b.** False

2. Chapter 3 of this book, on "models for software architecture," has nothing to do with user interfaces described in this chapter.

    a. True   **b.** False

3. User interface refers to static components and their layout, not dynamically displayed information.

    a. True   **b.** False

4. The MVC model suggests the separation of the user interface from the logic of the software system.

    a. True   **b.** False

5. Which of the following is true for implementing the separation of the user interface from the logic of the software system?

    a. Increases reusability.

    b. Eases maintainability.

    c. The same contents can be accessed by different kinds of user interfaces.

    d. The business logic and the user interface can be modified without affecting each other.

6. The look and feel of a user interface can be defined by using engineering rules.
    a. True   b. False

7. A customizable user interface is not a good style since it will confuse users.
    a. True   b. False

8. The usability of a user interface is enhanced by consistency and integration.
    a. True   b. False

9. The acronym SAPCO describes
    a. the structure of user interfaces
    b. the market values of user interfaces
    c. the satisfactory principles of user interfaces
    d. the development process of user interfaces

10. The Java programming language supports graphical user interface components, layout managers, and event listeners, all needed for designing and implementing user interfaces.
    a. True   b. False

Answers to the Self-Review Questions

1. b 2. b 3. b 4. a 5. all 6. b 7. b 8. a 9. c 10. a

13.11   Exercises

1. What are the differences between the static and dynamic graphical user interfaces?
2. What are the special features of the technique of multitouch sensors?
3. Why is the MVC model important for designing user interfaces?
4. List as many as possible existing user interface examples that implement consistency and integration principles.
5. The Eclipse Modeling Framework (EMF) is a methodology for developing customizable and integrated software tools and their user interfaces. What are its major points?
6. What techniques can be used to involve users in planning, requirements, design, construction, product evaluation, and deployment of a user interface?
7. Why do we need to apply component-oriented philosophy to designing user interfaces?

8. Estimate the usability of an example software system referring to different users with different experiences and capabilities.

9. Is Java programming language suitable for designing and implementing user interfaces?

10. Search your own name by using a search engine. Do you satisfy the returned information?

13.12   Challenge Exercises

1. Implement the user interface of the TI-83 Calculator, selectively implement certain computational functions, and link the functions with the user interface.

2. Design and implement a website for yourself. Pay attention to its user interface and the internal structure of the information that you would like to display with embedded hyperlinks.

3. Define some specifications or conventions for implementing a well-accepted, dynamic style of user interfaces.

4. Make comments and suggestions for the EMF model and draw patterns for designing customizable user interfaces.

5. Predict the evolution of graphical user interfaces in the future.

References

Budinsky, Frank, David Steinberg, Ed Merks, Ray Ellersick, and Timothy J. Grose. *Eclipse Modeling Framework*. The Eclipse Series. Gamma, Erich, Lee Nackman, and John Wiegand, eds. Boston: Addison-Wesley Professional, 2003, 2–44, 238–240.

Han, Jeff. *Unveiling the Genius of Multi-touch Interface Design* (TED 2006), 9 min., 32 sec. From *TED2006* in Monterey, CA, February 2006. http://tedblog.typepad.com/tedblog/2006/08/jeff_han_on_ted.html.

Rosenfeld, Louis and Peter Morville. *Information Architecture for the World Wide Web: Designing Large-Scale Web Sites*. 2nd ed. O'Reilly Media, Inc., 2002, 4–5, 211–242.

Torres, R.J. *Practitioner's Handbook for User Interface Design and Development*. Software Quality Institute Series. Prentice Hall PTR, 2001, 248–253, 263–274.

Suggested Reading

Sun Microsystems, "The Java Tutorials." http://java.sun.com/docs/books/tutorial/.

CHAPTER 14

Product Line Architectures

Objectives of this Chapter

- Advance the concept of systematic reuse and its particular implementation using product lines
- Discuss design considerations for product line architectures and component bases
- Demonstrate the enabling technology

14.1   Overview

Today, organizations are emphasizing component-based development (CBD) to achieve the elusive goal of *systematic reuse*. The idea of systematic reuse has gained success in commercial products, creating a plethora of technological solutions to build software out of "reusable" components such as OMG's CORBA, Microsoft's COM and .NET, and Sun's JavaBeans, mainly due to "flexibility through a capability of composition."

This current focus provides a renewed interest in devising a framework for incorporating processes, methods, and technology to engineer robust applications by interconnecting prefabricated components. One result of such an approach is the notion of *product line* software architectures and their supporting library of reusable components, or *componentbase*. This chapter presents product line architectures and component bases as a way of institutionalizing systematic reuse.[1] It discusses motivation, benefits, and technical support for the modeling and development processes.

The concepts of product line architecture (PLA) and of *reusable* componentbase (CB) have become dominant themes for addressing systematic reuse. These two themes implement two critical design features necessary for systematic reuse to work: *design-for-commonality* and *control-of-variability*. Design-for-commonality forms the basis for reusability and standardization by identifying those *crosscutting aspects* that are typically present in the systems in a given domain. Design-for-variability anticipates variation without compromising commonality, capturing the way these aspects may vary from one product to another and providing plug-in compatibility via standard interfaces to achieve control-of-variability.

A domain is an area of expertise with particular specialized tasks organized into systems where all tasks work towards a common goal, such as MS Office Suite. A PLA provides a common architecture framework as a design model that standardizes and maximizes the reuse potential of *all* software artifacts generated during the development process of systems within a given domain. At the same time, it clearly identifies variation points. These artifacts include requirements, designs and patterns, and the actual software components.* A reusable *componentbase* specifies common functionality across families of systems with direct control of variability.

14.2   Introduction and Motivation

In today's post-PC era, new artifacts and systems are increasingly software-driven. Plummeting hardware costs are leading to rapid growth in many new application areas all of which depend on well-engineered software for their continuing functioning; they require more software to be built and in shorter time frames. However, for many such systems each time a new product is built, routine functionality is custom written repeatedly from scratch. Typically, development takes place according to the *standard stovepipe approach*. This conventional approach contributes to higher demands for more software since quality and productivity suffer.

For some time now there has been an explicit recognition of the need for building software based on reusable components, paving the way for systematic reuse. The goal of systematic reuse is to produce quality software products consistently and predictably by moving toward an asset-supported development approach. In short, we need to move our focus from engineering single systems to *engineering families of systems* by identifying reusable solutions within a collection of related products. These collections are called software *product lines*.

Product line is defined as a collection of applications sharing a common, managed set of features that satisfy the specific needs of a selected market to fulfill an organization's mission.[2]

14.2.1   Software Reuse and Product Lines

Earlier definitions of software reuse include the following:

> "Re-use is considered as a means to support the construction of new programs using in a systematical way existing designs, design fragments, program texts, documentation, or other forms of program representation."[3]

---

*We use the term *components* in its most widely understood form to include requirements, software and hardware architectures, as well as blocks (both hardware and software code modules) and their test harnesses.

"Reusability is the extent to which a software component can be used (with or without adaptation) in multiple problem solutions."[4,5]

From these definitions, we can highlight three important aspects:

1. **Reuse is not an end in itself but a means to an end.**

   Systematic reuse refers to the organized creation of *common* assets with *controlled variability* that forms the basis for building systems in a domain of expertise by assembling them (systematically) from these reusable assets.

2. **Reusable assets are not limited to code components.***

   Reusable assets include any artifact produced during the development cycle and serve as templates for the generation of the various work products during product development. To assure higher probability of success, assets should be organized around ongoing business activities or domains, such as specific mission areas, areas of expertise, or core competencies (e.g., command and control, automotive, web development, etc).

3. **Software components may need adaptation.**

   Assets must adapt to particular problem solutions at reuse time. This process requires original design effort only once, and it can be applied in two ways:

   • *Adaptive design:* use known, established solution principles adapting the embodiment to the requirements. It may be necessary to perform *original design* on some individual parts or components.

   • *Variant design:* arrangements of parts or components and other product properties (size, etc.) are varied within the limits set by a previously designed product structure.

From this discussion we can also see that reuse actually occurs both within and across product lines, a notion discovered earlier and associated with the concepts of *horizontal* and *vertical reuse.* The notions of horizontal and

---

*Earlier definitions of an **asset** focused more on code. There are several problems with this view. Yes, code from one project can be saved in a "reuse" library in the hope that it will be useful in the future; but *unplanned, miscellaneous collections of code components will fail to achieve high-leverage reuse.* They would be difficult to locate, understand, and modify, since typically, design information is unavailable and adaptability is not designed-in.

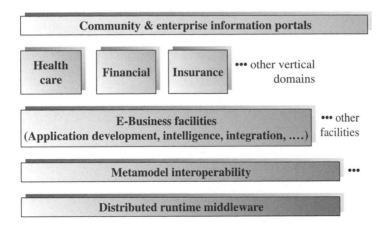

Figure 14.1
OMG E-Business Integration high-level Architecture (modified from [4])

vertical reuse have been formally incorporated in the CORBA software construction technology. The top layers of the CORBA architecture specify standard objects that can be shared by applications across domains; they are known as the *Horizontal CORBA Facilities*. Standard objects that are reusable within products in a given domain are referred to as the *Vertical (Domain) CORBA Facilities*. This is illustrated graphically in Figure 14.1.

Horizontal reuse refers to the use of an asset across several distinct domains or different product lines. Typically, assets reused in this way tend to be quite general with very specific functionality since they are, by definition, domain-independent assets. Variant design, instead of adaptive design, is best applied in this case. *Vertical reuse*, on the other hand, refers to the use of assets specially designed for a given domain or group of products; these assets are, therefore, product line specific. Assets that cross several domains take advantage of "economies of scope," a benefit that comes from developing an asset used in multiple contexts.

Systematic reuse needs to be planned for and means more work up front. It requires a consolidation of understanding of software systems in a domain in order to exploit commonality and anticipate diversity or variability. This commonality is expressed through a common architecture (PLA) with specific variation points clearly specified to accommodate adaptation. For example, taking a product that was built for a specific customer, with its own architecture rather than a PLA, and adapting it for a new customer, would likely result in an inferior product: one that contains undesirable features while lacking other desired features. This is not systematic reuse,

Figure 14.2
Ad-hoc reuse

but *ad hoc reuse.* To illustrate this point, Figure 14.2 depicts a situation in which a design (i.e., an architecture) of a fighter plane was "reused" to produce a commercial airliner, with the unfortunate consequence that the new product ended up without space to store your carry-on luggage, since this was a feature not present in the original fighter jet design.

Systematic reuse occurs when reusable assets are planned and created as a separate activity from product development, a process known as *product line engineering.*[6] Systematic reuse requires more "original" engineering design work, by focusing first on identifying as much commonality and flexibility as possible; these are then optimized out by reducing unnecessary variation and by providing specific variability control mechanisms. Thus, by planning ahead in support of the future development of multiple systems, an organization:

- reduces cycle time and cost of new products by eliminating redundancy and by producing them from common assets;

- reduces risk and improves quality by using trusted components;

- manages its legacy assets more efficiently;

- evolves a common marketing strategy and strengthens core competency around strategic business investments and goals; and

- makes decisions based on the (worth of) the asset base and the strategic goals.

This approach represents another evolutionary step in the development of the software field. It is a move in the right direction toward the more encompassing aim of attaining industrial-strength software engineering, a necessary condition that naturally leads to systematic reuse as in other engineering fields.

14.2.2 Methodologies, Processes, and Tools

A technological solution to the systematic reuse problem covers anything that can be used to help you produce software. This includes methodologies and accompanying processes, techniques, and tools.

A *methodology* refers to a specific approach to developing software as an overarching set of guiding principles, or a way of doing business for building software. Methodologies also have an impact on an organization and the way people work in teams. For example, achieving systematic reuse requires making reuse an organization-wide strategy, not a project-centered one. The entire organization may need to be redesigned to align with the "domain-model building and product construction processes" that are needed to support systematic reuse as illustrated in Figure 14.3. In a reuse-based methodology, products are "derived" from generic or *solutions* models.

A *process* specifies a list of activities and the work products produced, so that if followed carefully, it increases the likelihood of producing better software. The Software Engineering Institute at Carnegie Mellon University

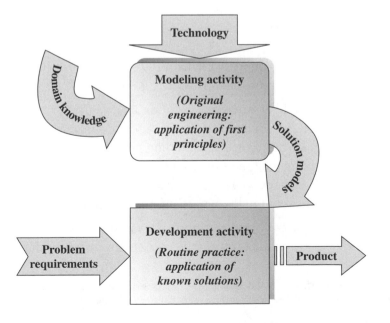

Figure 14.3
Modeling/development duality

has put extensive effort into this area with significant results. The process models produced cover the entire spectrum ranging from the corporation as a whole with the Capability Maturity Model for Software (Sw-CMM)[7] to the Personal Software Process (PSP) and the Team Software Process (TSP)*.[8,9] More recently industry is also focusing on process, although at a higher level than the CMM, and we see efforts on the Rational Unified Process (RUP). On the process front, the focus of systematic reuse is to provide specific activities for: (1) design-for-reuse—the creation of reusable assets; and (2) design-with-reuse—the creation of individual products out of these reusable assets.

The *techniques and tools* directly support the production of the various artifacts by packaging known best practices. The current focus is mostly on object orientation, as explained earlier in this book, and modeling techniques and tools are all gravitating around the object-oriented paradigm. One such tool (and language) that has become an industry standard is the Unified Modeling Language (UML). In fact, UML actually encompasses OO techniques with more traditional techniques, some seemingly orthogonal to others, such as state diagrams and flowcharts (known as activity diagrams in UML).

The *platform* is a set of subsystems and technologies that provide a coherent set of functionality that any product supported by that platform can use without concern for the details of how the functionality provided is implemented. Product line designs should strive to be platform independent as much as feasible, although this is a relative concept. The actual products, however, are platform-specific products. A product line can be supported by one or more platforms.

A model of the architecture is a description or specification of that system and its environment. *Product line architectures* capture common high-level structures of related products for building products, identifying common assets, and defining the means for connecting these assets. They allow integration of optional/alternative components. There is a strong relationship between a component model and architecture constraints.

Product line engineering results from using a domain-driven, model-based methodology for building software. A model-driven approach to software

---

*The Capability Maturity Model, Sw-CMM, the Personal Software Process, PSP, the Team Software Process, and TSP are all service marks of Carnegie Mellon University.

development prescribes certain kinds of models to be used, how those models may be prepared, and the relationships between the different kinds of models. Product line engineering is a model-driven approach because it provides a means for using models to direct the course of understanding, designing, constructing, deploying, operating, and continued evolution and modification of the software systems within the given domain. A PLA provides structural organization of the assemblage of components that are needed to build products in a domain. This structure is a standardized topology of how components are connected and how they interact to provide functionality for applications in the domain. The PLA is a generalized architecture for effective reuse across a given domain.

The Object Management Group (OMG), formed to help reduce complexity, lower costs, and hasten the introduction of new software applications, has introduced the notion of the Model Driven Architecture (MDA) framework. The approach starts with the well-known and long-established idea of separating the specification of the operation of a system from the details of the way that system uses the capabilities of its platform. MDA provides an approach, and enables tools for:

- specifying a system independently of the platform that supports it;
- specifying platforms;
- choosing a particular platform for the system; and
- transforming the system specification into one for a particular platform.

PLA documented using DMA specifications will lead the industry towards interoperable, reusable, portable software components and data models based on standard models. PLA together with MDA allow for long-term flexibility to be maximized:

- *Implementation:* since the PLA is less platform-specific, new ("hot technology") infrastructure can be accommodated.
- *Integration:* integration bridges can be automated.
- *Continued evolution:* access to systems specification and design for future features make "maintenance" simpler.
- *Testing and simulation:* models can be used to generate valid requirements and simulate (executable specification) target system.

14.3　Product Line Engineering: Design-for-Reuse

In this section we focus on the process needed to support product development following a product line approach. The process is multiplexed to correspond to the various product lines. This approach achieves design-for-commonality and control-of-variability by establishing a *reuse infrastructure*; that is, an overall framework that integrates the corresponding set of modeling, planning, and asset construction activities necessary for systematic reuse, and that, at the same time, allows the effective assimilation of technology. Fundamentally, it has the effect of reducing variance and increasing homogeneity, two essential aspects observed from disciplines that have moved into industrialization. Modeling is an important practice in increasing homogeneity. The domain modeling process primarily includes domain analysis and architectural design to produce a generic problem description.

It is clear that two sets of complementary activities are required: modeling generic solutions and product development by applying these solution models. Generative product development can be applied, whereby the developer states requirements in abstract terms and a generator produces the desired system or component. The causal relationship between building *model solutions*, on the one hand, and constructing actual products from these models, on the other, directly supports the modeling-first/development-second duality, whereby development focuses on setting problems in terms of known solutions and not building products from first principles. This approach provides a sound basis for industrial-strength software engineering. Within the duality of modeling development, products are created by instantiating models and by integrating prefabricated artifacts. We refer to this methodology or approach as model-based development.

In this way, one part of the development process (front part) is a development-for-reuse process for creating reusable software assets. The complementary back-end part refers to a development-with-reuse process to create specific systems with these prefabricated assets. The former is like performing *original engineering* (using first principles) to new tasks and problems that are realized by synthesizing new solution principles and sometimes by inventing completely new technology; this process requires careful technical and economic analyses. This development-for-reuse process creates reusable software assets by carefully analyzing the features provided by a family of systems in a domain, and subsequently designing a generic architecture (PLA) and the components implementation, that is, a corresponding CB. It primarily involves an investment for future work (efforts to create assets for future software development), and it basically focuses on building "generic" models, even at the code level.[10] Thus, the focus is one of analysis and design of variability within a set of products and the analysis and design of commonality across products. This takes special consideration of contextual differences to allow an asset to cater to the variability found in the various products, while designing for commonality across products.

14.4   Product Development: Design-with-Reuse

The latter, back-end development process is referred to as *routine practice*, involving the application of known solutions to solve reoccurring problems, thus becoming more of a routine activity mapping from needs to solutions rather than a synthesis activity of building from scratch. The process is also referred to as a *development-with-reuse* process to create specific systems with prefabricated assets. The actual development process follows any established framework, as for example the one illustrated in Figure 14.4.

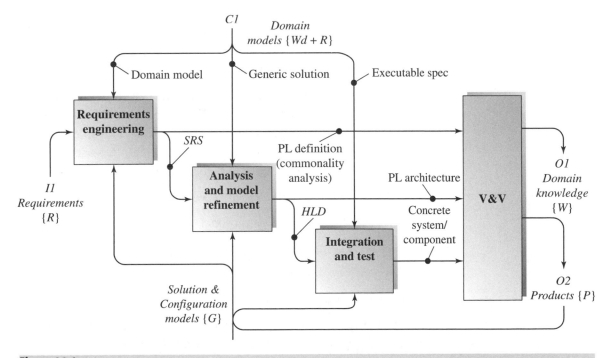

Figure 14.4

Product development activities

In order to describe the process more clearly, we use the formalism introduced by Gunter et al.[11] in their reference model for requirements engineering to label the various artifacts produced during the process of PLA generation and product instantiation. In this model, the primary information elements manipulated are in the Domain Knowledge {W}, which encompasses known facts about the domain environment or outside *W*orld. The domain modeling activity (see following) is constrained by the chosen scope {d} thus subsetting the domain knowledge to the specific set of products {Wd} based on strategic goals and organizational mission. The *R*equirements {R} define needs from an end-user point of view of a specific product. The resulting specification {S} is produced as a precise description of {Wd} from where an optimal *P*roduct {P} can be built. The target platform, or *M*achine, {M} provides the specific computing environment(s) on which the delivered products and assets will execute.

The various representations of W, R, and S contain models from different viewpoints. Each of these models highlights different aspects of the world, needs, and requirements, and they are collectively referred to as *domain models*. Domain models describe typical systems features, including functional and nonfunctional, as well as mandatory and optional features. A domain model formalizes knowledge about existing systems and requirements for new systems, all represented using information modeling techniques such as object models (use cases are very useful here) and feature models. They may also form the basis for business process reengineering.

Models are subject to validation and verification before being put on a baseline. Model V&V, as well as product V&V, are carried out through a continuous cycle. One of the most critical questions is to be able to define correct, unambiguous, and useful mappings between all these sets of conceptual elements and generated artifacts. For example, it follows that

- $S \subseteq R \subseteq Wd$, and that $S \Leftrightarrow M * P$, where
- {W + R} = abstract problem model,
- {S + M} = concrete problem model,
- G = generic solution model, and
- P = concrete solution model.

A complete analysis of these equations is beyond the scope of the current chapter. Interested readers should look at Sw-CMM.

In what follows we describe the basics of the essential activities grouped into three main, natural phases known as product line analysis, product line design, and product line implementation.

14.4.1   Product Line Analysis: Domain Models

Analysis in product line engineering is different from more conventional software engineering approaches, since we must conduct a special, more comprehensive study of the products in the domain. To address the question of what components are needed requires special, broad analyses of the products in the problem domain, a process known as domain analysis. We do this to identify the components that are typically "present" in those products and, particularly, the way that these components vary from one product to another. The idea is to be able to anticipate change and to build adaptation capabilities into "standard" components.

Domain analysis is a top-down activity for the identification of commonalties across products in a domain and results in the definition of *product line features* documented by *domain models*. See *Software Reusability*[12] for a survey of DA methods. A method specifically designed for DA is the Feature Oriented Domain Analysis (FODA) method developed at the SEI. This method defines a process for domain analysis that supports the discovery, analysis, and documentation of commonality and differences within a domain. The feature-oriented concept is based on the emphasis the method places on finding the capabilities that are usually expected or desired in applications in a given domain.

A FODA domain model captures the similarities and differences among domain assets in terms of a set of related features. A feature is a distinctive aspect, quality, or characteristic of the domain asset. The features identified by the FODA method can be used to parameterize the product line architectures and the corresponding domain components. The features differentiating domain entities arise from differences in capabilities, operating environments, domain technology, and implementation techniques, that is, a range of possible implementations within the domain. A specific product implementation would thus provide a consistent set of feature values describing its capabilities.

Recently, and due to the popularity of use case modeling, researchers and practitioners have been linking the notion of features to use case models. Groups of use cases can be used to model features. The mapping covers all possibilities for features modeling. Thus, some use cases can be optional while others can be alternate; scenarios within a particular use case may also be optional or there can be alternate ones; the same goes for the flow of events within a particular scenario, that is, it can vary or may be optional. Interested readers should look at the work of Eriksson.[*]

Section 14.5 contains an example of a product line analysis of the domain of traffic management.

14.4.2   Product Line Design: Design-for-Commonality and Control-of-Variability

Domain design focuses on a common architecture of related systems in such a way that design models become the means for system construction and for incremental growth. This common architecture is a PLA, a high-level architecture with an explicit identification of the points of variation (*hot spots*) and corresponding component flexibility, thus focusing on design-for-commonality and control-of-variability.

As defined in this book, the architecture design process produces architectures that specify products and components. It refers to "modularizing" for component-based development, thus increasing the probability that significant portions of the products can be built from standard parts (components) as specified in the design model. The resulting designs make tradeoffs between function (domain model) and form (domain design), and between generality and specificity. The architecture model proposes a "best fit" high-level architecture style(s) for the kind of problems in hand. The design contains details of specific behavior and systems properties (such as timeliness, and other SWaP[**] constraints) complete enough that they can be subject to analytical tools.

Design-for-commonality forms the basis for standardizing assets to build products in a domain of expertise by encapsulating common features of related products, and by defining a common architecture for related products. In this way, design-for-commonality translates into a:

- a common structure of related products (PLA);
- a specific design created by instantiating a common design;

---

[*]Magnus Eriksson, Jürgen Börstler, Kjell Borg. "Software Product Line Modeling Made Practical." Communications of the *ACM,* Vol. 49 No. 12, 2006: 49–54.

[**]Size, weight, and power.

- a clearly coordinated role in meeting a common need; and

- a product implemented by the identified reusable components.

Control-of-variability is the basis for providing flexibility in the assets to meet requirements for a variety of products without compromising commonality. It requires careful design to include appropriate levels of parameterization, generalization and specialization, and extension. Like commonality, adaptability must be engineered a priori, and thus, analysis must explicitly identify variations that anticipate adaptations. Control-of-variability results into:

- a specification of optional components;

- clearly specified alternate structures; and

- parameterized context dependencies.

Optional parts are very important. Possible combinations of optional features must be supported by the PLA and the flexibility incorporated in the component design, otherwise it may be impossible to reuse an asset "as-is" because commonality and specificity are mixed. This would make it necessary to modify the asset when reused in the new context, and this should obviously be avoided whenever feasible.

As we saw earlier in this book, components interact via *architecture connections* specified by protocols. Thus, connections are relations among components. This happens at two levels, namely at the static level as context dependencies, and at the dynamic level for control and data flow. Rapide,[13] an architecture description language, makes this distinction explicit: an Object Connection Architecture specifies collaborations as runtime message exchanges, whereas an Interface Connection Architecture defines connections between the components of a system using only the interfaces. The design activities are supported by system/software architecture technology, most notably Architecture Description Languages or ADLs. Component design is supported by Interface Definition Languages or IDLs.

Finally, the quality of the products is maintained through rigorous analysis and prediction, continuous improvement and refinement, and through designed experimentation and feedback from observations of actual systems generated from the generic solutions (the PLA/CB). The Attribute-Driven Design (ADD) method is a method for designing the software architecture of a product line to ensure that the resulting products have the desired qualities. The ADD method is based on the following:

- Both functional and quality requirements must be specified. The method insists on an explicit statement of quality requirements.

- The ADD method is a recursive decomposition method. At each stage in the decomposition, the elements of the next level decomposition are validated against both the functional and quality requirements. The steps at each stage of the decomposition are:

  1. Choose architecturally significant requirements, that is, the combination of quality, business, and functional goals that "shape" the architecture.

  2. Choose patterns and children component types to satisfy drivers. Choose the solutions that are most appropriate for the high-priority qualities.

  3. Instantiate children design elements and allocate functionality from use cases using multiple views.

  4. Identify commonalities across component instances.

  5. Validate quality, functional requirements, and any constraints.

  6. Refine use cases and quality scenarios as constraints to children design elements.

- The relationship between qualities and the architecture patterns that achieve those qualities can be codified and catalogued.

The ADD method has been used for application domains ranging from information systems to embedded systems.

14.4.3   Product Line Implementation: Configuration Model and Componentbase

The domain implementation includes selection of suitable target platforms, the partitioning and allocation of functionality among hardware/ software components, and the implementation of the various components that populate the system architecture. The implementation activities define the *solution space* with all their possible combinations. Domain implementation also includes a process for the creation of reusable software (code) components and their storage and retrieval in the domain library. Domain implementation is supported by component composition technology, most notably Module Interconnection Languages such as Ada and Java.*

Design models describe the generic *solutions* that are the result of PLA design. Implementation models include *configuration* models with specific information to support adaptation. A configuration model maps between the problem models and solution models in terms of product construction rules. These rules translate capabilities into implementation components, and describe legal *feature* combinations, default settings, etc. For example, certain combinations of features may be not allowed; also, if a product does specify certain features, some reasonable defaults may be assumed and other defaults can be computed based on some other features. The configuration model isolates abstract requirements into specific configurations of components in a PLA. The *domain libraries* contain generic solutions and components that for a given target platform M satisfy the set of needs described by reference requirements or domain model. It involves the use of product line languages, code generators, and component libraries.

The *componentbase* specifies common functionality across families of systems with direct control of variability. There are different ways to control variability: class hierarchies, generators, generic parameters (templates), libraries, configurations, etc. Components in this way imply some form of code, and, from this viewpoint, architecture components are relevant at two levels: at the static or source-management level, and at the dynamic or execution level. Quite explicitly, the term component is being used to refer to this static nature as the "unit of software deployment," whereas "objects" capture software's runtime behavior. Thus, "components and objects together enable the construction of next generation software."[14] Several definitions of this kind of components abound; they address granularity, contextual dependencies, and explicit, as well as implicit, interfaces.

---

*Nonmodular languages such as C and C++ make use of environment provided capabilities such as UNIX header files to support "composability."

Two fundamental component characteristics that affect composition ability and reuse payoff are *scope* and *granularity*. A component's scope can be domain independent, product line, or product specific. A component's granularity has two dimensions, namely fine-grained (small-scale) and coarse-grained (large-scale) granularity. The former is typically found in domain-independent components, whereas the latter are typical of application subsystems, or semifinished applications (such as frameworks). Component functionality has less to do with the size of it, but reuse profit is directly proportional to size.

A *domain-independent component* has a general-purpose focus with broad applicability to many domains (across boundaries). These components are almost entirely abstract data types such as list managers, mathematical functions, user-interface toolkits, and database management systems. The term *horizontal reuse* commonly refers to domain-independent components. More recently, these issues have reached the programming level with the notion of "adapters" and aspect-oriented programming.

Product line components have more limited applicability and are especially reusable within a specific domain. The term *vertical reuse* is used to refer to these components. The semantics of the component are domain dependent and hence have little or no use outside domain. These are things like packages that compute taxes, flight control laws, scheduling routines, etc. Such product line components make certain assumptions about how they will be used, reducing generality but increasing its usability. This refers to the traditional conflict between design-for-reuse and design-with-reuse.[15]

Product-specific components may be reusable within a product line, but they are specific to a product. The semantics of the component are bound to a specific application type. The product line may dictate a generic architecture, and component roles will be developed to fit it. Typical product-specific components are entire architectures developed internally or in-house. This means that the organization is developing for reuse and providing services internally. Hence it does not have a company barrier between service providers and customers. There are also externally developed product line components. This means that the organization is developing for reuse and providing services on the external market and hence does have a company barrier between service providers and customers, which complicates communication.

Each component is a means of achieving one or more reusability features. They must have syntactically and semantically clear specification (separate from implementation) and independence from environment (e.g., parametric coupling). A component specification captures its functional description and operability (parameters, conditions, etc.). A description of the connections among the interface elements and level of parameterization and kind of extension (e.g., parametric polymorphism vs. inheritance) enhances adaptability. Users of higher-level components may instead develop their own lower-level components to create the parameters needed to instantiate the higher-level component.

14.4.4   Heuristics

Here are some guidelines to address many of the issues discussed. The tradeoff between generality vs. specificity is also related to complexity and specificity. The fundamental problem is to produce generic models that are useful, to the point where routine engineering can be brought to bear. The focus is in reducing complexity, uncertainty, and ambiguity at the same time that we strive to produce specifiable, adaptable concepts. The difficulty is in making feasible concepts work, resolving conflicts, and making all the pieces fit.

During analysis the greatest impact on the preliminary system definition (or product line specification) is at the interfaces. This focus allows us to highlight important distinctions with conventional development. These are:

- analysis identifies, most notably, the variability in the set of systems in the domain
- separates optional features from the essential, necessary ones, but anticipates new requirements
- no feature redundancy but provides alternate uses of needed features
- implementation features not imposed on existing technology

Design produces architectures to specify products and components in the form of a high-level design solution. An architecture model or high-level design for products in the domain is developed. Detailed design and component construction can be done from this model. The focus is on modularizing for a product line, that is, design for commonality and control of variability. This increases the probability that significant portions of the products can be built from standard parts as specified in the design model.

- Avoid constraining design unnecessarily. For example, hierarchies that are too shallow do not allow sharing and commonality suffers.

- Avoid simplifying design unnecessarily. For example, hierarchies that are too deep do not control variability effectively and also lose commonality.

- Enhance iteration between function (domain model) and form (domain design). Form follows function in the sense that product line analysis is feature-based whereas design is form-based. Product lines are designed from the top down, driven by function instead of form.

- Enforce strict layering. Objects enforce encapsulation by hiding local variables and local functions. The idea is to permit changes to an object's implementation without triggering changes to other objects (by keeping its specification "clean"). Design encapsulation, on the other hand, is the form of encapsulation that is required for software component technology. It is the hiding of design decisions within "layers." Unlike object encapsulation, design encapsulation is not (currently) enforceable by language processing tools. Interfaces across levels make the distinction between design encapsulation and object encapsulation clear: higher-level components utilize lower-level ones, hence users of higher-level component reuse the lower-level ones.

New capabilities offered to the user can be introduced through prototyping of new system components (possibly utilizing different implementation technology). Such prototypes coexist alongside the operational system and may get hardened through incremental reengineering.

14.4.5   Software Technology for Systematic Reuse

This section describes the technological aspects of systematic reuse processes. While we do not discuss specific technology in detail, we suggest a road map for its application in the various phases and outline problems that have surfaced, especially in relation to object-oriented technology and systematic reuse. We explicitly show the different kinds of models needed during modeling and development, at the same time that we show each of the different levels of abstraction needed for PLs. The models represent the different stages of product development ranging from requirements to implementation, whereas the levels of abstraction indicate the degree of domain information incorporated in the artifact being reused. In general, we need modeling methods and specification languages; architecture styles, frameworks, architecture description languages; and component meta-models, patterns, and component description languages. All these models then serve as the basis for requirements and design analysis for a specific product, and they support creation of component libraries.

Figure 14.5 illustrates this. In this figure we juxtapose software technology with product generation stages. The *x*-axis, "product artifacts," plots software technology used to model the different product artifacts generated during the production process; these models range from high-level artifacts

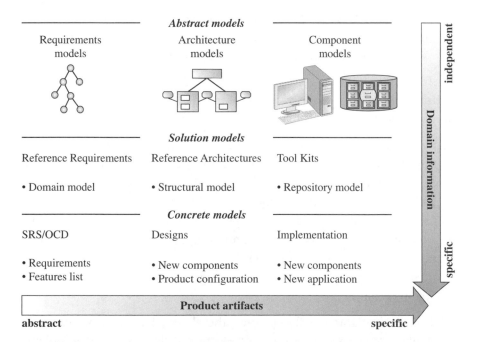

Figure 14.5

Integrated-MBSE: the relationship between the modeling and development activities is driven by technology and models, respectively. The former runs down from domain-independent models (top) to domain specific artifacts (bottom). Product development proceeds from high-level specifications (left), to the concrete realization of application systems (right).

such as requirement models to more specific implementations such as components and systems. Thus, product artifacts fall into three categories, namely requirements models, architecture models, and component models.

At the same time, the *y*-axis, development stages, indicates the level of abstraction of these models with respect to domain-information-dependency. That is, each product artifact model exists at various levels of abstraction ranging from abstract domain-independent models (for horizontal reuse) and generic solution product line models (for vertical reuse), to specific product configuration and implementation models (for system delivery).

These models are generated during domain engineering, and it is useful to distinguish two levels, namely *abstract models* and generic *solution models*. Abstract models provide basic modeling concepts in the domain and include things like reference requirements, product line architectures, and specific problem solutions (e.g., patterns). Analysis models include artifacts such as object and data models, whereas design models include architecture representations, patterns, and frameworks. The solution models become reusable assets that serve as templates for the generation of the various work products required during actual product development.

There are also *concrete models*, which result from the application of the abstract models to a concrete set of requirements by adding specific domain information.

In terms of actual software components, we can identify two kinds of object-oriented components, namely class hierarchies and frameworks. Class hierarchies (or class libraries) are product domain-independent components; they provide direct support for horizontal reuse and typically consist of a number of classes associated by inheritance. These domain-independent components are useful building blocks for different applications and even in different domains, but they are not easily adaptable and when reused, they may carry extra baggage (extra functionality) due to their general nature.

Object-oriented frameworks on the other hand, represent product line (partially complete) solutions to concrete, hopefully sharable, subproblems in the domain. They provide direct support for vertical reuse and typically consist of a number of abstract classes associated by message passing. They specify how to implement a product or a part of it by extending the framework with appropriate instantiations of some specific "plug-ins" and "hotspots"; the latter refers to variability identified in the requirements. More recently, the focus has been on higher-level abstractions called object-oriented *patterns* (specially designed patterns). These are abstract descriptions of solutions that work within a given context, allowing developers to reuse successful "working principles." In this sense, frameworks are concrete realizations of patterns, and patterns are abstract descriptions of frameworks. Collections of interrelated patterns form pattern languages, an "informal" communication tool to share architecture knowledge relating how the various individual solutions may work together to solve a larger problem. Variation points can be explicitly identified as abstract classes.

Although the principle of reuse is at the center of object-oriented development, and the technology *does* provide superior technical support for *code* reuse, object-oriented programming is simply not enough for large-scale systematic reuse.[16] Reusing code artifacts has the least amount of reuse payoff. Also, object hierarchies do not directly support the definition of families of systems. A more fundamental problem is that systems are not being designed for reuse; thus, because of object-orientation focus on code, it is not easy to design the system architecture a priori, that is, before components (e.g., classes) are built. For instance, architecture patterns and frameworks cannot be created before the actual components (classes) that they connect do exist. This, however, may not be a serious problem since we expect to have a library of components to begin with. The real question is the identification of the components in the first place and the way they fit together in an architecture. Also, objects in a class library are potentially reusable, but problems arise when we try to interface them with the outside world.

14.5   Sample Product Line Analysis

The following example of product lines is based on the Universal Traffic Management Society of Japan established in 1993 for the achievement of a safe, comfortable, and environment friendly automotive society. The following subsections refer to Figure 14.5.

14.5.1   WHY: Mission and Strategic Goals

Traffic management needs can be grouped as follows, each serving a different constituency:

- law enforcement and education
- managing traffic accidents or emergency cases
- managing traffic in large scale disasters

- managing drivers and driving licenses

- managing road usage (e.g., freight)

- managing nontraffic police activities

The traffic management dimension defines various business objectives or strategic goals, including secure and satisfactory traveling circumstances, optimum resource distribution, and public welfare. These translate into optimum allocation of traffic-related resources (traffic demand management), arrangement of rights of way in time division (traffic signaling), arrangement of rights of way in space division (route guidance or regulation), protection of people (pedestrians, physically impaired, and the aged), etc.

14.5.2   WHAT: Product Families

The achievement of the strategic goals can be met by the definition of the following products grouped into three product lines:

Product line 1: safety

- DSSS: Driving Safety Support Systems
- HELP: Help System for Emergency Life Saving and Public Safety
- FAST: Fast Emergency Vehicle Preemption Systems

Product line 2: control

- DRGS: Dynamic Route Guidance Systems
- MOCS: Mobile Operation Control Systems
- ITCS: Integrated Traffic Control Systems
- PTPS: Public Transportation Priority Systems

Product line 3: information management

- EPMS: Environment Protection Management Systems
- IIIS: Intelligent Integrated ITV Systems
- AMIS: Advanced Mobile Information Systems
- PICS: Pedestrian Information and Communication Systems

14.5.3   HOW: Asset Base

These products share the following common elements:

ACTORS

walking people	outside people (operators & administrators)
driving people	roads

TRAFFIC INFORMATION FEATURES

Information acquisition	Information dissemination
vehicle detectors	traffic information to drivers
weather and environment	traffic information to pre-trip drivers
travel time	travel information to all travelers
traffic information from video image	public transport information to travelers
traffic information from still image	Warning information
police communication	hazard information at dangerous places
strategy	warning information at roads
traffic planning	driving information about neighboring vehicles
control parameters	driving information on high-speed traffic

TRAFFIC MANAGEMENT FEATURES

Controlling elements	Controlled elements
route guidance	pedestrians (including wheel chairs)
arterial/wide area traffic control	the environment
intersection traffic control	public transportation (including taxis)
lane oriented traffic control	commercial vehicles
zone oriented traffic control	emergency vehicles
	grade crossing
	special vehicles (governor's, pope's)

Domain analysis will identify the various systems features, commonalities, and differences. The domain design will identify a high-level architecture with an explicit identification of the points of variation (hot-spots) and corresponding component flexibility.

14.6   Ultra-Large-Scale Systems

Software is moving in two directions at once. It is simultaneously becoming found everywhere and growing very, very large. Software is increasingly of public importance, and high-quality software is becoming critical to our daily lives, our safety and security, and the national and global economies. Software is also increasingly becoming very complex. Its systems are characterized by thousands of platforms, sensors, and actuators affecting decision makers and connected through heterogeneous wired and wireless networks. These systems are pushing fast and far beyond what can be comprehended, with thousands of millions of lines of code; hundreds of thousands of people employing the system for different purposes; the amount of data stored, accessed, manipulated in the billions (so-called data tsunami); thousands of connections and interdependencies among architecture components. They are being called *ultralarge-scale systems* (ULS).[17]

According to the SEI report, characteristics that will distinguish ULS systems from large monolithic systems include:

- *Operational independence of elements:* component systems are independently useful.

- *Managerial independence of elements:* component systems are acquired and operated independently.

- *Evolutionary development:* they are not created fully formed but come into existence gradually.

- *Emergent behavior:* behaviors are not localized to any component system.

- *Geographic distribution:* components are geographically distributed.

Furthermore, the characteristics of ULS systems that will develop because of their scale include:

- decentralization of data, development, evolution, and operational control;

- inherently conflicting, unknowable, and diverse requirements;

- continuous evolution and deployment; and

- heterogeneous, inconsistent, and changing elements.

Finally, the design of ULS systems

> "broadens the traditional technology-centric definition of design to include people and organizations; social, cognitive, and economic considerations; and design structures such as design rules and government policies. It involves research in support of designing ULS systems from all of these points of view and at many levels of abstraction, from the hardware to the software to the people and organizations in which they work."[17]

14.7 Summary

In this chapter we have argued for establishing a causal relationship between models representing reusable assets, created by applying first principles, and the application of these models to actually develop the delivered application, by the routine application of solution models. The formal interaction between asset producing and asset utilization activities, whereby products are assembled from prefabricated artifacts, is known as systematic reuse. We conjecture that the separation of models and product artifacts provides a suitable framework for integrating technology in the pursuit of systematic reuse. It is increasingly clear that developers require software models to be able to build new systems as variations of "old" systems. A prime example of this promising technology can be observed in the development of CORBA and its recent focus on domain technology. There are currently eight vertical-domain task forces and special groups, and a wealth of information can be found at OMG's website.* This in turn promotes the development of new, higher-level domains as illustrated in Figure 14.5. With these important efforts we are at the brink of finally beginning to have product line engineering handbooks, a most critical component of an industrial-strength engineering discipline for software.

Organizations must invest in creating models of the common capabilities of related software products. Organizations use these models as software assets supporting the creation of products that meet increasingly changing requirements. The former is a *development-for-reuse* process to create software assets, whereas the latter is a *development-with-reuse* process to create specific systems with these prefabricated assets.

---

*OMG CORBA Business Objects: http://www.omg.org/homepages/bodtf/

An important aspect to secure institutionalization of systematic reuse is the attainment of "economies of scope." Component-based development focuses on the structure of a set of components, embodying features within a domain, leveraging prior investment to the maximum degree in support of developing multiple products. Components, objects, and architectures will all be important parts of the next generation of software development technologies.

An *architecture style* is a description of component types and a pattern of their interaction. A style can be thought of as a set of constraints (on the component types and on the interaction patterns) in an architecture; for example, in the client-server style, clients are anonymous. Architecture styles are not architectures. However they represent, in a very high-level sense, families of related systems. A related concept is that of a *reference model*, which specifies a division of functionality into conceptual components, a standard decomposition of a known problem into parts that cooperatively solve the problem. They are characteristic of matured domains, such as compilers. A reference software architecture is a reference model mapped onto software components and their relations (mapping of functionality onto software components).

One problem in design is the management of complexity. Design principles deal with complexity and are also important for component-based development. These include decomposition and hierarchical structuring to increase understanding, cohesion/coupling to allow aggregation, encapsulation to support optional parts, and abstraction/hiding to support modifiability. High cohesion and low coupling are desirable properties in any system. Heuristics deal with design issues that cannot be specified exactly in algorithmic form.

Creating a product line architecture rather than single-product unique designs directly supports a desire to implement systematic reuse. When product lines are designed to support an organization's objective or mission, we are institutionalizing reuse. The approach allows engineers to come up with the "right" solution quickly and effectively by assembling applications out of "proven" components. This also represents a main motivation for component-based software engineering: a desire to modularize a system in such a way that there is a high probability that significant portions of the system can be built from "standard" parts—at least within an application domain.

Solution models represent both software and hardware architectures (components and their interfaces) suitable for solving typical problems in the domain, and include PLAs and component designs. A PLA depicts the structure for the design of related products and provides models for integrating optional/alternative components. Component designs specify the structure for the explicit variability of components across products; they serve as models for specifying and encapsulating commonality.

The notions of vertical and horizontal reuse have been formally incorporated in important software construction technology such as CORBA. The top layers of the CORBA architecture specify standard objects that can be shared by applications across domains; these are known as the Horizontal CORBA Facilities. Standard objects that are reusable within products in a given product line are referred to as the Vertical (Domain) CORBA Facilities.

Object-oriented technology does provide superior technical support for code reuse. However, it by itself is not enough for institutionalized systematic reuse. Interestingly enough, claims are being made that object technology is neither necessary nor sufficient for systematic component-based development. (It is worth emphasizing that component-based development seems to work with and without objects. For additional examples visit the SEI web page.*) One problem with object-oriented development is the low level of granularity of the assets being reused. Furthermore, the perceived benefits of reusing patterns and frameworks will not be materialized unless they are taken into account by the product development process. The reason for this is that, in contrast with functionally decomposed systems, object-oriented systems will not have high-level functions that map directly to the functional requirements. This information is not easily extracted from the code either since the focus there is on inheritance. The development process for product line components (frameworks) should follow the traditional domain analysis process. An important change in the traditional object-oriented analysis process to accommodate for systematic reuse is the need for a more formal variability analysis. Product line domain analysis must be done (not just domain analysis of one application domain) with emphasis on variability analysis. It is also important to keep domain-independent, product line, and product-specific components apart and possibly physically separate.

---

*http://www.sei.cmu.edu/plp/plp_case_studies.html

Object-oriented systems are typically monolithic pieces with difficult-to-detach "components." Current object-oriented component technology (including JavaBeans, ActiveX, COM) imposes severe constraints on the components, tightly coupling them to implementation infrastructure. Truly reusable components must be specified as free of constraints as possible.

In summary, object technology is in fact neither necessary nor sufficient for systematic reuse. The properties of adaptability and composability are not yet automatically achieved by applying object-oriented concepts. Identifying flexibility and designing mechanisms that control this flexibility are the real issues.

14.8   Self-Review Questions

1. The constituent parts of the architecture of a system are:

    a. its components, connectors, and the rules governing their interactions

    b. its connectors, concurrency, and the rules governing their interactions

    c. its classes, connectors, and the rules governing their interactions

    d. its classes, concurrency, and the rules governing their interactions

2. Domain analysis identifies the various common features in a domain and their differences.

    a. True

    b. False

3. Control-of-variability forms the basis for reusability and standardization by identifying those crosscutting aspects that are typically present in the systems in a given domain.

    a. True

    b. False

4. Product line processes are a way to institutionalize systematic reuse.

    a. True

    b. False

5. Design-for-commonality anticipates variation without compromising commonality.

    a. True

    b. False

6. A domain is an area of expertise with specialized particular tasks organized into systems where all tasks work toward a common goal.

    a. True

    b. False

7. The goal of systematic reuse is to produce quality software products consistently and predictably by moving toward an asset-supported development approach.

    a. True

    b. False

8. A software product line is a collection of components sharing a common, managed set of features that satisfy the specific needs of a selected system.

    a. True

    b. False

9. Reuse is not an end in itself but a means to an end.

    a. True

    b. False

10. Reusable assets are limited to code components.

    a. True

    b. False

11. Software components do not need adaptation.

    a. True

    b. False

12. Horizontal reuse refers to the use of an asset across several distinct domains or different product lines.

    a. True

    b. False

Answers to the Self-Review Questions

1. a 2. a 3. b 4. b 5. b 6. a 7. a 8. b 9. a 10. b 11. b 12. a

14.9 Exercises

1. Select an area of expertise (domain) you are familiar with and list five features that are common and that support horizontal reuse.

2. Select an area of expertise (domain) you are familiar with and list five features that are not common in all systems but that support vertical reuse.

3. Describe briefly the three main phases of product line engineering.

4. Using the definition given for artifact during product line engineering and corresponding product development, explain each of the following relations:

   $S \subseteq R \subseteq Wd$, and that $S \Leftrightarrow M * P$, where

   $\{W + R\}$ = abstract problem model,

   $\{S + M\}$ = concrete problem model,

   G = generic solution model, and

   P = concrete solution model.

5. Two fundamental component characteristics that affect composition ability and reuse-payoff are scope and granularity.

   a. What is a component's scope?

   b. What is a component's granularity?

6. Each component is a means of achieving one or more reusability features. They must have syntactically and semantically clear specifications (i.e., separate from implementation) and independence from environment. Show examples of component specifications using:

   a. parameters and conditions to specify variability

   b. inheritance to enhance adaptability

7. Provide examples of the application of two heuristic rules for domain analysis and three for domain design.

8. Discuss the impact of current software technology on the implementation of systematic reuse and product lines in general. For example, what are the advantages and disadvantages of object-orientation for large scale reuse?

9. What is model-based software engineering?

10. Establish differences between original engineering and routine practice.

14.10   Design Exercises

1. Perform a small-domain analysis for a domain you are familiar with using use cases and indicating:

   a.   optional use cases

   b.   alterative use cases

   c.   optional scenarios

   d.   alternative scenarios

   e.   optional activities

   f.   alternative activities

   (*Hint:* Use the approach described in "Software Product Line Modeling Made Practical."[18])

2. Using the ADD method, perform a product line design of the domain you used in the previous exercise. Follow the four steps specified by the method, namely:

   a.   Choose architecturally significant requirements.

   b.   Choose patterns and children component types to satisfy drivers.

   c.   Instantiate children design elements and allocate functionality from use cases.

   d.   Identify commonalities across component instances.

3. The *componentbase* contains components implementing common functionality across families of systems with direct control of variability. There are different ways to control variability, e.g., class hierarchies, generators, generic parameters (templates), libraries, configurations, etc. From the design you have performed in the previous question, identify components in each of the following levels:

   a.   domain-independent

   b.   product line specific

   c.   product-specific

References

[1] Díaz-Herrera, J. L., Cohen, S. and Withey, J. "Institutionalizing Systematic Reuse: A Model-Based Approach." (In Proceedings of the Seventh Workshop on Institutionalizing Software Reuse. Chicago, 1995).

[2] Cohen, S., Friedman, Martin, Solderitsch, and Webster. "Product Line Identification for ESC-Hanscom." (*CMU/SEI-95-SR-024*, Pittsburgh, Pa.: Software Engineering Institute, Carnegie Mellon University. 1995).

[3] Dusink, E.M. and Katwijk, J. van. "Reflections on Reusable Software and Software Components. Ada Components: Libraries and Tools." (In Proceedings of the *Ada-Europe Conference*, Stockholm. Ed. by S. Tafvelin, Cambridge University Press, Cambridge, U.K. 1987), pp. 113–126.

[4] Hooper, J.W. and Chester, R.O. *Software Reuse, Guidelines and Methods.* (Plenum Press, New York, New York, 1991.)

[5] Katz, S., et al. *Glossary of Software Reuse Terms.* (Gaithersburg, MD: National Institute of Standards and Technology. 1994)

[6] Weiss, D. M. and C. T. R. Lai. *Software Product-Line Engineering.* (Addison-Wesley, Reading, MA. 1999).

[7] Sw-CMM. Software Capability Maturity Model. http://www.sei.cmu.edu/cmm/.

[8] Humphrey, W. S. *A Discipline for Software Engineering.* Addison-Wesley, Boston, MA: 1995.

[9] Humphrey, W. S. *Introduction to the Team Software Process.* Addison-Wesley, Reading, MA: 2000.

[10] Díaz-Herrera, J. L. and V. Madissetti. "Embedded Systems Product Lines." (*Software product lines, ICSE Workshop.* Limerick, Ireland. June, 2000).

[11] Gunter, C. A., Gunter, E. L., Jackson, M. and P. Zave. "A Reference Model for Requirements and Specifications." (*IEEE Software,* May/June 2000), pp. 37–43.

[12] Arango, G. "Domain Analysis Methods." In *Software Reusability.* (Chichester, England: Ellis Horwood, 1994), pp. 17–49.

[13] Luckham, D., Kenney, J. J., Augustin, L. M., Vera, J., Bryan, D., and Mann, D. "Specification and Analysis of System Architecture using Rapide." (*IEEE Transactions on Software Engineering*, 21(4), April 1995), pp. 336–355.

[14] Szyperski C. "Component Software: Beyond Object-Oriented Programming." (Addison-Wesley, Harlow, UK. 1998).

[15] M. Becker and J. L. Díaz-Herrera. "Creating Product Line Libraries: a Methodology and Design Guidelines." *IEEE International Conference in Software Reuse*, Rio de Janeiro, Brazil, November 1–4, 1994.

[16] Díaz-Herrera, J. L. and B. Thomas. "Model-Based Systematic Reuse: an Analysis of OOT Support." (OOPSLA workshop #18 *Object Technology, Architecture, and Domain Analysis.* 1998).

[17] Peter Feiler, et al. "Ultra-Large-Scale Systems: The Software Challenge of the Future." Software Engineering Institute, Carnegie Mellon University. June 2006.

[18] Magnus Eriksson, Jürgen Börstler, Kjell Borg. "Software Product Line Modeling Made Practical." Communications of the ACM, Vol. 49 No. 12, 2006:49–54.

Index